THE PLOT TO STEAL FLORIDA

ALSO BY
JOSEPH BURKHOLDER SMITH

PORTRAIT OF A COLD WARRIOR

JAMES MADISON'S
PHONY WAR

THE PLOT TO STEAL FLORIDA

c. 1

BY JOSEPH BURKHOLDER SMITH

ARBOR HOUSE NEW YORK

 Published in the United States of America by Arbor House Publishing Company and in Canada by Fitzhenry & Whiteside, Ltd.
Library of Congress Catalogue Card Number: 83-70459

ISBN: 0–87795–477–1

Manufactured in the United States of America

10 9 8 7 6 5 4 3 2 1

This book is printed on acid free paper. The paper in this book meets the guidelines for performance and durability of the Committee on Production Guidelines for Book Longevity of the Council on Library Resources.

ACKNOWLEDGMENTS

First, I want to thank Donald I. Fine, the publisher, for his steady support of my project and his sound counsel.

The greatest reward of research is meeting the able, dedicated people who run research facilities. Elizabeth Alexander, director of the P.K. Yonge Library of Florida History, University of Florida, Gainesville, Florida, personifies the scholar-librarian. Dr. Steve Kerber, her deputy, is a true alter ego. Both of them helped me unsparingly.

Mr. Carol Harris, who is in charge of the Florida Room of the Jacksonville Public Library, Jacksonville, Florida, is another devoted librarian who delights in helping people exploit the resources at his command. I also want to thank Jackie Beardon, who is in charge of the Saint Augustine Historical Society library, and the staff of the periodical room of the Library of Congress.

Charles A. Shaughnessy, of the Navy and Old Army Branch of National Archives, Washington, D.C., carefully explained, and thereby made it possible for me to cope with the chaotic filing system our nation's early bureaucrats of the War and Navy Departments employed.

I especially appreciate the helpful leads provided by Professor Phinizy Spalding of the history department of the University of Georgia, Athens, Georgia. Shirley Joiner Thompson, a genealogist who knows on a first-name basis the families who lived on the Florida-Georgia border at the turn of the nineteenth century, graciously shared her knowledge with me.

Locally, there are many friends who helped and encouraged me. In particular, I thank Mary Holt Boswell and Captain George Davis, two people who love Fernandina and the Saint Marys River, who guided my footsteps; my friends and colleagues of the Beaches Area Historical Society, Jacksonville Beach, Florida, who helped me appreciate northeast Florida's past; and especially, the society's president, Jean McCormick, who first got me interested, and Suevan Shine, the society's archivist, who helped me with some research tasks.

Chore work merits equal gratitude. I gratefully thank Charleen Thornhill and Maria Smyth, my typists, Linda Overton, my copyist, and my wife Jeanne, my in-house editor. Although she thinks writing a book does about as much for a marriage as having an affair, she again served admirably in that role. Any felicitous phrases are hers.

Mike Wolan, a fine tennis pro, linguist and superb Latin teacher at the Bartram School, Jacksonville, straightened me out on the Latin motto of the flag of Florida rebels.

The essence of government is power and power lodged as it must be in human hands will ever be liable to abuse.

QUOTATION FROM THE **Writings of James Madison**, INSCRIBED ON THE WALL OF THE JAMES MADISON MEMORIAL BUILDING, LIBRARY OF CONGRESS ANNEX.

Contents

PROLOGUE 11
I MR. MADISON'S WRINKLES 19
II THE PROBLEMS OF A PRESIDENT 32
III HOW WEST FLORIDA WAS WON 51
IV A YAZOO MAN 69
V FRONTIER DIPLOMAT 80
VI SOUTH OF THE BORDER 90
VII MATHEWS GETS THE MARSHAL'S BATON 106
VIII FRUSTRATED BY FOLCH 120
IX A RIVER OF SIN 133
X A SECOND-BEST SOLUTION 147
XI WHO'S IN CHARGE HERE? 157
XII THE REPUBLIC OF ROSE'S BLUFF 174
XIII THE FALL OF FERNANDINA 185
XXIV ON TO SAINT AUGUSTINE 202
XV A HIGHER PRIORITY 215
XVI THERE MUST HAVE BEEN SOME MISTAKE 232
XVII FRONT BURNER, BACK BURNER 249
XVIII BLACK AND WHITE AND RED ALL OVER 254
XIX SOUND RETREAT 272
EPILOGUE 292
BIBLIOGRAPHY 297
INDEX 307

PROLOGUE

"The war . . . was chiefly remarkable for the vehemence with which, from beginning to end, it was resisted and thwarted by a very large number of citizens . . . who considered themselves by no means the least respectable, intelligent or patriotic part of the nation."

Those words weren't written to explain the reason for the controversy over the Vietnam War Memorial. As familiar as they sound, they're no comment at all about Vietnam.

They were written almost a hundred years ago by Henry Adams to describe a war that took place seventy years before he wrote them.

Those who ignore history think the Vietnam War was the first war when all the American people didn't rally around the flag with glowing and unquestioning enthusiasm. They believe Vietnam was the first war our nation lost. That's not so.

The first war in our history which featured articulate, strident, determined and able protesters, and the first war we clearly didn't win, was the very first war we fought after winning independence. It was the War of 1812.

From the outset opponents of the war insisted we were engaged in a struggle we should not have entered. We not only could not win battles consistently, but Washington was captured by the enemy and the capitol building and the president's house left in ruins. And the treaty ending the war was merely an agreement to cease fighting. None of the issues was decided. They were postponed.

So the War of 1812 and the Vietnam War are broadly analogous. There are some narrower similarities too. We began our involvement in Vietnam with covert operations in 1954, when the CIA covertly helped put Ngo Dinh Diem in power. A year before we declared war against England in 1812, we undertook a covert operation in Florida. As a matter of fact, we undertook two. One was a sort of success; the other was a failure.

Supporting Americans living in the Spanish territory of West Florida, in what is now Alabama, worked out with a little luck. Nearly everything favored its success. But when President Madison tried to instigate a covertly supported revolt by the persons of American origin who lived in East Florida, north of Saint Augustine and south of the border with Georgia, the operation failed.

The passage of time and the work of industrious national mythmakers have obscured the bitterness of the country's mood during the War of 1812 and all but obliterated the story of the covert operation in East Florida. Unlike the aftermath of the Vietnam War, when Americans nearly drowned in self-pity and remorse and demanded accusatory investigation of the government, especially the use of the Central Intelligence Agency in the conduct of foreign affairs, following the War of 1812 a totally different kind of reappraisal took place.

The enemies of the war shook their heads in disbelief; the only concession they made was to admit that the peace treaty saved James Madison. That was enough, however, and the nation turned to a new agenda. There are signs now that in the 1980s the recrimination and hatred of the Vietnam years are finally being forgotten. In 1815 these emotions disappeared overnight.

Thomas Jefferson and his two disciples, James Madison and James Monroe, were promoted to the pantheon of the Founding Fathers, the American nationalist religion's temple, while all of them still lived. To bolster this status, sculptors of the time portrayed them in the costumes of the heroes of ancient Rome, such as the toga-draped lifemask of Madison that J. H. I. Browere produced in 1825.

In reality all three of them were practical, pragmatic politicians. They all put on their togas one arm at a time. Nothing reveals that better than the kind of diplomacy they practiced and their use of covert manipulation to wrest territory from the crumbling Spanish Empire. James Madison, the father of the Constitution, was also the father of covert-action operations.

As for telling the truth to the American people, all three were Olympian when writing political philosophy. When running the government, their regard for the niceties of frank communication was Nixonian.

When Jefferson authorized negotiation for the purchase of New Orleans from France, he, his secretary of state, James Madison, and his special envoy, James Monroe, immediately launched a devious diplomatic ploy. As soon as Napoleon indicated he would sell all of Louisiana, they quickly made sure the eastern boundaries of that territory were left unclear. Their aim was to create a claim to Florida out of a mist of vague language.

Subsequent moves in their maneuvering matched the moral standard thereby established. These included, at a later date, a two-million-dollar bribe attempt to get France to put pressure on Spain to cede Florida, and Madison's changing dates on documents to help the cause along.

All diplomatic efforts to gain acceptance of the claim that the Louisiana Purchase included West Florida—the rich area of present-day Louisiana north of New Orleans, plus parts of the present states of Alabama and Mississippi—failed. So a covert-action operation was used. The area north of New Orleans was occupied in 1810 after the United States-sponsored rebellion of settlers there provided the excuse for our troops to move in. The remainder of West Florida was left dangling. So was East Florida—the present state.

James Madison determined to push on. As it would years later, one successful covert operation suggested another. Just as the successful Guatemala operation of CIA which overthrew the Arbenz government there suggested the same thing could be done to Castro at the Bay of Pigs, Madison thought he would try the same tactic in East Florida he had gotten away with in West Florida. Just as in the Bay of Pigs' case, it didn't work.

Again there is the same broad analogy between the failed Florida operation and the Bay of Pigs that there is between the War of 1812 and the war in Vietnam.

The CIA tried to run the Bay of Pigs operation with as many as possible of the members of the successful team that had run the Guatemalan operation. Madison tried to work the Florida deal with one of the players from the earlier effort. In both cases there was confusion about what was meant by certain key instructions, and in both cases the president and his key advisors waffled when push came to shove.

More important than any analogy is the way in which the failed Florida operation was forgotten along with all the other unpleasantness of the war years. James Madison's phony little war in Florida has been as overlooked as has his futile larger war against Great Britain. The most recent biography of James Madison makes no mention of the Florida adventure at all.

So when revelations of CIA's covert-action operations began to fill the press in the 1970s, these accounts either explicitly stated or strongly implied that such activity was foreign to our national tradition. Covert manipulation of other countries' business was portrayed as the invention of the too zealous cold warriors of the CIA. The forgotten Florida operation shows that use of such tactics is almost as old as the republic itself. And there is more the operation illustrates.

It set the style for filibustering in Latin America from then on. Filibustering is a nineteenth-century term for what was a main feature of United States activities in Latin America up until at least the destablizing activities of the CIA in Chile. There have been broad hints that it is Reagan Administration policy in Central America still. In between, it has been the occupation of many colorful characters, like William Walker, who, on a private-enterprise basis, dominated Central America in the mid-nineteenth century, and

Theodore Roosevelt, who used it as a public personage to create a country where he could build a canal.

The common pattern it established, from which the others were cut, consisted of a preliminary propaganda phase—working up excitement in and about the target—then the organizing of a "patriot government" opposed to the group we wished to get rid of, then an armed attack by the "patriots" on the nearest legitimate authority over which the targeted group held sway, then an appeal to the United States government to assume control and restore "order," a call which the United States government usually answered. Often, in came the marines.

When the call for United States assistance went out in the last half of the twentieth century, there were some modifications. The marines no longer came. They were replaced by economic aid and military-assistance missions.

Another pattern almost as methodically drawn was a design which the aftermath of such operations all too often followed. What follows these operations are events that are unforeseen, uncalled for in the script and all too often unfortunate. After the Bay of Pigs, Castro was stronger and more popular than he had been before.

After the Patriots War, as it is still known locally in Florida, relations between white settlers and Indians were worse than they had ever been. The Spanish governor called upon the Seminole Indians for help when he found himself in Saint Augustine besieged by a group of "patriots" accompanied by American soldiers.

The Seminoles had large numbers of blacks living beside their villages. These blacks were technically slaves, owned by the Indian chiefs. In reality they were as free as tenant farmers ever are. When the call went out to fight, they fought for their land like all farmers do. In short, most of the fierce Indian warriors who fought white troops and then white settlers were black, not red.

This was a matter of concern, perhaps of the greatest concern, to American settlers in Florida and to American farmers and planters in Georgia beyond the easily crossed Saint Marys River border. Almost half the population in rural Georgia were black slaves. A slave rebellion was a nightmare that ruined sleep on every remote farm, large plantation and in villages and towns of all sizes. None occurred, but the worry didn't go away.

Madison's larger war swallowed up his smaller one, and American troops were withdrawn. The patriots' only prize, Fernandina, the paradise port of smugglers across the river from Georgia, was returned to Spanish rule on May 6, 1813. The situation in Florida, however, got worse before it got better.

Remnants of the "patriots" in the spirit of the times plundered plantations of those they claimed had opposed them and wrecked their hopes. When the United States finally bought Florida in 1819, both the injured and the people who caused the damage joined in lawsuits to try to recover their losses from the United States government. Actually, the purchase of Florida was another neat trick of the kind of foreign policy management Jefferson, Madison and Monroe practiced. The United States merely agreed to assume the claims its citizens had against Spain. The ultimate outcome of the whole affair was simply more expense for the United States taxpayer.

In addition to rendering these larger, recurrent, frustrating patterns covert operations often present, James Madison's plan to stage a revolt in Florida affords anyone seeking to explain and understand it another molestation common to clandestine activity.

Clandestine activity, by its nature and purpose, thwarts historians. Successful or unsuccessful, good or bad, covert operations leave a limited paper trail. Such written records as there are, are often deliberately misleading. Orders to start rebellions in other people's countries cannot afford to be totally clear and explicit. Reading between the lines is where the true story is found. Still, even today, the key punch lines aren't taped, even by presidents inclined to do so.

"If I ever carried a marshal's baton in my knapsack out of the Oval Office, it was that day," Richard Helms said when Nixon ordered the operation to stop the election of Salvador Allende as president of Chile. That sums up the situation. *The word* is given by what is said, not what is written, when the ground rules for a covert-action operation are established. What was true for Richard Nixon was true for James Madison. What was true for Richard Helms was true for George Mathews, President Madison's special agent chosen to carry out the secret operation in East Florida.

This causes more problems than the difficulty historians have in verifying the details of the operation. Mathews was left with no defense when Madison decided to scrap the operation. James Madison was not only father of the constitution, and father of convert-action operations, he was the father of *plausible presidential denial.*

Plausible presidential denial is the doctrine by which all covert operations during the cold war were run. It means that these activities are to be conducted in such a way that the president of the United States can baldly declare he knows nothing of them when they go sour. This is standard operating procedure in running such operations designed to disrupt or destroy the defenses of another country, and has been long practiced by those adept at such activities. Nikita Kruschchev was stunned when President Eisenhower abandoned the script and didn't deny Gary Powers's U-2 flight.

Enough documentation of the plot to snatch East Florida from Spain survives so that it is possible to follow the course of events. But we will never know the exact words that passed the marshal's baton to Mathews's saddlebags any more than we know the words that put it in Richard Helms's briefcase unless he chooses to tell.

Piecing together the parts of the plot is like trying to follow clues in any adventure. We do the best we can and trust we can come close to understanding the motives of the principals.

CHAPTER I

MR. MADISON'S WRINKLES

In 1812 a sometime visitor to Washington called James Madison a withered little Applejohn. He went on, saying the president was "a short man, his forehead full of wrinkles, a face which has the appearance of a midnight lamp."

These were the words of Washington Irving, our country's first successful professional satirist, so the description may contain some striving for effect. Also, Irving was not friendly toward Thomas Jefferson and his followers. He lampooned Jefferson's erudition. Of Madison's predecessor he wrote, "Having acquired a smattering of knowledge, he was ever a great conner of indexes, continually dipping into books without studying to the bottom of any subject."

But after making allowances for bias and literary license, there is no doubt that Madison had enough problems to wrinkle his brow. Unfortunately time has dulled the effect of the midnight-lamp image. In 1812 it was meant to suggest a moody flickering candle threatening to succumb to the surrounding gloom. Madison had much to be moody about.

For one thing he had a wife who was seventeen years younger

than he was. This can put pressure on a man, especially one, like Madison, in his early sixties. And his wife was no ordinary woman.

Dolley Madison made the legend-in-her-own-time mark that Jacqueline Kennedy did one hundred fifty years later and for many if not all the same reasons. Her clothes were the talk of Washington, she lavishly redecorated the White House and her entertaining shocked the rural members of her husband's party. Like her twentieth-century successor, she had made quite a splash in government society circles while her husband was on his way to the top. Also, like Jacqueline Bouvier, her parents were what in her day were called "good stock." That meant they were counted among Virginia's gentry, but not among its top numbers. Marrying Madison was for her, too, a move up.

She was a striking-looking woman. The kind of woman at whom men always look twice. Most more often. "You are the most beautiful young lady in America," Benjamin Franklin told her when she was still an unmarried girl in Philadelphia. Franklin's assessment has to be given some weight. He was the great womanizer of his time.

Her type of beauty would not meet the standards of "the century of Svelte." She was not "bean lean, narrow as an arrow, pencil thin." Today she would be considered short and fat. She was about five feet two. James Madison was possibly five feet six. So in her high-heeled satin slippers, they looked each other in the eye.

Her ample bosom, however, assured her top marks from more than Dr. Franklin. Unlike today, when preternatural thinness is prized by the active, liberated woman, in the eighteenth century, woman's economic status was low. The marriage market was the only one she could enter. For the same reason *Playboy* and *Penthouse* girls get more masculine attention than *Vogue* and *Harper's Bazaar* models, eighteenth-century fashion strove to create the impression of enormous bosoms and bottoms. Dolley's natural endowment assured her fashion-leader status by the time her husband became president.

She was born on June 20, 1768 in a two-room log house at the New Garden Quaker settlement near present-day Guilford College in North Carolina, but her parents were both Virginians. Her maternal grandmother, Lucy Winston, was from a well-established Quaker family in Hanover county. Lucy's sister was the mother of Patrick Henry. But Quakers were not popular in colonial Virginia, where the Church of England was a bastion of society, which was why her father, John Payne, moved to North Carolina to pioneer a tract of land his father gave him. Dolley and her brother were born there.

Dolley was not, like Jackie, a nickname, although many biographers for years claimed it was. Her most recent biographer, perhaps because she herself is not only a careful scholar but a proud Virginian, found that "Dolley," spelled with an *e*, was the name given on the birth certificate.

When she was only ten months old, another gift of land, this time from her mother's family, enabled her parents to return to Virginia, where she grew up. Up to the age of thirteen, that is, which was early adulthood for an eighteenth-century girl.

In 1781 in the closing days of the revolutionary war, the ruthless British cavalry commander Colonel Banastre Tarleton brought the war to the Virginia countryside. Some planters panicked and had carpenters, hoopers and tanners make chastity belts for all the females in the family. The Paynes spared Dolley this indignity, but they decided to move to Philadelphia. Philadelphia was the Quaker capital of the colonies, and, of course, became the capital of the new nation.

Her father did not prosper in Philadelphia. In fact, he lost so heavily in land speculation Dolley had to go to work as a dressmaker and help her mother run a boardinghouse. Finally things got so bad for her father he was read out of the Quaker's Society of Friends for the sin of bankruptcy. The Quaker merchants of Philadelphia found few sins worse than that. Dolley's faith was badly shaken. After her brief, tragic marriage, it would be destroyed.

Despite her father's troubles, Dolley's good looks attracted young men as she matured. She met and married a young Quaker lawyer, John Todd. Marrying the young lawyer was an essential step back up the social scale. He had clients, and he owned his own house.

On February 29, 1792, Dolley gave birth to a leap-year baby. He became a man who forever acted as though he only had a birthday every four years.

The trouble Payne Todd brought his mother and stepfather was down the road. During the first year of his life, Dolley faced other disasters. She gave birth to another child, but then lost both this baby and her husband in the yellow-fever epidemic that struck Philadelphia in 1793.

Dolley abandoned the Quaker faith and, as she gradually overcame her grief, became a different woman. Her fifteen-year-old sister Lucy eloped with George Washington's nephew in the spring of 1794, and Dolley herself was out of widow's weeds and Quaker gray and seeing gentlemen. Aaron Burr was particularly struck by the young widow, but he already had a wife. Dolley wasn't interested in a relationship so chancy. She agreed to marry James Madison after a whirlwind courtship. He proved to be a better bet in nearly every way, though there seems to be one way that may not have worked out too well.

The sex life of the Madisons is a mystery. Although Dolley had given birth to two children by her first husband, she and Madison never conceived. Unfortunately their intimate letters were lost. In any case they probably do not contain what such letters might today. It seems safe to assume that whatever was said in them would not reveal anything about any birth-control techniques they used. There are, however, some clues.

When James Madison graduated from Princeton in September 1771, he collapsed. He remained at Princeton until the following April, too weak to go home. His most authoritative biographer, Irving Brant, says he suffered from a functional disorder known today as epileptoid hysteria.

Sufferers from this problem are usually adolescents with strong hypochondria leading to periods of weakness and showing symptoms of epileptic seizure. Epileptics suffering from the worst form of that neurological problem, grand mal, have severe convulsions and may urinate uncontrollably and foam at the mouth. There is no evidence James Madison ever did that. In the lesser form of epilepsy, petit mal, the person suffers transient attacks of impaired consciousness. Madison evidently did so suffer. He often complained of sudden feelings of weakness.

The strongest evidence of his difficulty is the list of drugs "For an Epilepsy" in his father's plantation records. There is some debate over whether epileptoid hysteria continues as such in later life, but Madison continued to complain of what could have been such symptoms. They could account for the face like a midnight lamp. And they may have affected his sex life.

One of Dolley's biographers flatly states that he was impotent. But this author gives no specifics and makes the statement in a context which suggests she may have meant infertile. Something happened on his wedding night, however, that was enough to have induced impotence at that important moment in his life.

Little Payne Todd always slept with his mother. That's where he slept the night Dolley and James Madison were married. He continued to join them in bed when they went off on their honeymoon at Madison's sister Nelly's.

Nelly, at least, was indignant. "Then, there was *that child* [her italics] who would have nothing else but to sleep in their bed with them, as he had every night since they had been man and wife."

Whether this induced impotence in James Madison for the rest of his life is speculation. But it is understandable. There are several other hints that may indicate something about his sexuality.

He was not able to take his bride home to introduce her to his parents until Congress adjourned in March 1795. Madison had been elected to the House of Representatives in the new government established by the constitution he had largely written and done so much to have ratified. He was proud of and fastidious in attending to his congressional duties. His father had been too frail to attend the wedding, and his mother did not come alone.

Dolley and Madison's mother Nelly immediately formed a close relationship. They had scarcely met when they were off together exchanging confidences, more like two college roommates than a mother- and daughter-in-law. Nelly seemed to welcome her new daughter-in-law in particular as another woman in whom she could confide things about her son.

Nelly informed Dolley that in his college years James had "never once committed an indiscreet act." And she added he would have been better off if he had. She seemed greatly relieved to find her forty-three-year-old bachelor son at last had a woman.

Finally there is an odd thing about a letter Dolley wrote on her wedding day. She had started the letter before the ceremony. Afterward she added a postscript. She had previously signed the letter "Dolley Payne Todd." The postscript read: "Evening, Dolley Madison! Alas! Alas!"

In any case, when they returned to Philadelphia after the honeymoon in September 1794, the Madison marriage immediately put on the public face by which it would always be remembered. No longer the quiet Quaker wife, Dolley quickly became a legendary hostess and incipient leader of women's fashion. Later in Washington she blossomed into the nation's trend setter in clothes and hairstyles. James, always known for his shyness, became famous for his quiet suffering through his wife's more lavish parties. He only unbent with a few friends at small dinners.

Dolley Madison once said she became famous for her recipes because she hated cooking and so learned to experiment in the kitchen. When Thomas Jefferson returned from being minister to France he had acquired a taste for food laced with wine. Dolley's experimental flair soon had her concocting recipes that used not only wine, but rum, applejack and whiskey. By the time the Madisons went to Washington, James as secretary of state and Dolley as the widower Jefferson's official hostess, she had perfected her style.

In the earlier Philadelphia days, however, she did not come up to French standards. A French aristocrat, Moreau de Saint-Mary, who visited Philadelphia, was unimpressed by the Madisons' table.

"At about two o'clock they dine without soup," he wrote. "Their dinner consists of broth, a main dish of an English roast surrounded by potatoes. Following that are boiled green peas, then baked or fried eggs, boiled or fried fish, the salad a thinly sliced cabbage, pastries, sweets to which they are excessively partial and which are insufficiently cooked."

The part of the long afternoon dinner hour he disliked the most was when James and his friends unbent. After washing down the entire meal with cider, beer and wine, the serious drinking began when the ladies left the table and withdrew to themselves.

"The bottles then go the round continuously, each man pouring for himself. Toasts are drunk, cigars are lighted, diners run to the corners of the room hunting night tables and vases which will enable them to hold a greater amount of liquor. . . ."

This does suggest a rather high degree of informality, but there were no powder rooms in eighteenth-century houses.

Serious American drinking was something no European visitor in the early days of the republic could understand or appreciate. When Frances Trollope visited America in 1827 she found whiskey-drinking to be a universal and daylong practice. She was startled to find the Americans could not take the time to be leisurely about it but, instead, swallowed their "universal drams" standing up. When she went to the theater, she was distressed to find the audience smelling of liquor and "inspired by this," yelling and even throwing things at the actors. Most of all she was so astonished to find people usually had a shot before breakfast that she wrote a satirical play, "Day of a Lady in the West," with an opening scene in which the father demands a drink before he gets out of bed.

After they got to Washington, Dolley's dinners became more splendid. Guests raved about her beef soup spiced with herbs, and her desserts "like apple pie in the form of a musk mellon, the flat side down, tops creased deep, and the color a dark brown."

And her husband continued to unbend with the boys. Samuel Harrison Smith, editor of the Jefferson administration's newspaper, the *National Intelligencer*, reported the good time had by all at a party at Secretary of War, ancient revolutionary war general, Henry Dearborn's house.

"After a few bottles of champagne were emptied, on the observation of Mr. Madison that it was the most delightful wine when drank [*sic*] in moderation, but that more than a few glasses always produced a headache the next day, [he] remarked with point that this was a very time to try the experiment, as the next day being Sunday would allow time for a recovery from its effects. . . . Bottle after bottle came in. . . . "

This is not to suggest that drinking was one of Madison's problems. It shows he shared the general capacity of his countrymen. As Smith commented regarding the experiment with much champagne on Saturday night, "Its only effects were animated good humor and uninterrupted conversation." He said nothing about anyone seeking vases.

The liquor might have helped Madison with his other problems as his fellow citizens thought it helped them cope with theirs. Dolley was expensive to keep.

In Philadelphia she was accustomed to buying twenty pairs of shoes at a time. They were her great extravagance. When Josephine became Napoleon's bride in 1796, she introduced the high-waisted decolletage to Europe. As soon as Dolley got wind of this, she followed suit. While others hesitated, Dolley quickly ordered dresses, hats and shoes in the new French fashion. Soon she was designing things she thought suited her best. Her emergence as a fashion leader was assured.

Vice-President Adams's wife, Abigail, was not only outraged but explicit in her criticism of the new style.

"The style of dress," Mrs. Adams wrote, "is really an outrage to decency. . . . A satin petticoat of certainly not more than three breathes gored at the top, nothing beneath but a chemise. Over this thin coat, a Muslim sometimes, sometimes a crape made so strait before as perfectly to show the whole form. . . . Not content with the *show which* nature bestows, they borrow from art and literally look like Nursing Mothers."

Dolley preferred clear colors, in particular pinks in a whole range of shades. She had a special fondness for off shades such as magenta and terra-cotta. But white was her favorite. Peale's well-known miniature shows her in a white gown, three rosebuds in her white turban. She completed her white outfits with white satin slippers, a white feathered fan and an ivory-handled white parasol.

She took the lead in hairstyles as well as in clothes. From her earliest days as Mrs. Madison, she broke with current hairstyle fashion. Ladies of that era wore powdered wigs. So did men. Neither President nor Mrs. Washington ever appeared in public without their white wigs. Nor did James Madison, for that matter, not until his dying day. Madison had a balding problem. But Dolley was very proud of her thick dark hair and chose to show it off. Soon, however, she became enamored of the turban. This is the picture of her most people recall, for example, in the James Woods portrait in 1817 as she and her husband were leaving Washington. White turbans, black turbans, gold, she wore them all, and they caught on.

By the time of her husband's presidency, she was the nation's last word in glamor. At a ball in 1816 people stood on benches to get a better look at her as she swept into the room in black velvet, gold trimmed, and a gold-laced turban. Setting off the whole outfit was a tiara with twenty-three sapphires.

At the beginning of his first term in 1809, when she entered the White House as the president's wife, and not merely an official hostess as she had been for Jefferson, she took friends around to show them how shabby it was. She also made a point of doing the same thing with congressmen. As a result one of the first bills passed in the new administration allotted funds to redecorate the President's Palace, as it was then called. By the time she was finished and left Washington in 1817, she had not only redone it but given it the name by which it would ever more be known—the White House.

Congress allowed $12,000 for repairs and improvements and $14,000 more for furnishings and ordered the high-fashion architect Benjamin Latrobe to undertake the job. According to the Bureau of Labor Statistics Handbook, 1975 edition (the last year such comparisons between modern currency values and such an early date are given), an 1810 dollar would amount to $3.25 today. The difference does not seem as great as it should be, but the dollar was exceptionally strong in 1810 because of the war in Europe. Therefore, Dolley received a total of around $85,000 to work with, A sum which in those days would have bought the United States Navy two warships.

Benjamin Latrobe was the principal exponent of Greek revival in the United States and the man who raised architecture to the status of a profession. He left his principal mark on the president's official dwelling when it was rebuilt after the British burned it in 1814. In 1809 he and Dolley frequently fought about the decorations. While Madison complained in the background about expenses, she fought with Latrobe over the place where he wanted to put the largest mirror and about the curtains.

She insisted on papering the main drawing room in yellow satin made available by Napoleon's Paris decorator and herself purchased red velvet drapes. Latrobe was horrified by the garish colors.

They agreed, however, on enlarging the central staircase and on adding new public and private rooms. An enlarged wine cellar for the president's large stock was mutually agreed upon. The thoughtful Dolley then saw to it that the first indoor water closet the house had known was installed in the presidential living quarters. By May 31 she thought the place presentable and launched the first of her Wednesday afternoon assemblies. The Madison era of Washington society had begun.

Beneath the social facade there festered a continuing wound to the spirits of Dolley and James Madison. The little boy who insisted on joining them on their wedding night grew into a troublesome adolescent, a worrisome young man and a complete delinquent by middle age.

In letters to and from friends, Dolley indicated that he was a strong-willed and wayward boy, frequently causing embarrassment. At age ten he was accustomed to running off to loaf at the stables rather than attend his stepfather's tutoring sessions. At the same age he rushed up and pulled the wig off General Van Courtland at the moment the gentlemen was paying "a flourishing compliment" to one of Dolley's younger friends.

The Madisons tried two schools for him when he was older. He didn't last long at the Alexandria Academy, a school George Washington had founded, at which they particularly wanted him to do well. Next they tried Saint Mary's Academy in Baltimore, run by a no-nonsense priest, Father Dubourg, who promised them he would not proselyte but would discipline him. It seemed to work.

He grew to be a handsome, athletic, six-footer, a giant to his mother and stepfather. He learned to speak French fluently and graduated in the spring of 1812. But to all the problems Madison had in an election year and those his foreign policy had gotten him into by that time was added the family worry caused by Payne's refusal to go on to Princeton.

He preferred to party about Washington, showing himself off to the girls in one of the new green jackets—called "lizards," because of their long tails that came to the calf of the leg, a leg usually encased in skintight trousers tucked into yellow boots.

When not involved with various young women, Payne was at the racetrack with cronies or playing cards for increasingly higher stakes while sipping one or the other of the favorite national beverages—whiskey, hard cider or rum. These habits would soon make him as much trouble to his mother and stepfather as the Johnson and Nixon siblings were to their brothers.

When Czar Alexander I of Russia indicated two years later to American minister John Quincy Adams in Saint Petersburg that he would be glad to try to mediate the war Madison had stumbled into with Great Britain the year Payne graduated from Saint Mary's, the Madisons thought they saw a way to deal with the Payne problem.

After all, French was the language of diplomacy and one thing besides drink and gamble the boy could do was speak it well. Madison made him an honorary colonel and shipped him off with the delegation headed by Treasury Secretary Albert Gallatin that he had decided to send to Europe to help Adams.

Payne Todd's European odyssey caused as much concern to his mother as the war and peace negotiations caused the president. And Madison was not spared the worry either. He learned from his harried diplomats that his stepson had run up debts, invoking Madison's credit with British bankers. The president, dipping deep into his personal funds, sat down and sent off a draft for $6,500, equal to 21,125 modern dollars.

What worried his mother most was what worries most mothers, a lack of letters from her son. In addition to not writing, Payne did not come home when he was supposed to, when Senator Crawford and Gallatin returned with James Bayard, a member of the mission who was dying. By this time Payne had wandered off to Paris and so had failed to catch the ship.

The reason for his Paris side trip was that Ghent, to which the negotiations had now moved, bored him. Also he had to leave Russia early because of his involvement with a young Russian countess whose father broke up the affair by sending his daughter off to a country dacha. Payne's heavy drinking began at that point. It was, of course, the kind of excuse alcoholics relish.

When he finally returned to the United States, he was in deep financial trouble. He had been sent off to Europe with $200 (or today, $650), for what had been expected to be a six-month stay. When he finally came back after over two years, he had spent on cards, assorted good times and art objects the equivalent of $32,500.

Things never got any better. He plagued the Madisons long after they had retired from Washington. They tried to set him up on a plantation overlooking the Shenandoah Valley, a few miles from their estate at Montpelier. He decided he would raise silkworms and failed miserably. He then thought he'd like to travel. His mother was shocked to hear in 1829, after another customarily long lapse in correspondence, that he was in debtors' prison. They paid his debts. The next year he landed in debtors' prison again, and again he was able to go free, thanks to parental assistance.

The saddest part of Madison's will is the codicil dealing with his stepson's problems. Madison entrusted Dolley's brother with the current equivalent of $65,000 in payment vouchers to cover Payne's "ruinous extravagance." He asked Dolley's brother to examine them and seal the packet and not to show it to Dolley until the will was read after his death. These remittances, he said, were exclusive of those made to her for the same purpose and those he had furnished her with the means of giving, saying "the sum thus appropriated probably equals the same amount."

In other words, Payne's expenses thus enumerated, which certainly did not cover all the smaller amounts doled out over the years, totaled $120,000. But until his death he had spared Dolley the truth. She thought they had been only half as much.

What else in their relationship was hidden, avoided or cast aside cannot now be uncovered. He may have always disappointed his ebullient wife in the bedroom. The manner in which he conducted the office of secretary of state and then president can scarcely be called forceful. He avoided confrontation, was more comfortable with covert than direct action, fretted whenever faced with a decision. How much if any of this might have been due to problems he had in bed is not clear, but it is clear that Madison was no macho manager of the nation's affairs. Evidence that impotence was the cause of his fretful, vacillating, inconsistent performance as president is only circumstantial. However, according to Robert A. Rutland, editor of *The Papers of James Madison*, there is another possibility, as documented in his letters. Madison had great trouble with his digestive tract—he suffered all his adult life from hemorrhoids.

In the midst of the war with England in August 1813, the war protesters of his day accused Madison of living on laudanum. In the midst of another unpopular war in the 1960s, presidents liked to make the same charge against the war protesters. In Madison's day laudanum was widely used in times of stress. Gentlewomen used it delicately at delicate times of the month. By whatever name, it is the same soothing product of the poppy.

If Madison occasionally had a bit of laudanum, it would be understandable. He can certainly be forgiven his furrowed brow on the basis of an accounting of his personal problems alone.

But the political problems he faced were even graver than those within his family circle.

CHAPTER II
THE PROBLEMS OF A PRESIDENT

The political headaches James Madison suffered began as soon as he was inaugurated. Although the inauguration ceremony in the Senate was a brilliant success for Dolley, the complaint was that Madison mumbled.

One of the ladies in the gallery noted that he was "extremely pale and trembled excessively when he first began to speak." He spoke for only ten minutes and he didn't say much. A not too friendly historian commented about his soft-spoken words: "The address suggested a doubt whether the new president wished to be understood."

According to this critic Madison straddled every issue. As for the big question of the day, the fact that England and France were seizing United States ships daring to try to trade with Europe where the two nations headed rival coalitions locked in the world war of their day, he could only say he deplored what was going on.

"How long their arbitrary edicts will be continued . . . cannot be anticipated," he said. He added, "Assuring myself that under every vicissitude the determined spirit and united councils of the nation will be safeguards to its honor and essential interests, I repair to the post assigned me, with no other discouragement than which springs from my own inadequacy to its high duties."

That was certainly a modest enough statement, and it was good his audience could not hear him very well. Far from being a "united council of the nation," his cabinet appointments were a disaster from which he did not recover until the end of his first two years in office.

Not that there were not enough ambitious men to fill the positions of top presidential advisers. There were too many. Congress, in 1809 when Madison took office, contained as many presidential candidates as it did in 1960. In addition to men like Henry Clay and John C. Calhoun, familiar figures in all American history books, there were men like John Randolph of Roanoke, probably the most colorful person ever to sit in the House of Representatives, with his hunting dogs tied to his desk, and William H. Crawford of Georgia, Senate leader of Jefferson's and Madison's party. Another man, less talented and now lesser known than even Crawford but then a power figure, was Senator Samuel Smith of Baltimore, Maryland. He, together with several other now forgotten politicians, combined to cause Madison grief in selecting his cabinet.

Madison's problem, in fact, arose in large measure because of his own and his mentor Thomas Jefferson's great talent in putting together their party. They had succeeded in assembling a sizable assortment of ambitious individuals of varying intellectual ability but with an aggregate of considerable political skill. The Republican party, which took that name from the fact that it strongly supported the republic founded by the French Revolution in 1789—and which also liked to be known as "democrats" for the same reason, confusing modern readers who know two different parties by these names—set the style for the American electoral success. The modern Democratic party, which likes to claim it is the direct descendent of Jefferson and Madison's coalition, certainly is in this important sense. When it wins, it does so by getting a wide variety of conflicting selfish interests to stick together at the polls.

This array of electoral allies broke ranks and jostled the new president as soon as he suggested a name for the top spot in his cabinet.

He proposed naming Jefferson's able secretary of the treasury, Albert Gallatin, his secretary of state. Samuel Smith and his cronies objected.

These men would come to be known as "the Invisibles" for their role in working behind the scene against most of Madison's measures throughout his administration. For one thing, they were a major stumbling block to schemes he had for extricating himself after he had begun his covert operation in Florida. The label today also aptly fits the forgotten-men status of these once powerful individuals.

Samuel Smith was a wealthy merchant with more than political ambition. He did all he could to urge on his beautiful niece, Betsy Patterson, who had caught the eye of Napoleon's youngest brother, Jérôme Bonaparte, a member of the French diplomatic mission in Washington. Betsy was a sensation.

The wife of the British minister gave a breathless account of Betsy's appearance at a ball during Jefferson's administration. "Few dared to look at her except by stealth. What a beatiful little creature! What classic features!"

Another contemporary woman explained why looking at Betsy was so dazzling. "Mobs of boys crowded round her splendid equipage to see an almost naked woman. . . . Her dress was the thinnest sarcenet. . . . Her back, her bosom, part of her waist and her arms were uncovered and the rest of her form was visible."

All this was not lost on Jérôme Bonaparte, and he married her. First he got her pregnant.

His brother was furious, claiming the marriage was illegal since Jérôme was only nineteen. The shrewd Smith had talked his brother-in-law Patterson, although both were Protestants, into having the marriage performed by the Catholic archbishop of Baltimore to guard against a papal annulment, which Napoleon could easily have arranged.

Napoleon had never objected to beautiful women before, but at the moment he was about to have himself proclaimed emperor and was busy turning his commoner field marshals into a court. He needed sisters-in-law with royal blood. He forbade Betsy to set foot in France.

Smith's political manipulation was more successful than his efforts to improve his family's social standing. He got Madison to name his brother secretary of state.

Robert Smith was a bungling incompetent who owed his career to his brother, Samuel, who had earlier succeeded in getting him named Jefferson's secretary of the navy.

In that position Robert Smith became involved in some shady business which came to Albert Gallatin's attention and which led to a more important reason than brotherly love for Senator Samuel Smith's bitter opposition to Gallatin's getting the State Department job.

Gallatin learned of undercover contracts between the Navy Department and the Smiths' mercantile firm in Baltimore. He was scandalized and told Samuel Smith this was the most outrageous conduct he had encountered as secretary of the treasury. He threatened Smith's reelection to the Senate in 1808. But Smith won and was ready in 1809 to shoot down Gallatin.

Smith's Invisibles blocked the confirmation of any cabinet members. To unblock them, Madison suggested making Robert Smith secretary of the treasury in exchange for letting Gallatin move over to the Department of State. Madison realized that because of Robert Smith's bumble-headedness Gallatin would, in effect, have to run both departments. Gallatin objected. He convinced Madison that if he must name Smith to any job, it should be State, since Madison himself had been secretary for eight years and could live with that arrangement.

Although not as powerful as Samuel Smith's pressure, other politicians demanded their due, other political chits had to be called in and the rest of Madison's cabinet, except for Gallatin, who was enabled to remain at Treasury by the deal with Samuel Smith, was as mediocre as Robert Smith. The fact that the country was on the verge of war, and had been for eight years, made no difference.

William Eustis of Massachusetts, whose only claim to any professional military competence was that he had served as a hospital physician during the Revolution, was named secretary of war. His brother-in-law was the Jefferson-Madison-party boss of New Hampshire. Paul Hamilton was given the job of secretary of the navy because he had been governor of South Carolina. That gave sectional balance to the selection of the New Englander as head of the other armed forces.

These three men were the foreign-policy establishment with which the Madison administration faced the diplomacy of Tallyrand, the army of Napoleon and the navy of Lord Nelson.

The man who should have been among them, James Monroe, was not there because of an unfortunate coalescing of the headaches of politics plaguing the president and deepening the wrinkles his wife added to his brow.

Monroe had allowed himself to be used by John Randolph in Randolph's attempt to scuttle Madison's presidential candidacy. Why he did is only hinted at in any surviving documents of the period. Jefferson and Madison had been associates from the time Jefferson served in George Washington's cabinet. The two of them jointly established their political party as Jefferson grew more and more opposed to Alexander Hamilton's concept of a strong federal government. Seven years younger than Madison, Monroe had always been the junior partner. And Jefferson made it plain, although he was careful never to put anything in writing, that he wanted Madison to be his successor.

In February 1808 Jefferson made a discreet attempt to let Monroe know he disapproved of Monroe's permitting his name to come up in the presidential contest. He pretended the reason he was writing was to give instructions about how he wanted some scientific instruments handled. Monroe had brought them home for the president in his luggage from his assignment as minister to Britain.

"I see with infinite grief a contest arising between yourself and another, who have been very dear to each other, and equally so to me," Jefferson wrote.

Monroe replied and unburdened himself. He had been upset by the fact that Jefferson two years earlier had sent William Pinckney to join him in trying to negotiate with England settlement of the impressment of American seamen. And he had been disappointed with the president's flat rejection of the treaty he had subsequently signed. He said he would be an inactive spectator in the presidential contest, but he did not promise to withdraw his name. Monroe's case against Jefferson was flimsy.

The Monroe-Pinckney treaty was signed in direct contradiction to the president's instructions, which stated in no uncertain terms that no treaty should be signed unless the British agreed to cease immediately taking sailors off United States ships on the grounds that they were suspected British deserters.

Monroe's move against Madison had to have had deeper motivation than the exchange of letters with Jefferson indicated.

It did. Elizabeth Monroe was a wealthy New York girl, but she was also a very plain one. She did not like Dolley Madison. In all their long association as wives of colleagues, the two women never addressed each other by their Christian names. Elizabeth Monroe helped her husband make his decision.

John Randolph himself was very persuasive. "Everything is made a business of bargain and traffic," he wrote Monroe, "the ultimate object of which is to raise Mr. Madison to the presidency. To this the old Republican party will not consent. . . . They are united in your support."

When Monroe demurred, Randolph renewed his pitch again, saying how united the old Republicans were against Madison because they "have beheld with immeasurable disgust the principles for which they had contended neutralized. . . . " He then alluded to Federalist-party-inspired slanders against Dolley Madison and her half sister. These implied that during Dolley's down-and-out days in Philadelphia after her father's bankruptcy forced the family to take in boarders, the two Payne girls had provided them the services that a certain kind of house typically provides.

Randolph had broken from Jefferson early in Jefferson's presidency. He was now seeking to widen the gap between them. Randolph claimed Jefferson had betrayed his party's principles. The party was dedicated originally to the idea that the national government should be small, inexpensive and less powerful than the states from whom the power to establish the union was derived. The federal government could do nothing not explicitly stated in the Constitution as an area for national action.

Instead of scrapping the navy as he promised, Jefferson sent it off to fight the North African pirates almost as soon as he took office. He did not make the government smaller. He even kept some of the Federalist appointees in their jobs. And in 1803 he purchased Louisiana from France. Nowhere in the Constitution was anything like the power to do that written.

Randolph tore up the president on these issues, and by 1808 he was ready to try to put his own man into the presidency. After Madison handily defeated his candidate, James Monroe, in that election, Randolph provided in the House of Representatives the kind of continuous opposition to Madison's measures that Smith and his group did in the Senate. Throughout Madison's presidency, Randolph heaped invective on Madison in speeches usually three hours long and loaded with sometimes brilliant but often vile metaphors.

For whatever reason the Monroe presidential bid was made in 1808, the result was that it drove apart for two years two formerly close and mutually understanding colleagues. During the interval Madison not only had to cope with a worsening situation in United States-British relations under the handicap of a lightweight team of foreign policy and defense advisers, he also became bogged down in a project he and Monroe had shared for years—the acquisition of Florida—without his old friend to help him.

Madison and Monroe first became interested in Florida in 1803. They both saw the opportunity to take Florida, arising from the great diplomatic triumph they had helped Jefferson make that year. For the next ten it would be one of their major concerns.

The most important act of Madison's tenure as secretary of state of Jefferson's presidency, and, for that matter, of any other presidency, was the purchase of Louisiana from France in 1803. As one older historian wrote, "The results of the Louisiana purchase were so far reaching as to defy analysis." Jefferson and Madison sent Monroe to Paris to help in the negotiations. The three of them shared in this great enterprise and shared the same vision of what it meant.

The purchase more than doubled the size of the country, adding an area of immensely rich resources and providing almost limitless room for expansion for the tiny new nation. It marked the beginning of the march from sea to shining sea, encouraging the kind of nationalist emotion that that phrase expresses and, more mundanely, made possible the chance to take territory from the collapsing Spanish overseas empire. In less than fifty years, the United States took from Mexico the territory that would become Texas, New Mexico, Arizona, Utah, Nevada, California and half of Colorado.

The opportunity to take Florida, however, was the immediate opportunity the Louisiana Purchase afforded. In fact, that was what Madison mainly had in mind when he urged Jefferson to send Monroe to Paris to reinforce the American minister in negotiating with Napoleon and the tricky Tallyrand. What he wanted was clear claim to New Orleans and a crack at getting Florida.

The familiar story of the Louisiana Purchase is the one that has Napoleon, badly in need of money to renew war in Europe, splashing in his bathtub arguing with his brothers, who opposed the idea of giving up the large territory, last of France's once impressive empire on the North American continent. Louisiana had been named for their greatest king, Louis XIV, and the French people would not stand for its being sold, Napoleon's brothers insisted.

"And you will do well, my dear brother," said Joseph Bonaparte, coming close to Napoleon's bathtub and leaning over, "not to expose your project to parliamentary discussion, for I declare to you that if necessary, I will put myself first at the head of the opposition which will not fail to be made against you."

"You are insolent," Napoleon shouted back. "I ought . . . " he rose halfway out of the tub and stopped.

Instead of continuing, he threw himself back down in the tub, drenching Joseph from head to foot.

Brother Lucien then tried to tell him the act was unconstitutional. No French territory could be ceded to any other power without the consent of the two chambers of the national assembly. The argument became even more heated as Napoleon scoffed at this idea.

"If I were not your brother, I would be your enemy!" Lucien told him.

"My enemy . . . !" Napoleon rose out of the tub. Grabbing his snuffbox, he shouted back, "You, my enemy! I would break you, look, like this box!" And he smashed the box to the floor.

The brothers, of course, were right. The French never forgave Napoleon. When his fortunes on the battlefield waned, resentment over Louisiana gave momentum to Napoleon's slide from the summit of power.

Henry Adams, who, using a manuscript of Lucien Bonaparte, wrote the scene of the Bonaparte brothers in moments of less than brotherly affection, was wrong, however, when he stressed that Jefferson and Madison were totally unprepared for the opportunities for expansion the treaty brought.

Jefferson and Madison fully understood the possibilities. New Orleans, about which negotiations that led to the purchase began, was vital for the livelihood of the growing number of people moving beyond the Appalachian mountains. That everyone appreciated. It was their best outlet to profitable markets. The alternative was to haul their products over the mountains then crossed by only two roads.

Long before he became president, in fact, Jefferson had shown he had broader strategic ideas about American western and southern boundaries. Jefferson hoped to see the new nation rid of the potential threat posed by European-held colonies on the Gulf of Mexico's northern coast. When and how to acquire the territory were the only matters that worried him. In 1790 the Spanish, tired of feeding their garrisons in Florida by depending on an uncertain subsidy from Mexico, threw open their territory to American immigration. Secretary of State Jefferson wrote a jubilant letter to George Washington.

"Governor Quesada, by order of his court, is inviting foreigners to go and settle Florida. This is meant for our people. . . . It will be the means of delivering to us peaceably, what may otherwise cost us a war. In the meantime, we may complain of this seduction of our inhabitants just enough to make [the Spaniard] believe we think it very wise policy for them, and confirm them in it. This is my idea of it."

In these words Jefferson revealed a great deal about himself, and foreshadowed what would be the basis for Madison's covert-action scheme for taking Florida twenty-two years later. Jefferson's approach to diplomacy always allowed for a generous portion of devious maneuver. It is not surprising to see him in this letter suggesting to President Washington that he misled the Spanish as much as possible in order to set up conditions Madison would later try to take advantage of. If enough Americans settled Florida, Jefferson calculated, some way could be found to take advantage of that fact.

Jefferson had not only studied the geography of the Gulf coast and recognized its commercial and strategic significance, he knew his history. He knew that the French and Spanish had traded these areas back and forth and that their boundaries were vague and had become confused in the process. Florida and Louisiana had been pawns in the settlements of European wars.

England was the big winner in the Seven Years War, the world war of the mid-eighteenth century. So in 1763, when it ended, France, the big loser, gave Louisiana to Spain. Spain gave Florida to England.

Spanish Florida had long been two widely separated areas of settlement, one in the east around St. Augustine, the other miles to the west at Pensacola on the Gulf coast. Two garrison centers of Spanish authority were required. Boundaries of the two jurisdictions, however, were indistinct. The British, characteristically, made administrative matters more formal. They created the provinces of East Florida and West Florida, dividing the total territory roughly in half at what is now the southwestern boundary of Georgia. The province of West Florida ran west from that point to the Mississippi River.

Jefferson also knew that until Louisiana was ceded by France to Spain in 1763, the French had governed it as though it extended to the Perdido River, just west of the Spanish settlement of Pensacola. When the purchase of Louisiana was being negotiated, he, Madison and Monroe put this knowledge to good use.

Before Louisiana could be bought from France, of course, France had to get it back from Spain, which Napoleon proceeded to do in 1800 while the United States was preoccupied by its most complicated presidential election. Because the Constitution did not specify that the electoral college was to vote separately for president and vice-president, Aaron Burr, Jefferson's vice-presidential running mate, was able to make sure that he and Jefferson both received the same number of votes and were tied for election as president.

Tradition has it that Napoleon and Tallyrand, certainly two of history's craftiest diplomats, cleverly got Spain to agree to give Louisiana back to France by promising to make the king of Spain's son-in-law head of a small state Napoleon had carved out of divided Italy, catching the Americans off guard. Actually, they were up against three Americans who were not easily outdone at their own game.

Tallyrand was not wrong when he summed up the Americans' attitude towards expansion for his minister to Spain. In fact, he scarcely realized how determined these three Virginia politicians were.

He wrote in his instructions to his minister in Madrid, whom he charged with the task of talking the Spanish king into giving Louisiana back to France, "The Americans mean to rule alone in America. Moreover, their conduct ever since the moment of their independence is enough to prove this truth; the Americans are devoured by pride, ambition and cupidity; the mercantile spirit of the city of London ferments from Charleston to Boston. . . .

"Let the court of Madrid cede these districts [Louisiana and Florida] to France, and from that moment the power of America is bounded by the limit which it may suit the interests of the tranquility of France and Spain to assign her. The French Republic, mistress of these two provinces, will be a wall of brass forever impenetrable to the combined efforts of England and America."

Jefferson, Madison and Monroe were resolved to prevent any wall, brass or otherwise, from blocking the growth of their country.

The King of Spain signed the retrocession treaty, but then he began to worry that Napoleon would welsh on turning the Italian kindom of Tuscany over to his son-in-law. He did not sign the order actually surrendering Louisiana's garrisons to the French for two years. Meanwhile, Jefferson had settled into the presidency and had a chance to work on the situation.

By the time the news of the signing of the order reached Washington, Jefferson had a policy in place to deal with it. He gave orders to shore up Fort Adams, in Mississippi Territory, the closest American garrison to the Louisiana border. He ordered a recruiting drive to provide the needed troops and some to spare, and the purchase of five thousand new muskets and twelve new cannon, and for seven additional companies to be stationed at Fort Adams.

His next move was tinged with the same morality displayed in his and Madison's subsequent diplomacy. He ordered his secretary of war to instruct his Indian agents in Western Mississippi Territory to acquire more land from the Indians. His plan for doing this smoothly was to "establish trading houses among them and encourage their leading men to incur debt beyond their individual means of paying so that they might be induced to cede their lands to pay off their debt."

Things were thrown off track at this point when the top Spanish official in New Orleans closed the port to all foreigners. The president acted quickly. He appointed James Monroe to negotiate with the French and Spanish, and, in a secret accompanying legislative action, had Congress appropriate two million dollars "to defray any expenses which may be incurred in relation to the intercourse between the United States and foreign nations."

Before Monroe arrived in Paris, Napoleon had made up his mind to sell all of Louisiana. Events in Santo Domingo were one compelling reason. The successful slave revolt there, in which a French army and Napoleon's brother-in-law, General LeClerc, were slaughtered, cast a long shadow not only over the French dictator but over all the slaveholding states in America. It lingered on and affected the reaction of the Southern states to the rebellion instigated in Florida in 1811. Newspapers in these southern states like the Georgia *Argus*, Charleston *Courier*, Georgia *Journal*, Louisville, Georgia *Courier* and others continually reminded readers of Santo Domingo and cringed at the threat of slave revolt.

Realizing it would take at least fifty thousand men and more treasure in supplies than he cared to spend, Napoleon also understood Santo Domingo would be ruined by the campaign to win it back. Without Santo Domingo, the money-making sugar island of the new American empire he had in mind when he got Louisiana back from Spain, there was no purpose in keeping that remote area. Louisiana's role in his scheme was to supply Santo Domingo's food needs. No Santo Domingo, no Louisiana, he concluded.

In addition, like Jefferson and Madison, he had some longer range strategic ideas in mind. Selling the United States Louisiana would avert the threat of future wars with them, prevent driving them back into the arms of Great Britain, and help develop them into an ever growing, strong new nation capable of blocking the expansion of England.

By the time Monroe got to his hotel in Paris on Tuesday, April 12, 1803, meetings had already taken place between Tallyrand and Robert Livingston, and the offer had been made. There ensued some maneuvering by the American envoys, as much devoted to trying to see which of them, Livingston or Monroe, would get the most credit for arranging the final deal with the French, as to dealing with Tallyrand.

But vanity did not distract the two men from securing what Jefferson and Madison prized most, a vague clause on the boundaries of Louisiana and West Florida.

Madison made clear in his letter of congratulations to Monroe and Livingston that using the treaty they had just signed as a means of getting Florida was a major concern. There was no question they had made an excellent bargain. For $15 million or, adjusted to modern dollars, $42.9 million they had increased the size of the country more than eight hundred thousand square miles. Skipping lightly over this, Madison closed his letter by asking if the boundary with Florida had been left in doubt.

In two subsequent communications to Monroe and to the American minister in Madrid, William Pinckney, he made even clearer just how he felt about Florida territory and the importance he gave to acquiring it.

In a letter to Pinckney, he informed him that the negotiators in Paris had failed in their original mission, which had been to acquire New Orleans and the Floridas. "The Floridas are not included in the treaty, being, it appears, still held by Spain," he wrote, and he urged Pinckney to get busy discussing their possible purchase from the Spanish government.

On the same day he sent instructions to Monroe. They indicated some disappointment with the outcome of his mission in Paris. "It is thought proper to observe to you," he wrote, "that although Louisiana may, in some respects, be more important than the Floridas, and has more than exhausted the funds alloted for the purchase of the latter, the acquisition of the Floridas is still to be pursued. . . ." He ordered Monroe to get over to Madrid to help Pinckney as he had Livingston.

In the arguments he gave Monroe to use with the Spanish court and the comments he made in explaining them, Madison revealed the philosophy that guided all his subsequent actions in Florida. It would justify in his mind the covert-action operations he was to authorize later. Madison showed he was an early devotee of the *doctrine of manifest destiny*, as it would be labeled some forty years later when it became the slogan for challenging Great Britain over Oregon and fighting Mexico over Texas.

He told Monroe to point out that the cession of Louisiana had separated the Floridas from the rest of Spain's holdings in America. Therefore the Floridas were now of less value to Spain but they were of great value to the United States because of their geography and the rivers in the United States which flowed into the Gulf of Mexico.

It was also in the best interests of Spain to sell the Floridas because they were a drain on her treasury in time of peace and couldn't be defended by Spain in case of war. Failure to sell would be "a source of irritation and ill blood with the United States."

Further, he pointed out that Great Britain had designs against the Floridas and would acquire them sooner or later unless Spain sold them to the United States. Certainly Spain's interests would be better served with the Floridas in American rather than British hands.

"What is it Spain dreads?" Madison said to Monroe. "She dreads . . . the growing power of this country and the direction of it against her possessions within its reach." Not only does this accurately forecast future measures Madison will take, he also brags a little bit: "Can she annihilate this power? No. Can she sensibly retard its growth? No." Therefore she had better sell the Floridas lest she bring upon herself "prematurely the whole Weight of the Calamity which she fears." Above all, he assured Monroe, the Floridas would inevitably be American soil one day "because their position and the *manifest course of events* [italics, mine] guarantee an early and reasonable acquisition of them."

Nevertheless, he forgot about destiny for the moment and ordered Monroe to get on with the negotiations promptly. Madison explained he had obtained some funds for him to work with. "Although the change of circumstances [the acquisition of Louisiana] lessens the anxiety for acquiring immediately a territory which now, more certainly than ever, must drop into our hands, and notwithstanding the pressure of the bargain with France on our treasury, yet, for the sake of a peaceable and fair completion of a great object, you are permitted by the President, in case a less sum will not be accepted, to give two million and a quarter of dollars" to close the deal.

Spain spurned the offer. Madison then turned to other measures to bring true his prediction that the Floridas "must drop into our hands." For two years he continued to press without success the claim with Spain that Louisiana extended east until it nearly reached Pensacola. Frustration mounted. Finally he and Jefferson tried an end run around Spain and around Congress.

"The conduct of France and the part she may take in the misunderstanding between the United States and Spain are too important to be unconsidered," Jefferson wrote in his message to the opening of Congress in December 1805:

> At the date of our last advices from Paris . . . we have reason to believe that she was disposed to effect a settlement on a plan analogous to what our Ministers had proposed (to Spain) and so comprehensive as to remove, as far as possible, the grounds for future collision and controversy on the eastern as well as western side of the Mississippi. The present crisis in Europe is favorable for our pressing such a settlement and not a moment should be lost in availing ourselves of it.

What Jefferson and Madison had in mind was bribing France to pressure Spain into settling the Florida question on their terms. They went about the matter with characteristic finesse.

In his message the president sought funds for negotiations without being specific as to exactly what they were to be or to whom the money was to be paid or for what. He did not want to say that the funds would be used to purchase West Florida since he and Madison had been claiming since 1803 that the United States had already bought it when they bought Louisiana. He did not want to tell Congress in his State of the Union message that he and his secretary of state estimated they would need $5 million at least, and that half of that, they figured, would be the amount required to bribe Napoleon and Tallyrand.

Instead, he allowed a few of his most loyal leaders in the House of Representatives in on the scheme and they proposed two resolutions. One permitted his diplomats to offer to trade some of the vast western part of Louisiana for West Florida, or, as it was more delicately put: "Resolved, That an exchange of territory between the United States and Spain is deemed, by this House, to be the most advantageous mode of settlement . . . and that any arrangement . . . which shall secure to Spain an ample barrier on the side of Mexico, and to the United States the countries watered by the Mississippi, and to the eastward of it, will meet the approbation of this House."

The other resolution read: "Be it enacted, etc., that a sum of two million dollars is hereby appropriated towards defraying any extraordinary expenses which may be incurred in the intercourse between the United States and foreign nations." That was the bribe money.

John Randolph smelled a rat and found it lurking in the files of the State Department.

The administration had already received word from Paris that France would not consider pressuring Spain into any deal with the United States. Madison and Jefferson did not want to believe this, so they went ahead with their plan as though the information did not exist.

Randolph demanded the debate on the presidentially inspired confidential resolutions be made public. He wanted the public to know so that they might "acquire some principles by which to appreciate the conduct of members of this House." By making the matter public, people would see which members of Congress, by passing the resolutions, "would be willing to take the responsibility which properly belonged to another department of the Government; and to do all the dirty work which would otherwise have soiled their fingers." He correctly identified and chastised the secretary of state as the master of the department of dirty tricks.

Randolph's motion was defeated. And the resolutions passed.

The reports from Paris were accurate, however. Napoleon refused to go along with the plan, although Madison's minister kept doggedly at his assigned task. No progress was made on boundaries and the long-standing claims for damages at New Orleans were still pending. Madison and Jefferson became more and more frustrated and were ready to consider war against Spain.

At the end of August 1807, Jefferson wrote Madison, "While war with England is probable, every thing leading to it with any other country should be avoided, except with Spain. As to her, I think it is the precise moment when we should declare to the French government that we instantly seize on the Floridas as reprisal for the spoilation denied us, and that if by a given day they are paid to us we will restore all East of the Perdido [East Florida] and hold the rest [West Florida]." He suggested the matter be taken up at the next cabinet meeting.

Within two months, however, the war in Europe took a turn that was a deciding influence on the course he and Madison took. They had, of course, not been wrong in estimating the importance of using France to help them achieve their goal of acquiring the Floridas. Napoleon had been de facto ruler of Spain since 1795. In October 1807, Napoleon decided to take one step further. He got the weak Spanish king, Charles IV, to let him move troops across Spain and conquer Portugal. He did not stop there. French troops continued to pour over the Pyrenees and possess the entire Iberian peninsula.

In Spain the people blamed the feeble old king and his favorite minister, the vain adventurer Godoy, for the invasion. And in the recriminations that followed at the court, Crown Prince Ferdinand took up the popular cause. Riots broke out. When the news reached the Spanish colonies in America, a good many people saw opportunities for advancement. In all of them, mixed marriages between Spaniards and Indian princesses that began when Cortes was given Malinche, daughter of an Aztec vassal, had produced a special class condemned to perpetual middle-management status. Not all were descendants of *conquistadores* and Aztec nobles, and some rose to top management, but all *criollos* were jealous of the ruling class who came over from Madrid to run colonial churches, army and government.

March 17, 1808, the old Spanish king abdicated in favor of his heir. On the pretext of mediation, Napoleon got his hands on both Charles IV and Ferdinand VII. Charles was given a pension and Ferdinand made prisoner at Tallyrand's chateau. Napoleon put his brother Joseph on the Spanish throne. The *criollos* then began rebellions with the perfect excuse that they opposed the Bonaparte usurper and supported martyred Ferdinand.

Jefferson and Madison rethought their policy.

By summer 1808 the Spanish newspaper in New Orleans was claiming the United States was collaborating with Napoleon, because the American trade embargo against Europe, declared the year before by Jefferson to try to keep the United States out of the war there, weakened the Spanish colonies' resistance to Napoleon by ruining their trade.

William C. C. Claiborne, a shrewd Jefferson protégé who had been moved from governor of Mississippi to New Orleans by the president, wrote Washington about this and asked for advice. The reply he got set policy for Florida from that point on: "The truth is that the Patriots of Spain have no warmer friends than the Administration of the United States," replied the president.

> If they suceed we shall be well satisfied to see Cuba and Mexico remain in their present dependence but very unwilling to see them in that of either France or England, politically or commercially. We consider their interests and ours as the same, and that the object of both must be to exclude all European influence from this hemisphere. . . .

The true meaning of these tranquillizing words was not lost on Claiborne. He told the Spanish vice-consul in New Orleans that the president had instructed him to say that the United States was not collaborating with the Bonapartes, wanted the Spanish Americans to win, would assist them in any way possible—therefore they should not even consider asking the British for any help—and would be glad to receive an envoy from them in Washington to discuss the matter further.

Men as shrewd as Claiborne from that point on were equally adept at expanding on this policy statement. If the *criollos* of varying degrees of Spanish blood could contrive their independence from Spanish authority on the ground of patriotism, others with no Spanish blood at all could do the same.

With this rationale, James Madison moved from the diplomacy of secret bribes to covert action to achieve his goal of acquiring Florida.

CHAPTER III
HOW WEST FLORIDA WAS WON

The operational climate in West Florida, as twentieth-century intelligence officers would put it, was highly favorable for covert political-action operations. People who either would stand still for or actively support such a move by the United States were steadily growing in number. The area was already seething with plots, making it difficult for the legitimate authorities to concentrate their retaliatory efforts. The legitimate authorities, moreover, lacked the muscle to crush the subversion quickly and efficiently. And they lacked the leadership to do so effectively. The agent pool the American operation had to draw on to pull off the coup d'etat was large and full of able, fast-footed operators. They were so fast footed, they usually were some steps ahead of their official case officers.

Every year more and more Americans came down the rivers whose headwaters rose in their own territory and emptied into the Gulf of Mexico in land belonging to Spain. In the same way they had overwhelmed New Orleans at the mouth of the Mississippi, they were coming down the Biloxi and Pascagoula Rivers. Their barges floated down the Alabama and Tombigbee, flowing into the Mobile River, and sailed down the Mobile to the gulf.

In August 1809 Vicente Folch, the governor of West Florida, wrote to his captain general in Cuba saying that between two and three thousand boats annually descended down the Mississippi into the westernmost part of his domain, where they sold their produce and their barges. Each boat was manned by four persons, which meant a reverse current of six thousand men returning overland through Baton Rouge. He could keep them out, he said, only by erecting two new powerful military posts on the Nictalbany and Chifonte rivers that flowed into Lake Pontchartrain north of New Orleans. Another tide of these undesirables passed through Mobile and even Pensacola. If he attempted to force them back, he would only cause them to combine in armed bands with Indian recruits. If a single Indian were killed, a war with the savages would result. Given the on-duty strength of his military forces, he concluded, it was better to alllow them the free use of West Florida. This was one of the inconveniences brought upon the Spanish administration by the cession of Louisiana.

In addition to the invasion by these boat people, many of whom were at least were transients, years earlier the Spanish had actually welcomed settlement by Americans. In 1789 and 1790 Governor Esteban Miro instituted a policy of offering generous land grants permitting colonists to bring in personal goods duty free, and even permitting them to practice their heretical Protestant religion. He hoped to attract people of substance and, with them, to erect a barrier against future illegal immigration. At the same time the governor of East Florida adopted a similar policy—in his case, in an effort to bring in some people who would raise food for his garrison in Saint Augustine.

So by the time James Madison began to contemplate covert action, he had a substantial agent pool in place in the territory he planned to subvert.

On January 9, 1809, not quite two months before he took office as president, Madison had received a letter from John Adair. Adair had been a senator from Kentucky but was forced to resign his seat because of his connection with Aaron Burr in Burr's scheming in the area four years earlier. He was, therefore, a source somewhat biased in favor of adventurous activity in West Florida. Making allowance for this, his conclusions still may be accepted because he knew the territory so well. According to Adair, five-sixths of the wealth and population of West Florida were located in the District of Baton Rouge between the Pearl River, the river that subsequently became the boundary between the states of Mississippi and Louisiana, and the Mississippi River. And nine-tenths of the people there were Americans. The Spanish garrison, home based in Pensacola, consisted of between three hundred and four hundred men without adequate clothing, rations, money or credit. The people of West Florida, he said, "were as ripe fruit waiting the hand that dares to pluck them."

Adair certainly described the Spanish garrison correctly. Both Floridas were outposts of the empire Spain had established in the New World in the sixteenth century, an empire of which Mexico long had been the heart. By 1809, however, the fortunes of that country were in decline and the first stirrings of the "patriotic rebellion" against Spanish authority would break out in another year. The subsidies which provided the funds for the Florida frontier posts were levied on Mexico. They were never paid promptly even in the best of times. The condition of the troops available to defend West and East Florida in 1809 was only relatively worse than usual when Adair described them.

The colonial Spanish army also had some structural weaknesses. The officers were mostly *criollos* or foreign-born adventurers for whom the army offered a chance for social advancement. The brightest and best of them achieved it. But top rank in the Spanish army was reserved for sons of nobles, the *peninsulares*—men from the Iberian peninsula. Becoming governor in a far-off frontier post like East or West Florida was as high as many of the *criollos* got. Not great jobs, but titles and honors went with them that meant equal status with *peninsulares*.

Enlisted men and noncommissioned offers were recruited from the lowest classes of Spanish society and from derelicts and drifters, mostly Mexicans, Cubans, Italians and Germans. A deep chasm separated them from their officers. However, while the *criollo* officers were motivated by the honors and social standing they could achieve, the enlisted men were in the army in order to have something to eat. They competently performed what they had to do for that privilege. Those who found themselves in West Florida, however, did not have much to work with. Not only was food scarce and clothing, too, but they had a difficult senior commander.

Vicente Folch was not a *criollo*. He had been born near Barcelona in the Catalonian province of Tarragona, March 8, 1754. His parents were provincial nobles and he bore a fine Catalonian name. He was every inch a *penisular*. He studied mathematics and engineering at the military academy in Barcelona and in 1771 entered the army as a sublieutenant and was appointed to practice as an engineer. After serving in Africa and participating in the siege of Gibraltar he sailed for colonial service in America in 1780. In 1784 he married the daughter of a successful Havana merchant, and in 1787 he was stationed near the mouth of the Mississippi. That same year the governor-general of Louisiana, which was then still Spanish territory, secured his appointment as commandant at Mobile. The governor-general was his uncle. So began Folch's long years of Florida service, leading to his becoming governor of all West Florida.

Folch was proud and stubborn and always conscious of his prestige. He disliked *criollos* and foreign-born officers. He had some good reason to distrust the latter.

The year after he arrived at Mobile, he wrote his important uncle a sad letter. Perhaps because the governor-general was who he was, the letter appears in official files: "When I returned from a trip which I took at the end of May, one of my Negros told me the following story: My master, although I am a slave, I cannot allow what is being done to you; while you have been away, Señor Rigolen has gone to bed every night with my mistress. . . ."

After making inquiries which satisfied him that the slave was on to something, Folch worked out an elaborate plan to trap the bedmates. He faked another trip, taking along his storekeeper armed with the necessary equipment to effect a successful entrapment, such as a ladder for climbing back over the stockade in the dead of night. And "using the countersign which had been arranged so that we could be recognized," he was able to surprise the pair.

He brought the faithful storekeeper and additional witnesses into the bedroom. "Hearing the breathing of the two culprits, they understood the case exactly."

Then he brooded over the fate of military men whose situation far from any available "mother-in-law, sister-in-law or aunt" to watch over her virtue "leaves his wife in great danger because the vile seducers always attack the most defenseless." His wife told him she had not been seduced, however, but *forzada*, "forced." "Of which she tries to give strong proof," he noted. Meanwhile he kept her in jail and petitioned his uncle to expel the foreigner, a Frenchman, from the domains of Spain forever.

After that he never got along well with his subordinates. But he did fancy himself a diplomat, and, indeed, he proved to be a good one. Aware of his weak situation and the poor condition of his command as well as the problem of the swarming Americans, Governor Folch traveled to New Orleans in April 1809 to talk with his American counterpart, Governor Claiborne. He was on a diplomatic fishing trip, testing some bait.

Folch told Claiborne that the Spanish American territories would continue allegiance to Spain as long as the followers of King Ferdinand VII continued to resist Joseph Bonaparte successfully. Upon the capitulation of these Spanish patriots, however, Folch said the American colonies would refuse to submit to France and the independence of Mexico and Cuba would be declared immediately thereafter. The Spanish American territories would thereupon seek assistance from Great Britain and the United States in order to gain their independence and sustain it. Ties with the United States would be preferred to ties with Britain, however. Also, it had been decided that the Floridas should be ceded to the United States when the final crisis of the fight for independence occurred. The Floridas, Folch added, were by nature detached from the rest of Spanish American provinces and "must therefore from the course of things fall very soon into the possession of the United States."

Claiborne took the bait. When he reported this conversation to President Madison, he said he had assured Folch that the United States "would be well satisfied that Mexico and Cuba should remain part of the Spanish dominions" if Spain successfully fought off France. It would, however, "be cause of great regret to see those colonies fall politically or commercially into the hands of either England or France," and that "it was certainly interesting to the United States that all European influence (and more particularly as regards England and France) should be banished from the continent of America."

Claiborne realized that what Folch was saying was exactly what Jefferson had told him the year before was United States policy on the subject of Spain's American territories. Then Claiborne had gone beyond the words of the president's policy statement when he told the Spanish vice-consul in New Orleans the United States would support the Spanish colonies' rebellion. When he heard Folch spouting American doctrine on hemisphere relations, he didn't have to.

The following month, Folch was back in New Orleans spreading the same word. In a letter dated May 9, 1809, Claiborne told the president that the Spanish governor had been in town for ten days preaching the president's favorite line on Latin America. This time Folch did not confine himself to private diplomatic conversation. He went around the city to dinners and luncheons and told all he met "his wishes for the independence of Spanish America" because, he claimed, he had word that Spain had capitulated to France and the hour to act was at hand.

Folch was playing a game with the Americans that spring. Claiborne had described him years before, when they first met, as a man of "more temper than discretion, more genius than judgement." Folch was using excellent judgment for anyone in his position, although he certainly was not being discreet. He was playing from weakness. He had no big cards. There is no evidence, however, that he knew in the early months of 1809 just how weak his hand was.

He would soon find out.

The small, ill-furnished garrisons of Florida supplemented their strength by forming a militia from among the residents. Its value was dubious. The militia furnished its own equipment and supplies, and drilled infrequently. It was officered by leading citizens, merchants and planters. They enjoyed the honor their commissions conferred and in East Florida seemed interested in little else about their military role. Folch certainly knew they were not to be relied upon in West Florida either. Less than a year after he went about New Orleans talking up Spanish American independence, he would learn that militia officers could be not simply unreliable, but treacherous.

On April 20, 1810, Samuel Fulton wrote a letter to President Madison. Samuel Fulton was the adjutant general of the West Florida militia. He had been in the area for years, first in the service of the French, then as an aide to Governor Claiborne in the early years of Claiborne's administration, then as a landowner in the Baton Rouge district where he was now one of the top officers in the Spanish West Florida militia.

In his letter to President Madison, Fulton said that Spain would have to yield and remain under the yoke of the Bonapartes and that this would necessitate some changes in Florida. If the American government wished to take possession of the territory, he might be able to render it effective assistance and he would be glad to do so.

This was sedition if not treason to his Spanish superior, Governor Folch. When Madison decided it was time to act, Folch would quickly discover there were many more men like Fulton—officers of Folch's militia ready to help separate him from his province.

The same month Fulton wrote to Madison offering his services to subvert Spanish West Florida, Madison summoned Claiborne to Washington to talk over the situation and decide what to do about West Florida.

Direct invasion of the Floridas by United States forces was clearly the quickest way of gaining control of the territory, but this would raise serious diplomatic and domestic political problems. Claiborne and Madison agreed a more prudent course would be to take up the banner being waved by Spanish Americans in Venezuela and elsewhere and start a similar "patriotic movement" in Florida. There were plenty of Americans living in West Florida and East Florida who were willing to call for such action. One was Samuel Fulton. Claiborne had talked to others before leaving for Washington. Encouraged by this knowledge, Madison and Claiborne made a plan.

According to the scenario Madison and Claiborne developed, after declaring their independence from Spanish authorities Florida "patriots" would request support and assistance from the United States, just as Folch had suggested the Mexicans and Cubans should do, and then invite the United States to take possession of their territory.

Under Madison's direction Claiborne drafted a letter on June 14, 1810, outlining the operation and assigning the mission to William Wykoff, one of the men he had talked to before the conference in Washington. Wykoff was a member of the Executive Council of New Orleans Territory, a colonel in the territorial militia, a local judge and a farmer.

As in any covert-operational plan, the letter first set forth the reasons for taking action. Spain had succumbed to France, the letter stated, and Venezuela had already taken steps to gain independence and would soon be followed by other Spanish American colonies. The United States, however, could not tolerate Florida's becoming independent because the United States already claimed that territory.

"You know that under the Louisiana Convention we claim as far eastward as the Perdido," Claiborne wrote. "The claim never was, and never will, I trust, be abandoned. But I am persuaded under present circumstances it would be more pleasing that the taking possession of the country be preceeded by a request from the inhabitants. Can no means be devised to obtain such request?"

He cautioned Wykoff to be alert to the threat that other local factions, the pro-French, the pro-British, the truly loyal adherents of Ferdinand VII, posed for the operation. He urged Wykoff to have the agents of the Americans "silence the other factions."

He also advised Wykoff to explain to his operators not to get any big ideas. Claiborne told Wykoff to make plain to them that "to form themselves an independent Government is out of the question! Waving other considerations, the paucity of their numbers, their insular situation and circumscribed limits forbid the idea; a connection with France is opposed by all honest prejudices and would be attended with ruin, and as to the protection of Great Britain it could not fail to prove them a curse, for during the contest with the United States, which in that case must ensue, Florida would be the seat of war, and its entire conquest could not be protracted beyond a few months."

He then turned to operational details. Wykoff was to contact the gentlemen the two of them had discussed in their earlier conversation about the possibility of mounting the operation. Wykoff was to recommend to them they take some specific measure that would give their invitation to the United States to intervene a semblance of a popular and democratic request. He told Wykoff to be willing to accept whatever these men thought was the best approach and cover they could devise. He had, however, a best-case example in mind.

"Were it done, through the medium of a convention of delegates, named by the people," Claiborne wrote, "it would be more satisfactory."

"In the event that a convention is called," he went on, "it is important that every part of the District as far east as the Perdido be represented, and therefore I feel felicitous, that you should be at some pains to prepare for the occasion the minds of the more influential characters in the vicinity of Mobile. Whether this can be done, by yourself in person or by some citizen of Baton Rouge of *your confidence*, is left to your discretion."

Wykoff was reminded that the operation was confidential, his channel of communication with Claiborne was to be through the secretary of state and operational expenses would be reimbursed.

Claiborne's concern that Wykoff might have some trouble getting the operation off the ground or that the operators might need to be motivated and would have to be convinced to adopt the device of a popular convention as cover for their plot was needless worry. The men Wykoff and Claiborne had talked about as possible recruits had the operation in motion before Claiborne got back to his post.

The leading American planters in the Bayou Sara region, the western part of the District of Baton Rouge bordering the Mississippi River, went into action in May 1810, a month before the governor wrote the Wykoff instruction. They knew that Folch was absent in Havana, and they thought they had a weak opponent in Carlos De Lassus, head Spanish official in the district. They also had a few specific complaints about taxes, exorbitant fees and even higher bribery charges made by De Lassus's local subordinates, and they felt the local military commandant was slipshod. These grievances they could use to demand a public meeting and to propose a committee of public safety. This was the embryo from which Claiborne's convention idea could grow to full life size.

At the same time another political storm was battering De Lassus in Baton Rouge. Two Frenchmen from New Orleans began to hold nightly assemblies among the French settlers in the community under pretext of helping them defend themselves against alleged plots of the Spanish authorities against them. And De Lassus was also informed that additional French emissaries had arrived in New Orleans to raise a revolt in West Florida to capture Baton Rouge and Pensacola. These threats he considered more serious than the situation in Bayou Sara. When his beleaguered military commandant there wrote him that an anonymous petition calling for a popular assembly was circulating in his area, De Lassus decided to send him two Americans he trusted, Philip Hickey and George Mather, to suggest that the commandant call people together and let the trusted Americans read them a report about the danger the French posed for all of them in all the Baton Rouge District.

De Lassus's course of action was doubly unwise. It supported the popular meeting idea, whose proposers actually were planning subversion, and one of the Americans he chose for the mission, Philip Hickey, was one of the conspirators; he had written the anonymous petition calling for assembly.

In any case, with the same gun-jumping reflex that characterized the entire West Florida operation, before Hickey and Mather got to Bayou Sara a group of leading American militia officers had already talked the Spanish commandant into having the meeting.

Within weeks another meeting had taken place which elected four representatives to a proposed convention of all six subdistricts of the District of Baton Rouge. On July 6, 1810, the people of the city of Baton Rouge met to add their representatives to those already chosen. Among the names found in the report of this meeting are some familiar ones—Samuel Fulton, George Mather and Philip Hickey.

Not only were the conspirators who ran the operation which created the Baton Rouge Convention of 1810 fast movers, they were astute manipulators. The job of slipping West Florida out of Spanish hands that James Madison wanted done was accomplished with a few swift, adroit twists of the knife in Carlos De Lassus's back.

First they trapped him into concurring with their call for a convention to meet on July 25, 1810, by a clever paper which firmly supported him and his administration, listing the business of the meeting merely as a simple review of grievances to be mutually settled. When they met, they quickly showed their hand, and a generous portion of gall, after first ceremoniously swearing their allegiance to Ferdinand VII.

They complained, for example, that the legal system was defective because it used the Spanish language, which the majority of inhabitants did not understand. They criticized the defenses of the community, insisting that a larger militia was needed to protect the citizens from foreigners, deserters, refugees and French exiles. And when they came to making specific proposals of what was to be done about these grievances, they boldly proposed what amounted to a takeover of the government of the district by the convention.

Since the convention "had been created by the whole body of the government of Baton Rouge, and by the previous consent of the Governor," they declared the convention was therefore "legally consitituted to act in all cases of national concern which relate to this province" and to establish the judicial system to raise revenue for all necessary governmental functions, including paying the governor's salary. Not to leave anything out, the convention authorized itself to define its own powers regarding anything not covered. The convention also decided when and where it would meet again.

De Lassus recognized what was being proposed was the complete overthrow of traditional Spanish authority. He was an officer of a royal government. Admittedly the question of who was the rightful royal ruler was up in the air at the moment, but authority in Spain did not come from popular assemblies or conventions.

His answer was as disingenuous as their demands. He told them he had been happy to approve their meeting as the faithful vassals of Ferdinand VII which their oath of allegiance adjudged them to be. He appreciated their offer to share with him any responsibility for necessary changes in the administration, but as chief executive he alone was responsible under Spanish law, so he could not approve their generous offer. As for the ill-concealed bribe, he could not accept the compensation they mentioned, his salary from the royal treasury being sufficient for his needs.

But De Lassus knew his position was weak. He had a garrison insufficient to defend the fort at Baton Rouge, and the fort itself was almost completely broken down. He had absolutely nothing with which to undertake repairs. Storehouses were empty, the government owed its employees and contractors, and his treasury was bare. He actually could well have used the salary the convention offered. Under the circumstances, a well-worded letter was all he could come up with. He had to permit the convention to meet again.

The convention reconvened on August 13. The members did not like De Lassus's letter and became bolder still. They demanded that the governor arm the entire militia and place it under the convention's command without consulting his superiors, thereby promoting "public security and good administration of justice." They proposed for these purposes a plan under which the convention was to determine the size, organization and rules of conduct of the militia and appoint its superior officers. The convention also would appoint civil commandants for all the subdistricts of the District of Baton Rouge, establish a high court having final jurisdiction in all civil and criminal matters, appoint a land officer to grant titles to land to all who had not received them from Spanish authority and establish a tax system, appoint the collector and reserve for itself the final decision on the disbursement of all funds.

This was just short of a declaration of war. And the leaders of the convention were careful to report what they had done to the United States government through a channel Madison had provided, making clear that they were ready to ask for assistance, which they hoped would be swiftly forthcoming.

The channel of communications from the convention to the president was Governor Holmes of the Mississippi Territory. A few weeks after Madison had cleared Claiborne's instruction to Colonel Wykoff, he asked Secretary of State Robert Smith, "Will it not be advisable to appraise Governor Holmes confidentially of the course adopted in West Florida and to have his cooperation in diffusing the impressions we wish to be made there?" Smith wrote Holmes suggesting he "keep a wakeful eye" on events south of his border in West Florida.

Smith informed Holmes that he was being given the special mission of "proceeding without delay into East Florida and West Florida for the purpose of diffusing the impression that the United States cherish the sincerest good will towards the people of the Floridas as neighbors . . . and that in the event of political separation from the parent country, their incorporation into our Union would coincide with the sentiments and policy of the United States."

He was to report all intelligence he could on the political factions in Florida and he was instructed to keep his militia ready "for any service it may be called for." Later Madison sent off to Holmes a copy of the Claiborne instruction to Wykoff just to make sure Holmes got the point.

The rapid-fire action of the Florida conspirators made it unnecessary for Holmes to take a trip to Florida to diffuse any impressions, but he took his intelligence-collection assignment seriously. He sent his own man to cover the second session of the convention that took place in August. He had received a good report on the first meeting, on the basis of which he had informed the president that his appraisal was that the convention members were ready to take the next steps the operation called for—a declaration of independence and a call for United States intervention. He was ready for the feelers the August session put out.

Much to the surprise of the conspirators of the convention and to Holmes, De Lassus ducked the open challenge to his authority and agreed to meet convention representatives to discuss the plan of government they proposed. He was stalling for time while he asked Governor Folch, now back from Havana, to send him troops. Holmes reported to Madison that the agreement would not last.

The convention representatives chosen to discuss the convention's proposals with De Lassus intercepted the letter meant for Folch. Declaring themselves betrayed, they ordered their friends in the militia to take the fort of Baton Rouge.

On September 23, 1810, they did. They had no trouble accomplishing this military feat. The fort was a farce. There were large gaps in the stockade which constituted the fort's main defense. As there was no outer ditch, attack was possible from any direction. There were twenty cannons, or apparent cannons, defending the fort. Some of them were painted logs. Most of the real cannons were unloaded except when they were used for ceremonial salutes. There was not enough powder available to keep them ready for full service.

Shouting "Hurrah, Washington" and demanding that the few defenders lay down their arms, eighty rebels streamed through the undefended gate and numerous gaps in the stockade at two o'clock in the morning. One Spanish officer and one soldier were killed, and the action was over.

The attack succeeded so quickly that De Lassus was not even able to get from his house to the fort before it fell. He was about a block away when the attack began. Several parties of rebel horsemen met him before he could go any farther and captured him.

Governor Holmes was not greatly surprised when on September 24 he was given the report that indicated an immediate rupture between the convention and De Lassus was about to occur. Among the papers with the report was probably the order to attack the fort.

At midnight on the twenty-fifth, he got the news that the fort had been taken and that the convention forces of some 250 men were preserving order there. Accompanying this report was a signed petition asking that an American military patrol be sent to help.

Another report of the capture and another request for a patrol followed. This one touched on a familiar theme that would be heard again later in East Florida. The report expressed the fear that the Spaniards would stir up a slave revolt and that the blacks might not only rampage through West Florida but spread their terror into Holmes's home territory, Mississippi, and cause a "Santo Domingo" there. It would be years before American slaveholders forgot what Toussant L'Ouverture had done to the French.

Following this double appeal, Holmes ordered the colonel commanding American forces in his territory to employ one or more companies of regular troops to protect American interests on the border. Holmes needed no further urging to provide military assistance. He had been told to be ready and he was.

Meanwhile the convention reconvened again as soon as the attack succeeded and, after three days' deliberation, issued a declaration of independence for West Florida and shipped copies of it off to Governor Holmes and Governor Claiborne. The declaration was accompanied by a note which complied with the next step called for in the president's operational plan.

"We, the Delegates of the People of this State, have the honor to enclose you an official copy of their Act of Independence . . ." the note read, "with the expression of their most confident and most ardent hope that it may accord with the policy of the Govt., as it does with the safety and happiness of the People of the United States to take the present Govt. and People of this State under their immediate and special protection as an integral and inalienable portion of the United States."

On October 3 Holmes transmitted this note to the State Department. He also enclosed a copy of the Declaration of Independence the convention had written and a letter from its president. In his covering letter Holmes added the sort of comment successful operators cannot resist making. He noted "through this application [for admission to the United States] the views of our government have been in great measure realized."

Madison was pleased and agreed with Holmes's assessment. As soon as he had the word, he took the final step the plan called for. On October 27, 1810, he issued a proclamation authorizing Governor Claiborne to take possession of West Florida and govern it as part of the New Orleans Territory.

> Now be it known that I, James Madison, President of the U.S. of America, in pursuance of these weighty and urgent considerations, have deemed it right and requisite that possession should be taken of the said territory in the name and on behalf of the United States. William C. Claiborne, Governor of the Orleans Territory, of which the said territory is to be taken as part, will accordingly proceed to execute the same, and to exercise over the said Territory the authorities and functions legally appertaining to his office. And the good people inhabiting the same are invited and enjoined to pay dire respect to him in that character, to be obedient to the laws, to maintain order, to cherish harmony, and in every manner to conduct themselves as peaceable citizens, under full assurance that they will be protected in the enjoyment of their liberty, property, and religion.

The proclamation had scarcely been made public when the French minister to the United States, General Louis Turreau, was knocking on the State Department's door. Turreau had arrived in the United States six years earlier with instructions from Tallyrand to curb American pretensions to West Florida. Tallyrand reminded him that nowhere in the document had France ceded West Florida to the United States in the Louisiana Purchase agreement. Turreau had told Madison when Madison was secretary of state that France considered American claims to West Florida totally false. Now, in 1810, the French minister's intelligence had informed him that the Americans had inspired the revolt in Baton Rouge and he demanded an explanation.

Turreau was granted an interview by Secretary of State Robert Smith on October 31, four days after the proclamation had been written. "I swear, General," Smith declared, "on my honor as a gentlemen not only that we are strangers to everything that has happened, but even that the Americans who have appeared there either as agents or leaders are enemies of the Executive, and act in this sense against the Federal Government as well as against Spain."

Before the meeting, Madison had moved to cover his secretary of state's bold lie. Whether the idea came to him during a daily laudanum fix or whether it was born out of years of pushing the phony claim to Florida is impossible to determine, but the president doctored the record. He knew that official papers were routinely published in the press, in *Niles's Weekly Register* and elsewhere. So he withheld the enclosures Governor Hodge had sent along with his October 3 letter.

Over fifty years ago a historian studying the manuscripts of correspondence in State Department files discovered that Madison submitted the Declaration of Independence and the other communications from the Baton Rouge Convention as attachments to a follow-up letter Holmes sent on October 17 that did not arrive at the State Department until early November. And that is the way they were printed in the official American state papers to which the press of his day and posterity would have ready access. Secretary of State Smith's "honor as a gentleman" was safe.

Madison was not only busy establishing the ground for the use of the technique of plausible presidential denial in October 1810, he was acting to push the success in Baton Rouge as far as he could. The instructions he had the secretary of state send to Governor Claiborne to govern the latter's occupation of the new territory made clear that what he was proclaiming to belong to the United States was the entire province of West Florida to the doorstep of Governor Folch in Pensacola.

Governor Holmes might declare that "the views of our government have been in great measure realized" and Madison might proclaim all of West Florida to be United States territory, but both knew that such was not the case. A group of bold operators had seized the District of Baton Rouge; the rest of West Florida had not been won.

East of Baton Rouge Governor Folch still held sway, although his position was precarious. Some of the Baton Rouge Convention conspirators had their eyes on Mobile and were mounting filibustering expeditions to add it to the area under the convention's control. And when Governor Claiborne had moved troops into Baton Rouge, in accordance with the instructions the secretary of war sent him implementing Madison's proclamation, he officially turned his attention to Mobile and Pensacola. The fall months of 1810 were filled with political, paramilitary, diplomatic and intelligence activities as various individuals visited Mobile and the area surrounding it.

Among the persons who passed that way was a short old man who spoke with an Irish brogue so thick it was difficult to understand and who insisted on wearing one of the three-cornered hats that everyone wore when George Washington was president. Now thirty years later they were out of style in the eastern-seaboard cities and particularly out of place on the frontier. He was another special presidential agent. His assignment was to report on the political climate of the area, the strength of the Spanish government in West Florida and to give an assessment of the chances that East Florida might be as ready for a coup d'etat as West Florida so evidently was. He was also supposed to try his hand at diplomacy. He was to find out Governor Folch's reaction to the suggestion that the United States annex East as well as West Florida.

The man in the three-cornered hat was General George Mathews of Georgia. His West Florida mission to Pensacola and Mobile in 1810 grew into an even more delicate trust. He became the case officer of the operation to subvert East Florida.

CHAPTER IV

A YAZOO MAN

On the same day, June 20, 1810, that the secretary of state wrote Governor Holmes about keeping a "watchful eye" on things in West Florida, he wrote another letter. This letter was addressed to William H. Crawford, the senior senator from Georgia.

He enclosed a copy of the letter he had written Holmes outlining United States policy towards the Floridas and he informed Crawford that the president had instructed William Wykoff and Holmes to incite and encourage rebellion against the Spanish authorities there. Then the secretary told Crawford the president wanted his help in selecting yet another special agent to help carry out the same mission in East and West Florida.

"The enclosed letter of instructions [to Governor Holmes] will afford you a view of the policy of the President in relation to the Floridas," Secretary Smith wrote. "It is his wish to have the advantage of your cooperation so far at least as in selecting a gentleman of honour and discretion qualified to execute a trust of such interest and delicacy."

The president and Smith were in a hurry. The letter went on to say that since it would take a great amount of time if, before getting down to business in Florida, the Senator's selection for the job had to go through the normal process of being named a special presidential agent he was sending along the official forms already presigned by the president making the appointment legal. These documents left blank a space for the special-agent's name and another for the amount of compensation to be paid him. The president, said Smith, "reposed the fullest confidence" in Crawford and requested he fill in the blanks according to his best judgment.

William Crawford, the man in whom the president reposed so much confidence, is another now nearly forgotten, one-time giant American political figure. But if anyone had asked who in 1824 the most likely nominee of the Jefferson-Madison party was to be, and therefore surely the next president, politically wise Americans would have said William Crawford. By then Crawford controlled the congressional caucus of his party, and up until that time this caucus was the major mover in naming the party's presidential choice. Madison and his successor, James Monroe, both had gotten the nod that way. Unfortunately Crawford suffered a disabling stroke before the campaign got under way and never had a chance.

But in 1810 he was well on the way to building his strong political position. He was Madison's main lieutenant in the United States Senate. His qualifications for choosing a special agent for the mission the president had in mind were not based on his political skill, however, but on his understanding of the subject. Crawford was a rural Georgian, and rural Georgians had a special feel for the physical and human geography involved. There were only one hundred thousand white people counted in the census of 1810 in all of the state, and most of them lived in the coastal areas. Only a small band of determined people had settled the interior and pushed on westward.

Like most of these Georgians, William Crawford had been born in Virginia, in Amherst County, in 1772. Also like most of them he was descended from Scotsmen, in his case from John, the Earl of Crawford, who had emigrated to Virginia in 1643. Crawford's family moved to thirty miles above Augusta in 1779. Like nearly all of them, he was educated at a field school where he himself taught younger boys when he was only sixteen. But he managed to read law, and in 1799 he opened a practice in Lexington some sixty miles west of where he grew up.

His potential clients were few and had little in the way of fixed assets. In 1798 in Georgia there were only 15,781 white males listed as over twenty-six years of age and as heads of household. Of the homes these men owned only four buildings were worth between $6,000 and $10,000 ($19,500 to $32,500 in current dollars), the top category given. There were only fifty-one houses in the next category, $3,000 to $6,000 ($9,750 to $19,500). Approximately 12,500 of these men had houses worth less than $100 ($325). The amount of land associated with these modest dwellings was another story. The smallest of these houses valued at less than 325 modern dollars, log cabins of between 100 and 199 square feet, had an average of 192 acres associated with them. The largest, 400 square feet in size, had an average of 275 acres.

Land was the key to the story of Georgia, to the story of the frontier, to the story of the young United States. With some nod to geopolitical strategy, it was also the key to the urge Madison had to obtain Florida. Crawford and the man he chose for the mission to Florida, George Mathews, understood this well.

George Mathews was also a Scot and was also born in Virginia in 1739, thirty-three years earlier than Crawford. His father had arrived in Virginia just two years before. Unlike Crawford, he grew up in Virginia, but he too had little formal education; in fact, there is no record of his having had any. His letters indicate that the formidable mystery English spelling presents to everyone was something he certainly never solved.

Early in life he performed a typical frontier duty. He fought the Indians. On the eve of the American Revolution, he was fighting them on the Ohio and the Kenawha Rivers. This was recognized as qualifying service to earn him a commission in the Virginia militia that went off to war with George Washington.

During the American Revolution, he fought as a colonel of the Third Virginia Regiment at the battles of Brandywine and Germantown, at which last engagement he was captured by the British. He escaped from a prison ship in New York harbor and joined General Nathaniel Greene in the southern campaign of 1780. But it was as a man in search of cheap land that he first appeared in Georgia.

Two strong currents running throughout American history converged to bring him there. Georgia claimed to own a huge amount of land, and after the Revolution the first-elected Georgia legislators busied themselves passing a flurry of acts to give it away to the returning veterans of the war. Indeed, gifts of land to veterans of the Revolution gave them an even greater break than the cheap-mortgage provisions of the GI Bill of Rights gave veterans of World War II. The Georgia legislators in 1781 prepared land warrants by the hundreds. Their postwar euphoria was so great that they not only rewarded veterans but they declared, "As many persons were daily absenting themselves from the State, and leaving their fellow citizens to encounter the difficulties of the war with Great Britain, all who remained behind should be entitled to two hundred and fifty acres of good land which were to be exempt from taxes for ten years."

When Mathews heard what was happening in Georgia, he sought to cash in on his fine war record. He and a group of fellow officers from Virginia asked that a tract of twenty thousand acres be laid off and reserved for them under the sweeping provisions of the Georgia Land Act, which authorized the flood of warrants. His petition for one single immense tract for his group was not approved but he managed to get enough land to satisfy him and make himself a man of substance in the community and be named a brigadier general of Georgia's militia. In 1786 he was elected governor.

During his term in office he first became familiar with the opportunities and problems of the transappalachian territory, which his new state claimed on the basis of its original colonial charter. He worked closely with John Server, the governor of the short-lived state of Franklin carved out of the western lands ceded by North Carolina to the United States, in trying to obtain land-settlement agreements with the Creek Indians.

North Carolina might heed the call of the new federal government to cede its colonial claims to vast areas of largely unsettled land in order to help the infant nation pay the debts incurred by the War of Independence, but Georgians had other ideas about their rich colonial inheritance. When James Oglethorpe was granted his charter by King George II, he was given all the territory between the Savannah River on the north and the Alatamaha River on the south "and westward from the heads of the said rivers respectively in direct lines to the South Seas." The Alatamaha River empties into the Atlantic at the northern tip of Saint Simons Island. Below that, in Oglethorpe's time, the area was claimed by the Spanish as well as the British. Oglethorpe did his best to push his claim south. He crossed the Saint Marys River and made settlement on the Saint Johns River in Florida, naming the largest island lying between them "Amelia" for the daughter of his king. He never ventured to try to settle his holdings stretching to "the South Seas," however. In 1763 the question of any such venture was settled. When Florida was ceded by Spain to England in that year, all questions of boundary were set at rest. The northern boundary of British Florida was set at the 31st parallel and down the Saint Marys to the sea. Georgia's land empire was limited on the west by the Mississippi. Relying on these facts, after independence the legislature of Georgia in 1783 passed an "Act for the opening of a land office," and all the land from the Savannah River to the Saint Marys plus the vast western territory, most of the present states of Alabama and Mississippi, was up for grabs. Small wonder that George Mathews came down from Virginia to seek his fortune.

After an uneventful term in Congress, to which he was elected in 1790, Mathews again became governor in 1793. "No other state had so much to impede its advancement . . . " wrote Georgia historian William Stevens in 1859, "yet, despite these impediments, the laying out of seven new counties in one year was a cheering token of prosperity." Governor Mathews was committed to expansion. In January and February of 1794, he toured the frontier. He found the area in dangerous proximity to Indians and recommended the United States secretary of war beef up the border. He suggested stations every twenty miles, garrisoned by an officer, sergeant and sixteen soldiers. The War Department paid no attention, and Mathews complained that lavish funds were being spent in the Ohio country while his area was being neglected. It was not being overlooked, however, by those with plans to make money from the well-known generosity of the Georgia legislature. Matthews's second term as governor of Georgia was marked by the greatest land-speculation scandal in early United States history.

The Yazoo land sale of 1795, taking its name from part of the area involved along the Yazoo River in present Mississippi, became a national issue which for more than twenty years agitated not only the citizens of Georgia, the speculators and those left out of the deal but Congress and the Supreme Court. It led to John Randolph's bitter break from the Jefferson-Madison party and to the landmark decision of John Marshall in *Fletcher* v. *Peck*, which gave such power to the contract clause in the Constitution as to make it the foundation upon which American corporate industry was able to become a giant and for years fend off all forms of regulation.

The Georgia legislature sold to four companies in an act passed in December 1795 a total of 35 million acres of land for five hundred thousand dollars—a land sale described by one contemporary as "a grant of land to a few individuals, containing more square miles than either of the German principalities and of greater extent than some European kingdoms." The same type of deal had been attempted six years earlier.

The idea of acquiring the mostly vacant western land claimed by the state of Georgia had been the dream of all the land speculators who, like Mathews, found their way into Georgia at the end of the revolutionary war. In 1789 a man named Thomas Washington, alias Walsh, set the first plan in motion. Washington "was a most extraordinary man, one who cared not for any of the obligations by which, in civil life, man is bound to his fellow. In the daily habit of speculation, he would unhesitatingly sell to any applicant, lands, houses, horses, carriages, and negroes, before he had a shadow of property in them." He was joined by such compatible characters as "one Sullivan, a captain in the Revolutionary army, who had headed a mob in Philadelphia which insulted the old Congress and had to fly to Mississippi for his life." Sullivan got a Virginia company involved. At the head of the Virginia Yazoo Company was a rather well-known person, Patrick Henry.

The deal these gentlemen cooked up called for the sale of 15 million acres for $207,000. Another company calling itself the Georgia Company then appeared and tried to make a counteroffer. This company was "composed of citizens who were unwilling to see such large tracts of land passing into the hands of Carolinians and Virginians," even if they included old heroes like Patrick Henry. They were too late. The legislature brushed them aside and gave the land to the outsiders. Then the South Carolinians and Virginians tried to claim the land by paying into the Georgia treasury "some small sums in paper medium." The sale was nullified. Washington, alias Walsh, was shortly thereafter arrested for forging a large amount of Georgia and Carolina paper money. For this crime he was convicted and hanged in Charleston in 1792.

Two years after the hanging other real estate con artists were back at work. In 1794 they carefully went about bribing the legislature. Making offers like a half million acres for free for supporting their scheme, they covered the corridors. Outsiders were again involved. "A United States Supreme Court Justice from Pennsylvania was seen in the lobby of the legislature with $25,000 cash in hand to do business."

Once again, an opposing local group tried to make a counteroffer. The Georgia Union Company addressed a letter to each member of the legislature proposing a price of eight hundred thousand dollars and pledging to set aside four million acres "for the citizens themselves." Again they failed.

Governor Mathews at first resisted the deal. In his veto he called attention to the ridiculous price and expressed concern that so large an amount of territory in the hands of a small group of individuals would create a monopoly in land, preventing or retarding population and the growth of agriculture.

The legislature quickly formed a committee to reason with him. In addition they boldly proposed a new bill and tacked the old one on as an amendment. The new bill was an innocuous act for the protection of the "frontiers of the State." No one was fooled. Immediately howls of indignation went up.

One of the first to see the governor about the matter was William H. Crawford. He stressed the unfairness of the obvious fact that the speculators would push up the price when reselling the land. William Stephens in his *History of Georgia* noted that many others objected to the bill "because they were thereby to a great extent debarred participating in the grand speculation of the several companies." How much of the flood of righteous indignation that burst upon Mathews when he changed his mind and signed the new bill was honest outrage and how much the wrath of the real-estate speculators who were scorned is difficult to judge. The two Georgia companies who failed to win approval for their counterproposals in 1789 and again in 1795 were made up of many of those "debarred participation in the grand speculation." A scorned maiden has no greater fury than a con artist in real estate.

In any case, a new legislature was elected by popular demand. The new legislature met in January 1796, the constitution was rewritten and Mathews found himself out of office under its redefinition of the term of governor. By February 13, 1796, the land sale had been rescinded.

Two days after the bill rescinding the sale passed, the legislature adopted a report which suggested that the act selling the land to the four companies be expunged from the record and burned.

"A fire shall be made in front of the State House door and a line to be formed by the members of both branches around the same," the legislature decreed. "The Secretary of State . . . shall then produce the enrolled bill and the usurped act from among the archives of the State and deliver the same, to the President of the Senate, who shall examine the same, and shall then deliver the same to the Speaker of the House of Representatives for like examination; and the Speaker shall then deliver them to the Clerk of the House of Representatives, who shall read aloud the title of the same, and shall then deliver them to the Messenger of the House, who shall then pronounce "GOD SAVE THE STATE! AND LONG PRE-

SERVE HER RIGHTS! AND MAY EVERY ATTEMPT TO INJURE THEM PERISH AS THESE CORRUPT ACTS NOW DO!!!!"

Georgia tradition has it that after this elaborate ceremony was duly enacted, it was decided that common fire would not do. Someone got a sunglass and drew down fire from heaven to start the blaze which destroyed the accursed document.

The fire consumed the documents but the controversy burned on for the next fourteen years, and longer. In 1798 in the immediate aftermath of the drama Georgia yielded its western land to the federal government. It was to become part of the Mississippi Territory, and a six-man commission, three named by the president and three Georgians, was appointed to settle all conflicting claims. After some further haggling, the commission finally was named four years later by Thomas Jefferson. James Madison, secretary of state, Albert Gallatin, secretary of the treasury, and Levi Lincoln, attorney general, were Jefferson's logical choices.

The commission agreed to pay Georgia $125 million for the land, decided that Congress would confirm the titles of all those living in the area prior to 1795 and agreed to extinguish all Indian titles there and those still remaining in the area to the south between the Alatamaha River and the Saint Marys. There remained the claims of those involved in the Yazoo sale to be dealt with. The speculators had moved quickly to sell as much of their prize possession as possible. The commission proposed to set aside five million acres for the purpose of settling the claims of those with Yazoo titles.

John Randolph hit the ceiling. Randolph had visited Georgia while the controversy was raging and had become convinced that the corruption involved was monstrous and never to be condoned. He moved to block the bill that was introduced in 1803 to settle the Yazoo claims, after the commissioners had carefully studied them and recommended they be pared down but paid.

Using his full vocabulary and purplest phrases, Randolph said that if Jefferson were to sign such an act, it would "tarnish the unsullied lustre of his fame," and he tore into all those who supported the bill. "His speeches were too personal, his allusions to brothel-houses & pig stys too coarse & vulgar," wrote a member of Congress who heard them. A Randolph biographer claims they were parliamentary classics.

In any case, Randolph succeeded. The bill did not pass, the claims remained pending, and he managed to hang the phrase "Yazoo man," which he coined, on a number of men for the rest of their lives. He even labeled Madison a Yazoo man when he was promoting Monroe's candidacy in 1808, because Madison had been one of the commissioners Jefferson named to settle the claims.

The issue was not settled during Jefferson's presidency. In 1810 John Marshall made his decision. The claims were to be paid, said Marshall, because they constituted a contract which the Georgia legislature could not break under the contract clause of the United States constitution, and the last settlements were made in 1814.

It was in the same year, 1810, that Marshall made his decision that the Yazoo man in the middle, George Mathews, was picked by William Crawford for the delicate trust James Madison had in mind. Crawford evidently accepted the facts as Mathews presented them to the Georgia legislature in his valedictory on January 14, 1796.

Mathews told the legislators in a special message to them that he doubted they could repeal an act "that has been so fully carried into effect . . . the companies having paid into the treasury the whole of the purchase money, and cancelled their mortgages." Foreseeing the long controversy, he said he wondered "whether the remedy would be worse than the disease," and warned that there would be "murmurs and well-grounded complaints against the repeal." Then getting to the heart of the matter as far as he personally was concerned, he said he would "defy the blackest and most perverse malice . . . to produce one single evidence of my ever having been interested in the sale to the amount of one single farthing." He added that his most serious objections in his veto had been satisfied in the bill that he had signed. "I think," he wrote, "that no man of cool, dispassionate reflection, would have refused assent to it for any reasons short of clear proof of corruption in its passage through the Legislature, and *no such information ever came to my knowledge*[italics, his]." He gracefully accepted the change in his term of office which the new constitution had made, saying "the time for which I was appointed Governor having now expired, I have to request that, should an opinion prevail in the Legislature, that the duties of that important office have been improperly conducted, a committee may be appointed to examine the proceedings had therein."

Perhaps Crawford appreciated the large amount of self-serving which was involved in many of the complaints about the Yazoo sale. His own anti-Yazoo petition contained hints that the greatest shame was not being in on the deal. That there was a lot of land around and that there would always be another day was a common feeling on the frontier. When it came to looking into how more borderland might be won, in Crawford's mind Mathews's experience with the problems and interest in the border areas of Georgia certainly qualified him for Madison's mission.

"Your letter of the 27 July has been forwarded to the President," Robert Smith wrote Crawford on October 2, 1810, "and I have great pleasure in assuring you that he is perfectly satisfied with the arrangement made by you in the execution of the delicate trust which we took the liberty of committing to your management. It was indeed a most fortunate circumstance that threw in your way General Matthews [*sic*] who well understanding the view of the executive cannot but be happy in promoting them."

No document exists that tells what circumstance threw George Mathews into Williams Crawford's way, or explains specifically how it was that Mathews understood the president's view so well. But by the time Smith wrote that letter, Mathews was already in Florida.

CHAPTER V
FRONTIER DIPLOMAT

The mission George Mathews undertook for James Madison in 1810 was not his first encounter with Spanish officials in West Florida. No records survive which show how many times he may have traveled along the border during the visits he made to the outlying reaches of his domain while governor. But correspondence exists showing in June 1797, the year after the Yazoo scandal broke over his governorship and left him a private citizen again, he journeyed to the border area. He was armed with a flattering letter of introduction from Timothy Pickering, John Adams's secretary of state.

His purpose on this occasion was to discuss the settlement of land titles with the Spanish authorities. Unfortunately the former governor who had signed the Yazoo land sale bill found that was all his border contacts could think about when he appeared.

Andrew Ellicott had been appointed the previous year as United States border commissioner in the Mississippi Territory. His job was to monitor all border problems arising from the claims and counterclaims between Spanish and American settlers. These had built up in the territory as it was exchanged back and forth between Spain and Britain before finally becoming the property of the new nation.

It was to Ellicott that Pickering addressed his letter introducing Mathews. Ellicott was to use his good offices to smooth the way for Mathews with the Spanish officials. Pickering even suggested that consideration was being given to naming Mathews governor of the new Mississippi Territory. All this was too much for Ellicott. He instantly disliked the Yazoo man.

He wrote Pickering that it would be extremely unwise to name Mathews governor. He evidently managed also to give the Spanish commandant an unfavorable rather than favorable impression of the former governor. The Spanish official, Ellicott reported, was suspicious of the visitor. Mathews, said Ellicott, was "brave, honest, but extremely illiterate." And Mathews returned home to Georgia without accomplishing anything.

More than ten years later, neither William H. Crawford nor James Madison seemed to mind that the old general spelled coffee and Congress with a *k*. Dressed in his out-of-fashion clothes, his three-cornered hat, knee britches stuffed into top boots, a shirt with ruffled front and ruffles at the wrists, the seventy-one-year-old soldier set out in the summer of 1810 for Mobile, Pensacola and points east. This time he was to have better luck. His appearance in the area again made certain people nervous, but he was able to gather some useful intelligence and to see Governor Folch in a meeting that meant much to President Madison.

Following George Mathews's path in the late summer and fall of 1810 is difficult. He left no detailed accounts of his travels. In keeping with the evident agreement Crawford and he worked out when Crawford offered him the president's commission, he used Crawford as his channel of communication. Crawford's letters to Washington give the only picture that exists of what Mathews was up to. There is also a letter from a key contact Mathews made in Saint Marys, Georgia, the border town across the Saint Marys River from East Florida. Buckner Harris wrote Crawford at Mathews's request providing the senator information for his report to the secretary of state.

Mathews decided to undertake the diplomatic part of his mission first. He planned to go to Pensacola in September and talk with

Governor Folch, but he learned that a severe yellow-fever epidemic had broken out there. He also learned that Governor Folch had left the city to go to Mobile to check on its defenses. Two separate American filibustering expeditions were being planned to attack that city. One was run in the name of the Baton Rouge Convention, the other by a longtime border adventurer from Mississippi, Joseph Kennedy.

Mathews caught up with Folch in Mobile and presented the views President Madison desired him to push. They followed the refrain sung before. The United States was the best friend of the Spanish colonies and firmly believed in and supported the colonies' determination never to become part of a Bonapartist Spain. Of course, the colonies were weak and needed a friendly power to assist them. This power, obviously, must not be Great Britain. The Americans must never allow any European powers to dominate them again. Why not consider merging Florida with the United States?

Folch had heard this often. He himself had hummed the tune in his meetings in New Orleans two years earlier with Claiborne and the local citizens. Folch listened now with new interest. He knew that he had neither the troops nor the funds to supply them with sufficient ammunition to withstand any sustained attack from the filibusterers. He planned to write Governor Holmes and Colonel Sparks, commander of the United States forces in Holmes's Mississippi Territory, to ask that these troops take action to break up the filibustering schemes "and cement the union of harmony that exists between their respective governments." He became considerably more attentive when Mathews went one step farther.

Mathews, following the same tack taken by the Baton Rouge Convention with Folch's subordinate when they generously offered to pay his salary, suggested that something could be worked out to alleviate the sad financial situation the Spanish governor faced. In particular, something could be done to alleviate the personal plight of Spanish officials suffering from the piling up of unpaid salaries.

The meeting ended, as so many similar diplomatic conversations do, without firm agreement but with firm impressions. Crawford reported to Washington that Mathews was convinced "if provision were made for Spanish officials the great obstacle to union would be removed."

Pleased with himself, Mathews said he next would go to Saint Augustine, to see the governor of East Florida. First, in order to get some orientation and to fulfill the intelligence-collection portion of his mission, he traveled via his home state and stopped at the Saint Marys River in Camden County, Georgia.

Saint Marys, the port town of Camden County, was prosperous in 1810, but its prosperity was due to its remote location and the inclination of its citizens to wink at the law. They, like the people in the port on the Spanish side of the river, enjoyed breaking the laws the United States government had enacted to deprive the warring powers in Europe of trade and to deprive the citizens of the United States of slaves imported from Africa. These laws and this prosperity was of very recent origin. Camden County had been established a scant three decades earlier and for most of its official existence had been a poor and empty place.

Camden County was officially founded in 1777 after word reached Georgia that Independence had been declared. Georgia was the last colony to join the rebellion against Great Britain. In January 1775, when a congress of Georgia colonists was called for the purpose of lending support to the twelve territories to the north who had elected a Continental Congress to oppose British administration of American affairs, only five of Georgia's eleven parishes sent representatives to the meeting. Only twelve years had passed since the part of the colony which became Camden County was finally declared unequivocally British territory. Most of the land in the area belonged to only a few royal grantees who were relieved to have a clear British title at last. They were content with the status quo. It was the bright idea of the real enthusiasts who supported the hotheads in Philadelphia to change the eleven parishes of Georgia into eight counties and name one for Charles Pratt, the Earl of Camden, who had been making speeches in Parliament sympathetic to the American colonists and critical of British colonial policy.

The American Revolution had ended before a settlement remotely resembling a town was established on the Saint Marys River.

In 1787 a group of men bought 1,672 acres of land from Jacob Weed for $38. Each of the twenty subscribers who had pooled resources to come up with the cash was to own four squares of four acres each, and they all agreed each would build within six months a log frame or brick house of not less that sixteen feet by twenty-four feet or forfeit their tract of land to the common lot. They called the settlement Saint Patrick. Among the founders were men who would become important to George Mathews, men such as William Ashley, Lodowick Ashley and James Seagrove. James Seagrove was sent to the state legislature as the first representative of Saint Patrick, and Nathan Ashley, father of Lodowick and William, became the first tax collector. In 1792 the name was changed to Saint Marys and in 1802 the town was incorporated.

Saint Marys' status as first town and county seat lasted only four years. Another small settlement named after the man in Washington, Jeffersonton, was established in a more central location in the county, and to please the big rice plantation owners Jeffersonton became the county seat.

There may have been a few rice planters, sufficiently important to bring about this change but the population of Camden County was small and lived in smaller homes. Among the heads of household in Camden County in the 1798 count, thirty-one had homes valued between $100 and $500 (325 and 1,625 current dollars), ten had homes valued between $500 and $1,000 ($1,625 and $3,250). Only two houses in the county were worth between $1,000 and $3,000 ($3,250 and $7,750). There were no houses worth more than that.

The reason surviving records show such results is that Camden County in the post-revolutionary years was a transitional territory. After the British surrender at Yorktown in 1781, when the outcome of the war became unmistakably clear, the American colonists on the losing side, the Loyalists or Tories (what they were called depended upon who was doing the name calling) in the southern states of the emerging American nation flocked to Florida. East Florida faced what for it was a population explosion in 1782 and 1783. The number of people seeking refuge from their exuberant, victorious neighbors who delighted in taunting them and at times were carried away to the point of throwing in some tar and feathers to add to their fun escalated monthly. In 1783 a total of 17,375 of them were in Florida.

The war itself did not cause nearly the distress which the peace did for these unfortunate people. Next to the dead and severely wounded, they were the war's most tragic casualties. They were forced to rely on charity in Saint Augustine or they squatted on the shores of the Saint John's River, building log cabins or houses walled and thatched with palmetto leaves. They filed claims with the British government in which they poured out their woes. "Lost capital and property in support of King and Country" read one claim. "Friendless and unsupported, the King's promises of support and protection broken, the National faith bartered for an inglorious peace" read another. They were overwhelmed when the peace treaty gave Florida back to Spain. They had been deserted, they felt, and their options were few.

Most chose to flee to the closest British possessions in the Caribbean they could find passage to. Some, however, chose Nova Scotia and some went back to Britain. During 1783 and 1784 they scrambled on board ships at Saint Augustine as fast as ships could be found. Many left from Saint Marys. The evacuation was so rapid and so complete that by the time the parish priest had completed his census in 1784, they were gone.

Of those who left Florida via Saint Marys, not all took ship for abroad. At least seven thousand went into the interior parts of the country and spread westward, and many remained in Camden County. This created a curious situation. As Camden County grew, it did so thanks largely to the influx of these temporary residents of East Florida, who, in a number of cases, left relatives on the other side of the Saint Marys River. A study of the records of East Florida and Camden County, Georgia, for the period when George Mathews came to assess the situation for President Madison shows that the population of the two areas shared 423 identical names. There were an additional 142 similar surnames in East Florida and Camden County.

The fluidity of population of this border area played a vital part in the plans of the president's agent in 1810 and for the following two years. East Florida north of Saint Augustine was hardly to be thought of as a Spanish province. It was a land of Americans. Some had been on one side and some on the other in the recent struggle against the English king, but nearly all were newcomers seeking their fortunes. They were neighbors and, in many cases, relatives; in others they were the same persons seeking their fortunes on both sides of the river which was easily and frequently crossed. The Saint Marys was not a physical barrier between them. It was only political and artifical, the kind of line politicians and diplomats who live far away are fond of drawing in their ignorance of the local scene.

Some of the persons who had roots on both sides of the river, like John Houstoun McIntosh, were rich. Others, like the Ashley brothers, aspired to be. They lived by their wits. One of their activities was running a ferry across the river. Another was poaching on the Florida side and illegally cutting lumber, which became the subject of an exchange of correspondence between Governor White and James Seagrove, the founding father of Saint Marys, who by 1810 was serving as a local judge.

Early that year Seagrove wrote to Governor White that the Ashleys were smuggling cattle and "harboring all the vagabonds and horse thieves that come into the country." Seagrove was writing, he said, in consideration of the mutual concern he and the governor shared for the peace and safety of the border. He suggested that White reply in English since Ashley was capable of murder. Why an English language communication was to be preferred he didn't say, but presumably so he would be able to understand White's reaction, since Seagrove couldn't read Spanish.

White acknowledged the communication, but in a note to Justo Lopez, the commander of Spanish forces on Amelia Island, he expressed doubt as to the character of Seagrove. There was a good deal of trouble on the border and the Americans usually blamed the Spanish. White was evidently wary of this uncustomary break in the normal tenor of communications from American officials.

A more typical letter was the one Buckner Harris, one of the residents living upstream on the Saint Marys, wrote to Governor David Mitchell of Georgia.

On September 11, 1810, Harris wrote the governor, explaining that he was in the lumber business and had been asked by some of his neighbors to forward their sworn affadavits detailing damage done to them. For example, the Indians robbed their house and stole chickens and horses. Harris did the letter writing because his friends couldn't; they signed the affadavits with their marks. Harris went on to say that he feared major trouble from the Indians. Among the damage they had done was to kill beef. They also killed a buzzard and left a bloody arrow, it being the custom of the Indians, Harris explained, when they were about to go on the warpath, "to procure Down from a Buzzard to Stop Blood. . . . " Furthermore, he wrote, the week before this occurrence three hundred Indians were in Saint Augustine receiving gifts from the Spanish authorities. Harris recommended that the governor send ten to fifteen militiamen and a few spies, which, he said, should be sufficient for the moment to check up on the situation.

Mitchell passed the Harris letter on to General John Floyd, commanding general of the Georgia militia, for action. "I have reason to believe," said Mitchell, "that the lower Indians have bad intentions towards us and that they are prompted by our neighbors in Florida. . . . "

Whether or not Floyd sent the men and spies is not recorded. But by the times these letters were written, George Mathews was in the area. And Governor White and his local commander on Amelia Island were worried about his actions. Indeed, they had been worried about the actions and intentions of the Americans of the likes of Seagrove, the Ashleys and Buckner Harris for some time.

In March 1810 Justo Lopez wrote his superior that some Americans had been in town talking with eight of the local inhabitants. Two men of Lopez's confidence discovered they had been talking about actions against the government of the province. White instructed him to prepare defenses in case of invasion and to continue to monitor the situation. Their correspondence thereafter shows Lopez continued from then on to watch closely to see just how the fluid citizenry of his domain and the new nation across the river were behaving.

When George Mathews boldly crossed the river to talk to the residents of Amelia Island, Lopez and his loyal citizens were ready for him. They flatly told Mathews they were perfectly happy with things as they were and with their lot as Spanish citizens.

He was not discouraged. Fresh from his rather fruitful talk with Folch in Mobile, he told them he intended to travel on to Saint Augustine to have a chat with Governor White. He said he would sound White out on the subject of cession of Florida just as he had Folch.

George Atkinson, a leading merchant and planter on Amelia Island, brought him up short. "As sure as you open your mouth to White on the subject, you will die in Moro Castle [the Spanish prison in Havana] and all the devils in hell can't save you."

Mathews retreated to Saint Marys and into conference with his contacts there, of which Judge Seagrove was the principal. He had been justice of the Inferior Court of Camden County from 1789 until January 4, 1810, when he resigned this position to which he had been appointed by the governor because he refused to serve on the same bench with the man named to replace a colleague. He also noted in his letter of resignation that he was sixty-two years old and ready to retire. By the fall of 1810 he had been relieved of his duties but he had not retired. His interest in public affairs in general continued, and his interest in particular in exchanging ideas about the fate of Florida with George Mathews was keen.

Mathews was seventy-one years old, nine years senior to Seagrove in age and more senior still in public service as a former governor and general. Seagrove, having been only a major, was impressed by Mathews and happy to serve. Since he was locally important, he soon had Mathews conferring with all the leading citizens—men such as John Houstoun McIntosh, Archibald and Jacob Clark, important landholders, and George Cook, John Floyd, Thomas King and William Johnson, merchants and landholders, who were able to give Mathews a thorough briefing on the situation south of the border.

While Mathews was absorbing their information, he received a message from Washington. His report about his meeting with Folch had kindled renewed enthusiasm for action in Florida. In early December what appeared to be a firm offer to cede West Florida arrived at the nation's capital. Madison, in his annual message to Congress on December 5, 1810, reported that West Florida was to be occupied by United States troops in accordance with his October proclamation. Two weeks later he had a bill introduced in the Senate incorporating West Florida into the Territory of Orleans.

He did not stop there. He was convinced that now was the time to strike. If action were taken promptly, East Florida could be taken too. He sent for Mathews to report to him right away. The old general had a lot to tell the president about the struggling Spanish colony across the Saint Marys.

CHAPTER VI

SOUTH OF THE BORDER

If Enrique White took James Seagrove's measure and found him wanting, Seagrove and his cronies in Camden County were equally aware of Governor White's shortcomings. They knew well what his problems were with his finances and his military establishment. And, of course, they knew a good deal about his non-Spanish subjects, their relatives, whom the Spaniards called *anglos*. George Mathews's head was full of such information when he left the Saint Marys border, heeding the president's order to report in Washington.

White had less than a year to live when Mathews started his journey north. He had been worn down in the service of His Most Catholic Majesty, the king of Spain. In an era in the long history of the Spanish Empire in the Americas when three-fourths of the army's officers were *criollos*, White only more or less fit in. Born in Ireland in 1742, he had enlisted in the Spanish army in his teens, an outsider to the noble-born Spanish officers, the *peninsulares*, just as were the *criollos*. But without any Spanish blood at all, he did not even qualify as a member of the *criollos* establishment. At the beginning of the nineteenth century, one American chronicler of Florida who knew White said he was "without the suavity so predominant among the higher classes." A fairer modern view described him as a "harrassed commander of a remote border province."

As a youth White had campaigned with the Spanish army in Africa, South America, Cuba and the Gulf of Mexico and, in 1765, became a cadet in the officer corps at age twenty-three. He slowly plodded upward, and after thirty-one years of service reached the rank of colonel in 1796. His fitness report upon his promotion to what was to be his final rank reads like a model of the kind of report superior officers give similar plodders today—officers against whom they have found nothing in particular to complain of but of whom they have no great expectations either: "He is intelligent and fit for command," reads the report, "fulfils all commissions well, an officer of known valor, much application, superb capacity, good conduct." That should get him a promotion, the rating officer surmises, but not a really important command, one where he might do some harm if his "superb capacity" really only amounts to "good conduct"—i.e., keeping his nose clean.

On June 6, 1796, he was inaugurated governor of East Florida, one of the two top posts of one of the two lesser subdivisions of the viceroyalty of New Spain. East and West Florida comprised one of the empire's two frontier outpost provinces, the other being the vast stretch of the southwestern part of the United States still remaining Spain's after the loss of Louisiana, an area almost totally devoid of white population. The important divisions of the viceroyalty were Mexico and Cuba, and the Caribbean and Central America.

The remark about White's "suavity" may have been prompted by the fact that he had always been a barracks soldier. A bachelor of fifty-four when he took command at Saint Augustine, he enjoyed the ceremonial activity his position afforded him but had no flair for social life. He got along with the few leading people of his colony, however, having met them earlier as a staff officer on courier runs from the office of the captain general in Cuba, who was the superior military official to whom the principal officer at Saint Augustine reported. He was a paternal disciplinarian to his subordinates, mistrusted the settlers living in the province outside Saint Augustine and was disposed to treat the Indians as rowdy children. And he lived with two continuing worries—a steady shortage of funds and a constant struggle to maintain his military force anywhere near the strength he was supposed to have on paper. Funds to pay for the public duties of his office and to pay, clothe and provision his troops and their dependents were, according to royal decrees governing the colonies, to be provided from the royal treasury. This subsidy was not derived from the general expense fund of the monarchy, however; it was derived from a tax on the city of Puebla in Mexico. This arrangement stemmed from the grand days of empire when Mexico was thought to be a bottomless mine of gold and silver and the *situado* for Florida something the people of Puebla would never begrudge. Florida, after all, protected the Spanish Main—the route the royal treasure ships traveled north from Vera Cruz, across the Caribbean, and up to Cape Hatteras, where they turned east toward Cadiz. According to the myopic misery of the mercantilist economics of the Spanish monarchy, Mexico was supposed to ship the mother country all its riches and pay for protecting the shipment as well.

By the late eighteenth century the basic assumptions of this policy had shifted from their comfortable moorings. Mexico was no longer as rich, and Spain had long since surrendered the seas to France and England. And the people of Puebla did begrudge making payments to support the outpost in Florida. The tax on Puebla to pay the *situado* was supposed to amount to 350,000 pesos yearly, and it was to be sent directly to Havana in order to expedite payment of Florida's expenses. Two-thirds of the amount was supposed to be paid in necessary supplies and one-third in cash to pay military and administrative personnel and their dependents. During the entire so-called second Spanish period of Florida history, after Florida was regained from Britain in 1783, the *situado* arrived in Saint Augustine sporadically at best. Hundreds of the thousands of pieces of official correspondence of the colony, the *East Florida Papers* as they became known when seized by the American government in

1821, are devoted to the subject. There is nothing sporadic about the appeals written by White and his peers in the governor's post. They went out in a steady stream.

The establishment White tried to maintain consisted of core-troop strength that was supposed to be 450 men. It never was. The main body of troops he commanded were known as the Third Battalion of the Cuban Infantry Regiment. The garrison's highest total strength during his term as governor was 349 men, of which the Third Battalion infantrymen comprised 187. In addition, there was a small artillery unit of 24, a staff of 10 for the commanding officer and a company of dragoons, 16 men and only fifteen horses. The dragoons were charged with the responsibility of defending and policing the province. Sixteen men on fifteen horses to cover the sixty miles from the Saint Marys River to Saint Augustine were hardly adequate, not to mention the rest of the province. Armed with sixteen-year-old flintlock pistols, Model 1752, a brass-butted arm that was sturdier than it was accurate, the garrison was not exactly a formidable force. A motley crew of recruits from Mexico, Cuba and Spain with a few Germans and Italians, their morale most of the time was below a standard White could accept. Desertion was a constant occurrence.

Flogging was the best means of keeping his men in line that White could think of, but sometimes he had problems with this stern morale booster. According to Spanish military law, doctors were required to be present during the floggings. Men who were severely flogged died. Four doctors during 1809 protested. They apparently did not like having to be associated with the business, but the best thing they could come up with to try to disassociate themselves from the act was to claim that the deaths were not a medical problem. The wounds were not the cause of death, they said; it was the emotion that killed, aggravated by the hot climate.

And flogging could not get at the heart of the problem—that the men went for long periods without pay or proper supplies. The same year the doctors tried to squirm out of their duty, the money situation was so bad that the commander of the Cuba battalion asked permission of Governor White to spend one thousand pesos belonging to a lieutenant who had died intestate so he could buy clothes for his men.

The officers had little reason to be any more spirited about their service than the men. For five years they had been on half pay. A deeper reason for their discontent, of course, was that the *peninsulares*, the noble do-nothing officers appointed yearly by the crown, blocked promotion to more promising positions. When posted to Florida, they knew their careers had reached a dead end.

In fact, the only aspect of his command that White could view with any kind of satisfaction was his fort. Fort San Marcos had been built over a period of twenty-three years and was completed in 1695. The stone fort had withstood attacks by the British governor of South Carolina in 1702 and by James Oglethorpe, the founder of Georgia, in 1740. After that it had never been seriously threatened by anyone. The fort had taken more than twenty years to build because the stone used was quarried on Anastasia Island offshore and had to be transported by boat and the canoes of the Indians who did most of the work. The discovery of *coquina*, a white rock made up of seashells united by a calcareous cement, had been the only reward of the Spanish search for mineral riches in this northern outpost of their American domain. Building the fort was not only a long process but a large enterprise. Master craftsmen and journeyman masons, stonecutters, lime burners, carpenters were recruited from Cuba and the other better-established colonies. To do the hard-hat work, Christian Indians were recruited from the missions, local Spaniards not on the military rolls were drafted, Negro slaves owned by the Crown and convicts from other Spanish settlements were hustled to the job. When finished, the fort's walls were twenty feet high. One side faced toward the sea and the other three sides were surrounded by a moat.

When Enrique White took over his command, the artillery he had to defend this position consisted of one 24-pound cannon, two 18-pounders, six 16-pounders, four 12s and two 8s, plus nine other pieces which were mostly mortars and swivel guns. The eighteenth-century classification of cannons in pounds referred to the weight of the cannonball. A charge of powder equal to one-third of the weight of the ball was required to reach a range of one mile. A 24-pounder, in other words, required 8 pounds of powder.

San Marcos was respectably armed for its day, provided there was enough powder on hand; frequently there was not. But the fort's impregnability could still remain intact. On its seaward side, guns of the naval vessel of that age had unrifled barrels, as did all cannons. The balls they could fire at the thick *coquina* walls might sometimes have enough force to stick in the naturally cemented seashells, but most bounced off and none could possibly penetrate them. On the land side, the fort was safe as long as the bridge across the moat could be hauled up. When Enrique White was governor of East Florida, it could not be. The bridge had been broken for ten years and there did not seem to be any money anywhere to fix it.

Enrique White didn't like to look at the broken bridge. He did not like what he saw in his province beyond it either. The civilian population of East Florida was small after the English Loyalist refugees from the Carolinas and Georgia left. It was also polyglot. The parish authorities began taking annual census counts as soon as the colony was returned to Spanish rule, and these records are complete enough to have enabled a modern French demographer to make a thorough analysis. The first census, taken in 1788-89 immediately after Spain took possession from the English shows East Florida populated by Scots, English, French, Swiss, Germans, Irish, Portuguese, Poles, Spaniards, Italians, Minorcans and "divers." The diverse population remains as much a mystery today as it was to the customs takers who were unable to decide just what the origins of these people were. The Minorcans are another story. They were present as a result of the high-powered promotional effort the British government made to sell its newly acquired colony. The first spectacular Florida land-promotion campaign did not begin with Henry Flagler, the man whose railroad created the Gold Coast in the early twentieth century. It begain in 1763.

The British government realized that Florida was too close to the Caribbean and the Mississippi Valley and the fleets of the Spanish and French who, although they had lost the recent war, were not above attacking the tiny outposts at Pensacola and Saint Augustine. So the British government launched a hard-sell program to populate Florida in order to defend it. Articles appeared in *Gentleman's Magazine* and advertisements in other English and Scottish periodicals paid for by the government-sponsored Florida Society with offices in London. The land-grant policy of the government was very generous. Persons with connections at Court and in ministries petitioned for and were given grants ranging from 5,000 to 20,000 acres. Between 1764 and 1770 a total of 2,856,000 acres in East Florida was granted in 227 orders from the Privy Council. Members of the nobility, army and navy officers, members of Parliament, physicians and merchants were among those seeking Florida acreage. But only two men tried to colonize.

One was Denys Rolles, a second son whose brother had, under the medieval right of primogeniture still prevailing in England at the time, received all the family estates at home. He petitioned for and received twenty thousand acres in 1764. But his unique plan to populate the acreage failed. As a commentator writing some fifty years later put it, "The object of the founder was singular, in one respect, which contemplated the practicality of reforming the morals of a certain class of unhappy females by transplanting them from the purlieus of Drury Lane to the solitudes of Florida." The ladies were not happy in Rollestown, Florida.

An ambitious Scottish doctor, Andrew Turnbill, had a less singular but still too ambitious plan in mind when he secured a grant of similarly large proportions in 1767. Dr. Turnbill planned to run a vast indigo plantation with natives of Minorca, alleged experts in indigo cultivation, as the labor force. Indigo commanded a very high price and was further boosted by a bounty from the English government. Turnbill brought at his own expense fourteen hundred Minorcans and other East Mediterraneans to New Smyrna, his colony south of Saint Augustine. After only a few years Turnbill's avarice and cruelty toward his colonists had reduced their number to six hundred and their patience to an end. They revolted and fled to Saint Augustine. Although five leaders of the revolt were executed, the rest were given land at the northern end of the town and by the time Enrique White was governor they had become the town's craftsmen. The Minorcans were the stonemasons, the bakers, rope-makers, roofers, blacksmiths, shoemakers and carpenters. Some were also fishermen and sailors. The most prosperous Minorcans owned schooners, brigs, sloops and other ships. They were also the most clannish group, speaking their own language, intermarrying and keeping their own councils. Governor White looked upon them with a suspicious eye.

The census reveals a total white population consisting of 632 heads of household, which, given the imbalance of the sexes characterizing all the colonial societies of that time, means the total civilian white population was approximately 2000. They must be labeled "white population" because there were also counted in the provincial census a total of 2,330 Negro slaves. That blacks out-numbered whites in Florida as they did across the Saint Marys River in rural Georgia is a key element that must be kept in mind throughout this story. It was always in the back of the minds of all the principal actors who took part in the plot to steal Florida.

The other striking feature of the first census taken under renewed Spanish rule was that less than thirty-five percent of the population lived outside Saint Augustine and that a great amount of land was in so few hands as to constitute a potentially rival power base. One longtime resident, Francisco Sanchez, owned one ranch of one thousand acres where he kept forty horses, eight hundred to nine hundred head of cattle and a slave labor force of thirty-four with an English overseer, plus several smaller ranches. Sanchez listed himself a bachelor to the census taker. He neglected to count his black wife and seven mulatto children.

The potential parallel power was not this rich landowner, who swore eternal loyalty to the Crown; it was the trading company established under British rule. Leslie, Forbes, Panton and Company owned 12,820 acres outright in the form of nineteen huge lots within a sixteen-mile radius of Saint Augustine. In addition, the company controlled six thousand acres as the authorized representative of several departed British planters and a large number of building land and houses in Saint Augustine itself. To this land should be added 262 slaves, 72 horses, 330 head of cattle and a white work force of traders with the Indians and others of 36 men, many of whom had wives and children. In the second half of 1784, many of these departed, weakening the size of the colony still more but lifting a mortgage from the shoulders of the Spanish governor somewhat. In the continuing absence of the *situado* credit from Leslie Forbes, Panton and Company carried the colonial administration along from day to day.

The colony did not prosper. In 1793, three years before Enrique White became governor, the census shows a total population of all inhabitants, including slaves and soldiers, of only 4,735 persons. Blacks, 1,661 slaves and 128 free individuals, outnumbered the white population in 1793 by more than 700.

To do something about this situation, in 1790 land was offered free to any white persons who came, agreed actually to settle and swore allegiance to the Spanish king. Three hundred sixty-six heads of families of foreign extraction swore such an oath that year. Between 1794 and 1811 the statistics of oaths taken show that 521 more such new settlers arrived. Seventy-nine of them were French, refugees from the slave revolt in Santo Domingo; Irish, Scots and English totaled 127. Italians, Germans, Swedes, Dutch, Swiss, Poles and Portuguese also came. There were even four more Minorcans who arrived to join this close-knit subcolony. But the vast majority were people from the United States, in particular Virginia, North and South Carolina and Georgia, although some trekked down from more northern states like Pennsylvania and Massachusetts. Even New Hampshire was represented.

These Americans, 318 of them arriving between the years 1794 and 1809, decisively changed the nature of Enrique White's domain. Together with their kindred from the British Isles, these *anglos* all but erased the Spanish culture. Not only did they speak another tongue, three-fourths of them were Protestant intruders in the territory of His Most Catholic Majesty of Spain.

The lists of oath takers make this plain, but they do not tell the whole story. That story is told in exchanges like the one between

White and Seagrove, arguing about illegal lumbering enterprises. The new settlers who swore the required oath were supplemented by an uncounted number of squatters who crossed the Saint Marys upstream and settled on the parts of the Diego Plains they could find not owned by Francisco Sanchez and elsewhere along the more than mile-wide Saint Johns River.

The Americans who came to Florida were perched on rungs of the social ladder from top to bottom. The squatters mostly were on the latter end, but among the oath takers as well there were a variety of comers. The Spanish traditionally listed all persons in the census according to social status, the two major divisions being "notables" and "populars," divided according to the amount of property each held. Notables were honored with the title "Don." Some sixteen percent of the Americans who arrived received this title, but forty of those who took the oath were not capable of signing their names. The majority of these illiterates came from Virginia and the Carolinas.

A good third of the oath takers, however, were already landholders in their old states. One was a doctor from New Hampshire. One man from Boston said he left behind two hundred acres. Another from Connecticut mentioned holding five hundred acres, a house worth one thousand pesos, six Negro slaves, three horses, forty head of cattle and one hundred pigs, which he planned to transfer to his new home. The wealthiest man of all was John Houstoun McIntosh of Georgia. His Georgia plantation consisted of fifteen thousand acres which he valued at seventy thousand pesos.

What impression this made on the Spanish authorities when McIntosh made this declaration on July 12, 1804, is not recorded. But it meant a good deal to George Mathews when he returned from Washington to the border on his second mission for James Madison.

By the time Mcintosh arrived, the colony was no longer the stagnant place it had been when the Spanish renewed their control. The rural population augmented by the influx of new settlers was growing steadily. In ten years' time it would reach more than seventeen hundred people, more than the entire white population of the colony in 1793. Agricultural products were grown which not only took care of the needs of the capital city but were exported. Trade with Britain via Amelia Island expanded rapidly after the Jefferson administration embargoed such trade directly from United States ports in 1804. Among the products most traded were hides from the large herds of cattle that grazed on the wire grass that abounded in the area ever since the Indians had cleared and burned the ground many years before.

Cattle raising in Florida began early in the history of Spanish occupation of the peninsula. The standard accounts of the second voyage of Ponce de Leon, discoverer of Florida, state that he brought calves to the new country in 1521. On the strength of this, Florida cattlemen today like to claim that Florida was the birthplace of the American cattle industry. Actually Ponce did not succeed in this venture. He was defeated and killed by the Indians. Whatever cattle he may have brought probably did not survive.

The great English buccaneer, Sir John Hawkins, pointed out in 1565 that Florida was the best place in the Indies to raise cattle. He'd already tried it on several Caribbean islands. But the first records that cattle were being raised in Florida is a list of ranches with their owners' names, dated November 29, 1700. It shows that twenty-five cattle-ranch owners in the vicinity of Saint Augustine and westward along the Saint Johns river paid the government taxes in kind amounting to 162 cattle. Farther west in central Florida were nine ranches supplying 60 head of cattle in tax payments.

The most important of the seventeenth-century cattle ranches was the *hacienda de la chua* ("ranch of the sink hole") in north central Florida, owned and operated by the Menendez Marquez family. The earliest reference to it is to its exports in 1675. The founder of the family was Pedro Menendez Marquez, first royal accountant of Florida and first royal governor. He was descended from the *conquistador*, Don Pedro Menendez de Aviles, founder of Saint Augustine, on both sides of his family; on the one, from a grandnephew of the *conquistador* whose legitimacy was uncertain, and on the other through females for three generations. The official accountant had the opportunity to acquire the funds to obtain the land and start the ranch. Pedro Menendez Marquez descendants passed that job and the job of treasurer along in the family for thirty-five years. The accountant and treasurer knew when boats were being dispatched for trade with the Indians and could take a cut of the deal. They also could speculate on certificates for back wages, which served as the principal medium of exchange. Also they had the privilege of traveling to Mexico to pick up the *situado* when paid, and the per diem for these trips nearly doubled their salary of 1,470 pesos. Finally while visiting the viceregal capital, they could use some of the king's money to buy goods they could trade on the side.

From the prices prevailing in the mid-seventeenth century, it is possible to estimate the capital needed to start a ranch. Cattle averaged twenty-one pesos each, a locally bred horse one hundred. A black or mulatto slave from New Spain, expert at handling cattle, cost between five hundred and six hundred pesos. In addition to the outlay for equipment and buildings (land could be had free by royal grant) a spread of two hundred head of cattle, five horses and two ranch hands could run to over six thousand pesos or four times as much as their legal annual salary.

In the twenty-three years it took to build the fort of San Marcos, Saint Augustine was a busy place. In addition to the increased numbers of soldiers, more slaves, convicts and artisans came to work on the fort. The levy of Indian labor from the remoter parts of the province was higher. The demand for foodstuffs rose sharply and the Menendez Marquez family was ready to take advantage of this.

The ranch of *la chua* began operating at full strength. Tomas Menendez Marquez, Pedro's descendent, resigned his commission in the army to devote full time to the operation. The cattle which browsed in the woods throughout the winter returned to the savannas in the spring, when they were rounded up into corrals for counting and branding, then driven to Saint Augustine, crossing the Saint Johns on flatboats operated by converted Christian Indians. In the city they were taken to the royal abattoir and slaughtered. The meat was delivered to the garrison and sold to citizens.

The tallow was then extracted, the hides tanned, and these ranch products exported, some by the yearly vessel licensed to trade with Spain, the rest to Cuba. It was a profitable business, a monopoly of Tomas and his brother, who were both on good terms with the governor.

But Don Tomas was not satisfied to deal solely with Saint Augustine. The Gulf of Mexico port of San Martin on the Suwannee River was closer to his ranch and closer to Havana. Also the pig-and-chicken trade of the Gulf was not as attractive to pirates as the treasure fleets which sailed up the Bahama Channel past Saint Augustine. So Don Tomas got himself a frigate for the coastal trade, which he claimed was only used to bring in necessities for his ranch household. The Havana record of cargoes and destinations shows otherwise. He was carrying on a profitable illegal trade, just as the new settlers of East Florida in the time of Enrique White were. Don Tomas had a three-cornered operation going—ranch products to Havana for rum, rum to Indian country for furs.

By the end of the eighteenth century, as the flow of new settlers moved into East Florida, the Menendez Marquez family and their ranch were gone, but their enterprising spirit lived on in other *Floridianos*, as the descendents of families from the first Spanish period were known. And the genes of the cattle bred for more than a century were still propagating themselves. Francisco Sanchez made out with his cattle and other items almost as well as had Don Tomas Menendez Marquez.

Francisco Sanchez's brother married the daughter of Diego Espinosa, uniting two families who between them controlled most of the land between what are today the Jacksonville beaches and Saint Augustine, an area named Diego Plains for Don Diego Espinosa.

Fresh meat as well as firewood for the residents of Saint Augustine and its garrison were supplied on contract and administered by the Spanish government. The Sanchez family held both contracts from the late 1790s through 1811, when Enrique White died. They traded rum, too, just as had Don Tomas, and rice and citrus fruit as well. These clever Spanish entrepreneurs, in fact, shipped most of their citrus fruit in *agria*—a concentrated form. Unfortunately, records of exactly how they managed to anticipate Minute Maid orange juice by 150-odd years have not yet been found.

When Francisco Xavier Sanchez died in October 1807, his estate was probably the largest probated in the entire second Spanish period in East Florida. It consisted of lands, slaves, cattle, townhouses and lots and commercial interests. The Sanchez townhouse in Saint Augustine was amply furnished in mahogany and had a staff of twenty-seven slaves. Another Sanchez house was rented to the lieutenant governor. Still another was rented to the garrison commander. Several other of his houses were used as retail stores for the sale of goods from the United States and Cuba. The lands of the estate outside Saint Augustine were located in both Diego Plains and along the Saint Johns River. The main Sanchez property on Diego Plains comprised six separate pieces of land including much adjacent pine land from which pitch and ship's stores were made. When Don Francisco died, he had over one hundred head of cattle at this main ranch, ten horses and two teams of oxen.

As did others who lived with black women, Don Francisco legitimatized all seven of his mulatto children in his will. Unlike other contemporaries who found themselves in the same situation, he remarried in the church after the death of his common-law wife in 1784. The new Señora Sanchez, Maria del Carmen Hill was the daughter of an upper-class South Carolina family who moved to East Florida in 1780, He and Marie del Carmen had six daughters and four sons. In the first years after their marriage in 1787, the whole brood of mixed-blood and all-white children lived together, passing their time between the big ranch on the Diego Plains and the large townhouse in Saint Augustine. Providing for all these children eventually contributed to the breakup of the large estate after Maria del Carmen died in 1813.

Of course not all planters and cattle growers were Francisco Sanchezes. And cattle growing in a land without fences led to a lot of straying, some brought about by cattle's inclination to wander in search of tastier fodder and some induced by human greed. "On the 18th day of February one thousand eight hundred and seven," James Lewis made his will, which he signed with his mark. A principal clause of the document was an agreement he made with one Isaac Wilkes selling Wilkes his cattle. It had to provide further for "John Forrester, by mutual agreement of buyer and seller," to go find Lewis's cattle "in whatever place they can be found in this province with my mark and brand." Forrester was to be paid the "sum of Eight Spanish mill'd Dollars for each head of cattle delivered."

The increasing general prosperity, especially the growth of trade with Britain, that centered on Amelia Island led to some new and interesting developments. For one, it made the men across the border with whom George Mathews conferred in 1810 more interested than ever before in East Florida. It also made the British traders pay special attention to the needs and tastes of the market in Spanish America. William Walton, Jr., of London published two volumes in 1810, *The Present State of the Spanish Colonies*, in which he gave advice on the subject.

"To make quick and profitable sales of goods in any part of the Spanish possessions in America, depends on the selection of the cargo destined for these markets," wrote Walton. "It is for want of these proper assortments that so many enterprizing merchants and adventurers have been injured. The real wants of the Spaniard," he continued, "are few, his prejudices many, he does not like innovation, and his luxuries are also confined. The Spanish taste varies from our own at home, the customs as well are different." He advised all piece goods be accompanied by bale cards "in order to avoid opening of the same, and they ought to correspond perfectly. It will be advisable also to sell by the package, as the shop keepers would cull your goods and leave many of little or no value or at least choose the most saleable."

"It is to be observed," he concluded, "that goods intended for the Spanish market, in their respective kinds, are required to be light, shewy, thin and low-priced and on a different principle of strength, and good wear to those which are intended for sale and consumption in Great Britain. They require the article to be dressy, not to last long; cheap and pretty, is their corresponding proverb." In short, they were to be treated and viewed as simple heathen—that is, non-British.

He then listed a "selection of a Cargo suited, on a general Scale, for the Spanish Settlements in America."

These included "Linens, Scotch and Irish" with the note "all as white as possible, for the Spanish American requires the commodity to flatter and please the eye more than the touch or feel, but at the same time seeks it cheap." He includes four hundred handkerchiefs "being intended for poor people to wear on the head, must be cheap." Three hundred silk umbrellas and three hundred silk parasols for the ladies in "shewy colors," are part of the selection. He lists everything from ten copper stills of sixty to one hundred gallons, to buttons, snuffboxes "if possible with a likeness of King Ferdinand," combs for the hair and "100 dozen assorted files, handsaws etc." And he includes an assortment of medicines such as "cream of tartar, rhubbard, glauber salts, nitre, ipe cacuanna, calomel mercury, and opium," noting they should all be ready for use, "powdered etc. as these operation are tedious in a hot country and require apparatus."

This English merchant was not aware as was George Mathews of the change that had taken place in the north central part of East Florida. Here the people were no longer so different in customs and tastes from those of "our own at home." The Englishman's American cousins had moved in. George Mathews hurried north in December 1810 to tell President Madison all about it.

CHAPTER VII

MATHEWS GETS THE MARSHAL'S BATON

James Madison was anxious to talk with his special agent because by early December several things had happened which moved Florida up on his agenda. He assumed that United States troops were about to occupy the Baton Rouge territory with no trouble and he had a report from Colonel John McKee, his agent for dealing with the Choctaw Indians, that was exciting.

Indian agents were important parts of the military and intelligence establishment in nineteenth-century America and especially so in the early years. They were in charge of the delicate and difficult task of negotiating the treaties by which the Indians were talked into surrendering their hunting grounds to the steadily growing number of settlers in frontier areas like Mississippi Territory. They were also the eyes and ears of the government in these remoter regions. How much intelligence work they did depended on the time and circumstances and on the character and inclinations of the agent. John McKee had a bent for such work. Funds for intelligence activities were earmarked for the Indian agent in an uncharacteristically vague category in the budgets of President Madison's careful Swiss secretary of the treasury, Albert Gallatin.

Gallatin, as any good Swiss banker would, regularly gave his budget estimates in figures down to the last penny, such as *Civil List*—$639,690.94, and *Naval Establishment and Marines*—$2,504,669.60. *Lodging, Indian Trading and Intercourse with Foreign Nations* was a category given only in round numbers, such as $142,000 in his budget proposal for 1812. It is always hard to put a specific price tag on the kind of intercourse intelligence agents have.

Whatever their precise relationship, Vicente Folch obviously considered John McKee the appropriate channel for his next move in the trials he was having with the eager filibusterers who were trying to take Mobile and the rest of West Florida from him. When the filibusterers burned a sawmill and a dwelling outside Mobile and then had the audacity to call for a joint conference to discuss the best method for securing the independence of West Florida, Folch wrote a desperate letter to his chief, the captain general in Havana, on November 30, 1810. He told him that unless he received relief and assistance by January, he would deliver his province to the Americans.

Then he called in John McKee and asked McKee to deliver another letter for him to the highest authorities in Washington. In this letter he made an apparently clear statement of his intention to surrender. He did, however, make the offer conditional on the actions of the captain general, the Marquis de Someruelos. "I have decided," he wrote, "on delivering this province to the United States under an equitable capitulation, provided I do not receive succour from the Havana or Vera Cruz, during the present month; or that his excellency the Marquis of Someruelos (on whom I depend) should not have opened directly a negotiation on this point." In his letter to Someruelos he had covered himself, warning "I have thought of addressing myself directly to the Executive power of the United States . . . proposing to treat for the delivery of the province . . . because, as our difficulties every day increase, the necessity of hastening their conclusion increases also."

McKee hurried to confer with the American commander of the Mississippi Territory. They agreed that in view of what Mathews had earlier reported and since Folch had given the American commander permission to use his troops below the border to restrain the filibusterers, the offer was the break the Madison administration had been waiting for. They ignored the qualification and McKee took off on the long trip for Washington.

Before McKee arrived, Madison had already drafted his State of the Nation message, giving important billing to Florida. He made public his hitherto confidential proclamation of October 27 and suggested consideration be given to legislation incorporating West Florida into United States territory. Accordingly, Senator Giles (who would later join the cabal the Smiths and others formed to harass Madison but who was at the moment an administration stalwart) introduced a bill on December 18 making West Florida part of Orleans Territory. True to Madison's long-cherished ambition, the bill extended the boundaries to the Perdido River, the gates of Pensacola.

The Giles bill touched off a bitter debate, during the course of which the outlines of the sectionalism which was to divide the country for the next fifty years and culminate in civil war became glaringly apparent. Just as apparent was the fact that senators were fully aware that the claim that West Florida had been included in the Louisiana Purchase was groundless. And the doctrine of *national-security interest* was invoked for the first time to cover up disclosure of information embarrassing to an incumbent administration. Senator Timothy Pickering's reference to the diplomatic correspondence which proved we had no valid claim to West Florida anticipated the Pentagon Papers by more than a century and a half. The Madison supporters reacted with the same ferocity that the Nixon administration displayed when the Pentagon Papers were published. And with the same self-serving skillfulness in identifying their own interests as the interest of national security. Pickering was given a vote of censure as a security risk.

Henry Clay led off for the administration. He made the extreme case for the alleged diplomatic claim and asserted that the act of October 31, 1803, by which the United States had taken possession of Louisiana, was still in force. He then claimed that an act of the following year passed in pursuance of this measure empowered the president to erect West Florida into a collection district for tax purposes whenever he deemed it expedient.

"These laws furnish a legislative construction of the treaty correspondent with that given by the Executive," Clay declared, "and they vest in this branch of the government indisputably a power to take possession of the country whenever it might be proper in his discretion."

He was stating a doctrine that would become the banner of southern and western expansionists and the bane of the old northeastern states, dividing them more and more hopelessly as the years went by. He also was foreshadowing the fate of every measure that subsequently had to do with the land within and bordering the Louisiana Purchase. As Henry Adams pointed out, "Fate willed that every measure connected with that territory should be imbued with the same spirit of force or fraud which tainted its title. By this doctrine every President past or to come had the right to march the army or send the navy of the United States at any time to occupy not only West Florida but also Texas and Oregon, as far as the North Pole itself, since they claimed it all. . . . as part of the Louisiana purchase."

Immediately, senators from New Jersey and Massachusetts were on their feet to attack the senator from Kentucky. Between them, Outerbridge Horsey and Timony Pickering effectively demolished Clay's claim. Before turning to the matter of title to the territory under the terms of the Louisiana Purchase agreement, Senator Horsey questioned not only the legality of the acts of Congress Clay used to support his argument but also the legality of Madison's October 27 proclamation. The Constitution gives the right to make laws and war exclusively to Congress, he said. Madison's Florida proclamation did both in open violation of the fundamental law of the land. "The proclamation makes war by directing the occupation of this territory by military force," Horsey declared, although he had to acknowledge the president's supporters who said the proclamation scrupulously avoided a direct confrontation with the Spanish and so was not an illegal declaration of war. The proclamation provided that in case of any place, however small, remaining in possession of a Spanish force, the commanding officer was not to proceed to employ force but to make immediate report thereof to the secretary of state. But "suppose while your commanding officer is making this report, the Spanish force sallies out and makes an attack upon your army . . . what are Governor Claiborne and his army to do?" Horsey asked, "ground their arms and surrender themselves prisoners of war; or are they, sir, to drop their muskets and to take to their heels? . . . They must either surrender, run, or fight. And who would doubt which of these alternatives the gallantry of an American army would impel them to choose!" To Horsey, Madison clearly had invented the undeclared war.

The president also had illegally unsurped the power of Congress to make laws, Horsey declared. By annexing the territory in question to the Orleans Territory, creating a governor, enacting territorial laws and appropriating money, the proclamation was, in fact, the Giles bill. The Giles bill did nothing more to establish a territorial government than had already been done by presidential proclamation.

"If the President has no power under the Constitution to issue this proclamation, I think it equally clear he had none under any existing laws of Congress," said Horsey, thus dismissing Clay's claim that the act of February 24, 1804, for laying and collecting duties in the territories ceded by France gave legality to the president's desire to occupy all of West Florida. The president admitted in his State of the Union message that this law and the earlier act of possession of Louisiana "recognized that at the time of their passage the territory was in the hands of a foreign power," Horsey pointed out. But he further states that those laws contemplate an eventual possession by the United States. The question was what kind of possession? Here Horsey argued that possession by force was never intended "by the express declaration of Mr. Madison himself, while Secretary of State."

Madison in a letter to the Spanish minister to the United States, dated three weeks after the act of February 24, 1804 was passed, assured the Spanish official that the "provisions relating to Louisiana 'would not be extended beyond the *acknowledged limits* [original italics] of the United States, *until it shall be rendered expedient by the friendly elucidation and adjustments* with His Catholic Majesty.'"

The senator from New Jersey then reviewed the question of the title to West Florida having been included in the sale of Louisiana. He carefully read the pertinent documents in the diplomatic history of the case going back to 1756, the beginning of the Seven Years War in the colonies between France, Spain and England. These documents showed no such claim could be sustained. That it was implied by Tallyrand when Monroe and Livingston negotiated with him, Horsey found unacceptable.

Pickering showed just how unacceptable, when he read the letter Tallyrand wrote on December 21, 1804, in response to Monroe's inquiry on whether West Florida was part of the Louisiana Purchase. In that letter, Tallyrand declared flatly that "West Florida had not been a part of the territory retroceded by Spain to France and consequently West Florida was not part of the territory purchased by the United States in 1803."

The administration supporters immediately flared up and demanded an official reprimand be voted citing Pickering for violating his oath of secrecy. Tallyrand's letter had been communicated to Congress by Jefferson in 1805, and an injunction to secrecy had been extended over the document. Five years had passed and the secrecy injunction had not been removed.

"If the president could not have some degree of serenity that the documents confidentially commited to Congress not be disclosed and on the preservation of which in confidence perhaps the safety of the nation depended, must not all reliance on the Senate be lost?" asked Henry Clay, sounding the sort of note that would become all too familiar in the 1970s debates.

Senator Dana of Connecticut replied, "I do not acknowledge the power of the president to lock our lips in eternal silence." Another senator declared he didn't know what all the fuss was about since the facts disclosed "had already been circulated in the newspapers." All the trappings of the national security debates of the Vietnam era adorned the Senate that day.

Pickering was censured by a party vote of twenty to seven. He did not mind; in fact he considered the vote a compliment because he read a document that he felt the administration should have been ashamed not to publish.

The security violation debate, meanwhile, obscured the central issue (as it usually does). It was plain that no convincing case could be made for West Florida's belonging to Louisiana either as a Spanish or an American province. If Mobile Bay and the Gulf Coast as far as the outskirts of Pensacola belonged to Louisiana, the territory that would later become the states of Alabama and Mississippi and was then claimed by Georgia had no outlet on the Gulf. Georgia would never consent to such a fate. William Crawford, the Georgia senator and Madison's floor leader in the Senate could not swallow that one. Giles's bill was silently dropped.

The Georgians in the House were even more adamant when, frustrated in the Senate, the administration had a bill reported in the House on December 27 admitting Lousiana as a state, with West Florida extending to Pensacola included. The Georgia representatives demurred, demonstrating downright delicacy for the rights of Spain. None of West Florida could be included in the new state, they said, because "it was yet in dispute and subject to negotiation" with the Spanish Crown. They proposed instead that West Florida be annexed to the Mississippi Territory or made a separate government.

Congressman Rhea of Tennessee objected immediately to this move to create a dangerously big state next to his. The debate in the House achieved no better results than the one in the Senate. The bill was referred back to committee and there the matter rested.

President Madison did not rest. By this time Colonel McKee had arrived with the letter from Governor Folch, and George Mathews was also in town. The president reviewed the situation, and decided to launch a new and bigger Florida project after considering all the good news about prospects there.

On January 2, 1811, the Senate slapped Senator Pickering's wrist. The next day Madison sent Congress a request for consideration of an urgent call for action in Florida. The message was marked Confidential, and he asked that it be considered in secret session. He wanted no new security leaks on this. He wanted a joint resolution authorizing the seizure of East Florida.

"I recommended . . . the expediency of authorizing the Executive to take temporary possession of any part or parts of the said territory, in pursuance of arrangements which may be desired by the Spanish authorities . . . " the message read. He then got to the point: "The wisdom of Congress will at the same time determine how far it may be expedient to provide for the event of a subversion of the Spanish authorities within the territories in question, and an apprehended occupancy thereof by any foreign Power."

He attached Mathews's report of his meeting with Folch and Folch's letter brought by John McKee to his message as proof of the need for quick and decisive action.

Congress obliged. On the same day they received his message, the House of Representatives considered the request and referred it to a select committee. Two days later this committee reported a bill "authorizing the President to occupy the territory therein mentioned, and for other purposes." And on that same day, the committee reported a text for a joint resolution. The Senate responded with equal promptness.

The request to keep the resolution secret by its nonpublication, however, required a total of thirty takings of the *yeas* and *nays* before it was agreed upon. On January 15, 1811, Congress passed the resolution that "the United States, under the peculiar circumstances of the existing crisis, cannot, without serious inquietude, see any part of the said territory pass into the hands of any foreign power, and that a due regard to their own safety compels them to provide, under certain contingencies, for a temporary occupation of said territory; that they at the same time declare that the said territory shall, in their hands, remain subject to future negotiation."

This resolution carefully threw in a cover, the fiction of a "foreign power" as a greedy onlooker waiting to seize what the president wanted. It also tried to meet any possible objections to the planned covert subversion operation by suggesting the matter might "remain subject to future negotiation."

Simultaneous with the passage of the resolution was passed "An act to enable the President of the United States, under certain contingencies, to take possession of the country lying east of the river Perdido and south of the State of Georgia and the Mississippi Territory, and *for other purposes* [Italics, mine]."

Those last three little words were fateful. They gave Madison blank-check authority for covert action. Whenever such action is desired by a government, some similarly vague set of words are used to authorize it. They avoid embarrassing questions, and they keep friend and foe equally in the dark. In 1947 when Congress passed the National Security Act establishing the Central Intelligence Agency, the Cold War was well underway. Congress knew President Truman wanted authorization to run covert-action operations to disrupt what he was convinced were Soviet plans for world domination. The Security Act of 1947 specified that the CIA was to "correlate and evaluate intelligence relating to national security, and provide the appropriate dissemination of such intelligence within the Government." It should also "perform *such services of common concern* as the National Security Council (NSC) determines can be more efficiently accomplished centrally, and *such other functions* and duties related to intelligence affecting the national security as the NSC may from time to time direct. [Italics, mine]." The words "such services of common concern" and "such other functions" were the keys which unlocked the door through which soon rushed a multi million-dollar covert-action effort complete with a new large office within CIA devoted exclusively to that purpose.

Congress's act of January 15, 1811, created nothing so large or expensive, but it authorized the launching of a covert-action plan to subvert the government of East Florida in order that the province could be acquired without further negotiation or a declared war against Spain. And while no match for our twentieth-century support for similar activities, it did provide $100,000 ($325,000 in current dollars), a reasonably substantial sum for that day.

The act contained several other carefully calculated phrases beginning with its title, which referred to "certain contingencies" under which the president was authorized to take possession of East

Florida. The first section of the act specified, without making exactly clear, some of these contingencies.

The president could take possession of this territory "in case an arrangement *has been* or shall be made with the *local authority* of the said territory [italics, James Cooper, *Secret Acts, Resolutions and Instructions under which East Florida was Invaded*, Washington, 1860]." The author of the pamphlet in 1860 wondered at the use of the past tense and who the local authority was. It is as evident now as then that more was implied here than stated. This section of the act went on to offer another completely different contingency under which the president was also permitted to seize East Florida. "Or, in the event of an attempt to occupy the said territory, or any part thereof by any foreign government," the president could act. And also he could "for the purpose of taking possession and occupying the territory aforesaid, and in order to maintain therein the authority of the United States, employ any part of the Army and Navy of the United States which he may deem necessary." The one hundred thousand dollars in operation funds were "appropriated for defraying such expenses as the President may deem necessary for obtaining possession as aforesaid, and the security of said territory, to be applied under the direction of the President, out of any moneys in the Treasury not otherwise appropriated."

Section 3 of the act authorized the president to "establish within the territory aforesaid a temporary government and the military, civil and political powers thereof shall be vested in such person or persons, and be exercised in such manner, as he may direct, for the protection and maintenance of the inhabitants of the said territory in the full enjoyment of their liberty, property and religion."

In this fashion Congress created a well-constructed framework for the operation. Filling in the details now had to be done by the president and the national-security council of his day. The National Security Council established in 1947 included the president, the vice-president, the secretary of state, the secretary of defense, the director of the Office of Civil and Defense Mobilization, the secretaries and under secretaries of such other departments as the president might select with the advice and consent of the Senate, and an executive secretary and "such personnel as may be necessary." Madison's security establishment consisted only of himself and the secretary of state, with some consultation with the secretary of war and the secretary of the navy.

Eleven days after Congress passed the secret enabling act, Madison and Secretary of State Smith had orders ready. George Mathews and John McKee were appointed commissioners for carrying out the program Congress had enacted. They were ordered to "repair to that quarter [Florida] with all possible expedition, concealing from general observation the trust committed to them, with the discretion which the delicacy and importance of the undertaking require."

The instructions, like the act by Congress, carried a double-barreled load. They instructed the commissioners what to do in case of a voluntary surrender of the province by the governor or "local authority" and how to act in case no such surrender occurred. In that case "should there be room to entertain a suspicion of an existing design in any foreign power to occupy the country in question," they were to keep themselves "on the alert, and on the first undoubted manifestation of the approach of a force for that purpose," they were to "exercise, with promptness and vigor, the powers with which they are invested by the President to pre-occupy by force the territory to the entire exclusion of any armament that may be advancing to take possession of it."

The instructions then gave these presidential agents considerable freedom of action. "The conduct you are to pursue in regard to East Florida," the instructions read, "must be regulated by the dictates of your own judgements, on a close view and accurate knowledge of the precise state of things there. Should you find an inclination in the governor of East Florida, or in the existing local authority, amicably to surrender that province into the possession of the United States, you are to accept it on the same terms that are prescribed by these instructions in relation to West Florida."

That paragraph revealed a great deal about Madison's reasoning in reaching the decision to launch his covert-action plan for East Florida. Folch's offer to surrender West Florida was an overriding consideration. If Folch were willing to act as he suggested he might, then the governor of East Florida might well have a similar "inclination." If not, the intelligence Mathews had reported about the state of affairs in East Florida made it clear that a "local authority" willing to offer up the province could be manufactured quickly. Therefore the two commissioners were given explicit instructions to see Folch and told how to handle the details of his surrender and to follow the same procedure for dealing with East Florida after they had obtained it.

In West Florida they were told to request Governor Folch to cede to the United States the portion of that territory still in Spanish hands. As a lure they were instructed to suggest that the United States would be willing to retrocede that territory to the lawful sovereign of Spain, King Ferdinand, then Napoleon's prisoner, when he was restored to his throne.

The commissioners were given several options to be used as circumstances warranted once they had gotten hold of Spain's province. They were to guarantee all bona fide land titles. They were to assure Spanish functionaries that they would be retained in office where no special reasons required their removal, and to assure local inhabitants that existing Spanish laws would be respected. They might advance a reasonable sum of money for the transportation of Spanish troops out of the province if Folch requested it and they thought it was necessary.

If they did not manage to get Folch to agree, then the same contingency applied in West Florida as it did in East Florida. If they could dream up a plausible case for claiming a foreign power was about to move in on the place, they should seize it. The actual words were "should there be room to establish a suspicion of an existing design of any foreign Power to occupy the country in question." It seems reasonable to substitute the shorter phrase, "dream up," for this wordy diplomatic language.

The instructions made plain how the commissioners were to proceed in both provinces in case, under any of the contingencies, they thought they needed military help. "If in the execution of any part of these instructions, you should need the aid of a military force, the same will be afforded you upon your application to the commanding officer of the troops of the United States on that station, or to the commanding officer of the nearest post, in virtue of which orders have been issued from the War Department. And in case you should moreover need naval assistance, you will receive the same upon your application to the naval commander in pursuance of orders from the Navy Department."

The orders closed with reference to financial matters. The commissioners were told the Treasury Department would issue the necessary instructions as to what they should do about imposts and duties to be levied in the territory they would add to the United States if their efforts succeeded, as well as what to do about any slave ships whose arrival was apprehended. Each commissioner was authorized eight dollars a day and expenses and they were given immediate authority to draw funds, two thousand dollars from the collector of customs in Savannah and eight thousand dollars from his counterpart in New Orleans.

Mathews kept his copy of these orders with him at all times. He seemed aware he might need them just in case the orders supporting his operation which the War, Navy and Treasury departments were supposed to issue got fouled up. He had no record in writing of the things that were told him in the president's office.

Only fragments of memory and secondhand accounts of the words in which what is expected of a covert operation and the men who are to carry it out ever survive. In the case of the 1811 East Florida mission of George Mathews, there is just the letter written by Ralph Isaacs, the man who accompanied Mathews on the operation, to James Monroe three years after it was all over.

Ralph Isaacs was a colonel in the militia of Mississippi Territory, where he bought and sold land and to where he returned and disappeared from history. He and Mathews had met during Mathew's first mission. He accompanied Mathews in 1811 as his secretary, a position in which he was invaluable. He was fond of the old Scottish speculator. Mathews was descended from the Scots whom Oliver Cromwell, after his conquest of Ireland, had settled in the north of that country to tame the natives. Isaacs's Jewish ancestors had wandered for centuries, unwanted strangers in many lands. Both had similar inbred strategies for coping with a world seen as a sea of mostly unfriendly faces. Without Isaacs the general could scarcely make himself understood in writing.

Mathews was told he should pursue the recruitment of suitable persons who could constitute the local authority mentioned in the written instructions and who would be willing to offer him their province. In playing this role, they would repeat the performance of the men who took over Baton Rouge. They should, therefore, be United States citizens who held property in East Florida and could claim to be local residents.

In order to gain their cooperation Mathews was told he could offer them generous rewards. The United States government would gladly give them title to large tracts of land in East Florida once the territory was the United States government's to give away. How these people were going to go about taking over control of the local government in order for them subsequently to ask, as the Baton Rouge Convention had, that the United States assume sovereignty over them, was left to be worked out.

This did not bother George Mathews. He had talked enough with Seagrove and his friends, he was confident he could work that matter out. With the written orders he had, not to mention what had been said, he could be confident. The words spoken to him, however, had been what the Spanish call *la media palabra*, the half word. By this they mean words from which meaning is implied. What is implied, of course, is malleable. The speaker can claim the implier implied too much. Unfortunately, the written instructions, too, although explicit enough on some points, in others were *la media palabra*. Mathews would find this out in time. In the winter of 1811 he made his way south unaware of it.

CHAPTER VIII
FRUSTRATED BY FOLCH

Mathews's orders were dated January 26, 1811. He lost little time getting back to his contacts on the Saint Marys, considering the transportation available to him. Together with McKee and Isaacs, he traveled on horseback along the one road that ran south from Washington. Although the thirteen colonies now had a federal government, they did little to improve the physical means of linking themselves one to the other. The ocean highway, forerunner of Highway 1, which orginated in Bangor, Maine, was as good or as bad as each state's attention to its condition determined.

Between Boston and New York was a reasonably well-kept road along which, three times a week, stagecoaches carried passengers and the mail, completing the journey in three days' time. From New York a stagecoach started every weekday for Philadelphia, taking almost two full days to make the trip. South of Philadelphia the road was tolerable as far as Baltimore, but between Baltimore and the new federal city of Washington it meandered through forests, the stagecoach driver choosing the track which seemed the least dangerous and rejoicing, in wet seasons, if he reached Washington without bogging down in the mud or upsetting the coach. South of the Potomac River the roads became steadily worse, and south of Petersburg, Virginia, even the mails were carried on horseback.

The three men on their secret mission made the best time they could. At some point Isaacs turned west for the Mississippi Territory and Pensacola, which he reached at four in the afternoon of February 25. Mathews and McKee passed through Charleston and at Savannah stopped to draw the two thousand dollars they were authorized to get from the collector of customs there. From Savannah they made their way through coastal Georgia, a land of rivers, smaller streams and low-lying swamp that was in spots almost impassable and the streams at times unfordable. At Browns Ferry the Savannah post road reached the banks of the Satilla River and from there curved through more of the same type of terrain for twenty miles until it reached the village of Saint Marys, where they arrived on February 23.

Mathews sat down to report to Secretary of State Robert Smith. His letter shows why Ralph Isaacs was so vital to him. Perhaps it also shows why, in addition to the obvious security considerations, it had been a good idea for President Madison to rely on oral briefings in dealing with the old soldier.

"I arivid hear on the 23rd instant from Chalstown," wrote Mathews in an uneven hand, "the rodes in the worst condition I evar saw them and the watar courses the most difiquil to cross. On my arivil hear I found the Gentlemen hows names I give you will disposed to sarve our Government but thar has not been one soldar arrived or one armed Visil or gun bobt in this rivar, from this cause its thought not propar to attemp eny thing at presint. I lave this tomorrow morning for Mobail and from the arrengmints I have maid will return hear by the 20th of April at which time I hope to have it in my power to carry the President wishes in to afact.!"

The letter is important for much more than to prove that when the border commissioner in Mississippi Territory called Mathews extremely illiterate in 1797, he was not exaggerating. It shows a great deal about the dimensions of the operation that had been discussed in Washington. Obviously, in the oral briefings Mathews had mentioned the men he had in mind to constitute the "local authority" that would give him East Florida. And the military support referred to in his written instructions in general terms had also obviously been talked about specifically. He evidently found that the orders of the War and Navy departments mentioned in his written instruction had either not been issued or not carried out. Not only did he indicate he had thought he would find some "soldars" to work with, he gave a little subtle nudge on the subject besides. He closed the letter by sending his "complimints to Doctor Eustis and Col Hamilton"—respectively the secretary of war and the secretary of the navy.

The letter also foreshadows some of his future problems caused by the calculated lack of clarity covert-operational approvals so often contain: " . . . Our Commihon only gives to West Florada while our Instruthon imbrace. East Florida wont it not be proper to forward a commthon for East Florada by my return hear. Should the President think this proper direct it to me hear to the care of the Post Mastor. . . . "

Mathews might not have known how to spell, but he knew that at a great distance from headquarters a man in charge of running a covert operation involving coordinated military support must have his authority firmly fixed.

He left Saint Marys the morning after he wrote the letter to the secretary of state. He and Colonel McKee probably skirted the great Okefenokee Swamp on their left as they moved by wilderness trails northwest to reach the main road again. On the night of March 9 they reached the small settlement known as the Creek Agency, where Benjamin Hawkins, agent to the Creek Indians, put them up and noted they seemed to be in good health despite their travels. After resting two nights they departed for Fort Stoddert, the frontier post on the border of the Mississippi Territory and West Florida.

From Washington to Fort Stoddert by way of Saint Marys, Georgia, was a journey of more than a thousand miles, the best part of which was the uncomfortable road running south from Washington by which they had reached Saint Marys. After leaving the Creek Agency, most of the route ran through uninhabited forests where the roads were really only footpaths and through Indian lands where there was always the chance they would meet marauding bands of braves bent on robbery or murder of the few white settlers around.

A road of sorts did wind its way from Augusta through Milledgeville, then the capital of Georgia, crossing the Chattahoochee River near the present site of Columbus, Georgia, and continued through Fort Mitchel and Fort Mims to Fort Stoddert. It was called the "Three Chopped Way" after the triple blaze on the trees along the route which enabled travelers to find their way.

Mathews and McKee reached Fort Stoddert on the evening of March 21. The fort had been built in 1799 and named for the man who was then acting secretary of war, Benjamin Stoddert. It was almost on the border of Florida. Fifty miles farther on lay Mobile. The fort was a hub of communications for the Mississippi Territory as well as a border outpost. The trail from Natchez on the Mississippi River entered the fort from the west and continued east and northeast to the Chattahoochee River and Georgia. Another road ran along the Tombigee River north of the fort and turned west, connecting the main trails to the western part of the territory and Tennessee.

Just above the fort, the Tombigee and Alabama rivers joined to form the Mobile River, which, a few miles below the fort, divided into an east and west branch both flowing into Mobile Bay. Fort Stoddert, therefore, was an official port of entry from the bay into United States territory as well as a communications and trade center. It was the most important post anywhere in the area, with five hundred regular troops and militia manning it and swarming with land speculators, traders, merchants and adventurers planning to take West Florida by force—the filibusterers, out of fear of whose schemes Governor Folch had put out his feeler which had brought Mathews and McKee to negotiate with him with Isaacs preceding them to Pensacola.

Three weeks before Mathews and McKee reached Stoddert, Isaacs had talked with Folch. Folch had been prepared for the arrival of the American negotiating team by a letter from Secretary of State

Smith written in January, less than a month before Isaacs arrived. The letter overlooked the conditional nature of Folch's offer, especially his suggestion that the whole of Florida might be exchanged for an equivalent transfer of territory in the vast unsettled western reaches of the Louisiana the United States had bought from France.

"I have it now in charge from the President to inform your Excellency that he is fully persuaded that such an arrangement as you have intimated for the delivery of the country, now under your jurisdiction, to the United States, will be advantageous to all parties concerned," wrote Smith. "He has accordingly appointed General Mathews and Col McKee to enter into the same with your Excellency and to receive from you possession of the country in the name of the United States."

Isaacs brought with him a personal letter from McKee to the Spanish governor outlining the proposition which his and Mathews's instructions presented as the American position on the subject of the transfer of Florida. Folch backed off as quickly as he could, revealing, once again, what a wily diplomat he was.

Folch explained to Isaacs that when he had made his proposal to McKee the preceding fall, he had acted under duress. He reminded his visitor that the rebellious forces stirred up by the filibusterers had been on the outskirts of Mobile. When he gave McKee the letter that McKee had taken to Washington the preceding December, the rocket that sent Madison into orbit over Florida, he had no money and no reinforcements for his miserably equipped handful of men.

Now, said Folch, he had received funds and men, and the American commander in Mississippi had generously helped in quieting the filibusterers.

Isaacs saw immediately what Folch's plan had been all along. By his clever moves, the enticing offer, and his concurrent request for help from the United States commander in Mississippi to maintain order in what he made appear to be territory that was on the verge of becoming part of the United States, he had succeeded brilliantly in achieving his goal. American troops had secured peace on the frontier. At the price of a small bit of American troop activity inside his territory to round up the revolutionaries, he had saved Mobile, Pensacola and the rest of East Florida.

Isaacs had three interviews with Folch before he gave up and wrote down a complete report for Mathews, including the above shrewd assessment of what had happened.

Folch told Isaacs that the October 27, 1810, proclamation by Madison and the seizing of the Baton Rouge Territory had tied his hands. He had letters from Spain and from his superior in Havana warning that these acts could cause hostilities between Spain and the United States. He said he had been ordered to hold Florida at all costs.

Issacs told him this was too bad because Napoleon's actions had so weakened Spain that it was unlikely the Spanish regency Folch represented could hold the colonies. Isaacs said he had hoped those colonies would unite with the United States in defying "the continental powers of Europe"

Folch replied that he too had once wished the same thing. Madison's proclamation, unfortunately, now prevented any such united front. He suggested that the United States might want to negotiate directly with the Spanish regency's national Cortes, representing the people, which was now assembled in Spain and which had sent him his orders not to surrender Florida.

Isaacs was badly discouraged and didn't have the heart to sit down and write his full report for a week after his final interview. He sent off his report to Mathews and McKee on March 31, 1811.

Mathews was shaken by this unexpected reversal, but he was not defeated. He abandoned his plan to return to Saint Marys by April 20 and decided to have a go at the governor himself. On the excuse of searching for fugitive slaves belonging to him, he entered Pensacola as a private citizen. In reporting this to the secretary of state on April 10, McKee tried to sound optimistic. "Mexico is in revolution, Cuba, if it escapes that fate, can't help him [Folch] because of its own great wants, only transatlantic aid can help and none is known . . . "

A week went by and no word from Mathews. McKee wrote Washington that he was sending a friend from Mobile to "impress on Governor Folch the idea that the United States is ready to negotiate on terms advantageous and honorable to him and his country."

Mathews was a stubborn Scot. In his first meeting with Folch they went over the same ground Folch had covered with Isaacs. Mathews did not give up. McKee did not hear from him because he stayed in Pensacola and saw the governor two more times. Whether the friend McKee indicated he was sending over from Mobile talked to Mathews and persuaded him to offer the "terms advantageous and honorable both to him and his country" or whether Mathews decided on his own to sweeten things, Folch later reported in defending his conduct to his superiors that the general made a generous offer.

Mathews told Folch that nine-tenths of the American people were solidly behind the Spanish who were resisting Napoleon and his brother, and that the Madison administration did not in any way support France. He brought forth the carrot Folch himself had stuck into his initial proposal to McKee in the fall of 1810, and which the American secretary of state had studiedly ignored in his letter to Folch in January notifying the governor of the Mathews-McKee mission.

His instructions, said Mathews, simply empowered him to receive the province from Folch upon condition of returning it when Spain terminated her contest with France. But if Spain then preferred, his government would exchange it for land in the western part of Louisiana or make some other suitable compensation.

Mathews also said he was empowered to render full inventories for all property delivered, to pay all arrears in the salary of the clergy and the civil officials of the province, to continue to give full pay to all who wished to remain in the province or to assume their transportation if they preferred to leave, and to assure the people full religious toleration and the continuance of such Spanish laws as were not contrary to those of the United States.

In making these offers Mathews was stretching his instruction as far as he could. He was authorized to inventory all items taken over from the Spanish, and to offer transportation to retreating Spanish troops to make sure they got out of the province. He could promise to permit citizens of Spanish descent to follow their religion unmolested and could say that laws not contrary to United States law would be respected.

But the matter of possible later negotiation for return of the province and any possible swapping of territory was touched on only very delicately in his orders. "And should a stipulation be invited on the re-delivery of the country at a future period," they read, "you may engage for such re-delivery to the lawful soverign." As for paying Spanish officers, Mathews perhaps could have extrapolated that from the references to reimbursement for "all ordinance and military stores." Certainly nothing indicated explicitly that he could either make such payments or take the initiative in offering to trade part of western Louisiana for Florida at some future date, unless both ideas were spoken of in *la media palabra* sessions he and the president had before he left Washington.

In any case, Mathews's diplomatic efforts were to no avail. Folch steadfastly held his ground and a deeply disappointed old man returned to Fort Stoddert on April 23.

Mathews did not know that Folch had been backed to the wall by his superiors. The Marquis de Someruelos had been furious when he received the letter Folch had written in December threatening to offer his province to the Americans if he didn't receive funds and reinforcements. Someruelos had not only told him to hang on, he severely reprimanded Folch and reported the matter to Spain, recommending court-martial. He did, though, send Folch fifty thousand dollars and more men, but he never accepted Folch's version of what had taken place, neither in the earlier loss of Baton Rouge nor in the negotiations with the Americans about the status of the rest of West Florida.

Mathews did not know that Folch had asked to be relieved of his command on April 3, before their conversations began. If he had, things might have worked out better for the next move he made. The day after he returned to Fort Stoddert he had conceived a scheme to take control of Mobile Bay, leaving the Spaniards surrounded in Mobile. For the next two weeks he explored the east bank of the

Mobile River and the bay area. He found a spot between the Perdido River and Mobile Bay of about forty square miles inhabited by fifty families and not occupied by a single Spanish soldier. On the eastern shore of the bay were excellent sites for military posts and good locations for commercial enterprises.

Since President Madison had always claimed that all of West Florida to the Perdido River had been sold to the United States in the Louisiana Purchase, Mathews thought the area east of Mobile bay should be seized at once and forts erected along the bay and river. The United States would thereby obtain all advantages expected from the surrender of Mobile hoped for in the aborted negotiations with Governor Folch, and could at the same time cut off communications between that port and Pensacola, the Spanish provincial capital. West Florida, except for the isolated Spanish community at Mobile, would be American without firing a shot.

This scheme necessitated the immediate occupation of the area by United States troops before Folch could move men into the area. Since his orders stated "if, in the execution of any part of your instructions, you should need the aid of a military force, the same will be afforded you upon your application to the commanding officer of the troops of the United States. . . . ," he asked the commander at Fort Stoddert to give him the men to do the job. The commander refused. Mathews showed him his orders and pointed out that the secretary of war had been told to inform all commanders they were to comply with Mathews's requests when made. Hadn't he received these orders? He had, the commander replied, but they had instructed him that he should obey the requests for assistance only in case of an attempt to pre-occupy the Floridas by a foreign power. This was the first time that Mathews learned there could be some confusion between the powers that had evidently been given him and the follow-up orders from authorities in Washington governing the vital matter of coordination of his operational plans with the military.

It would not be the last. By this time he was growing tired of the frustration, and he was already overdue to return to East Florida. His prospects there were better. There he had done all the groundwork himself, knew the key figures. There were no competing adventurers like those who were all over the place in West Florida, and he should be able to handle easily the commander of the small American border post at Point Petre outside Saint Marys. He was ready to abandon the disappointing diplomatic manuevering with Spanish officials and punctilious American army officers and get back to Georgia.

And he learned on May 14 that James Monroe, whom he had known well years before during the War of Independence, had taken over the State Department from Robert Smith. He quickly wrote a letter of congratulations to the man who was now the principal officer he would have to deal with in carrying out his operational assignment. "I will not recite all the motives I have for joy on this occasion," he wrote. "I find enough in the character and harmony it will give to our national councils and the advantage that will thereby be derived to the Nation." Actually Colonel Isaacs did the writing of this bit of buttering up, which far exceeded the old soldier's standards of spelling and sycophancy.

Five days later, on May 19, Mathews said good-bye to Colonel McKee, and he and Isaacs began the long journey back to Saint Marys, Georgia. The change at the State Department did bring more harmony and character to the nation's councils, but it turned out to have unfortunate consequences for the general's ambitious mission in East Florida. The small-minded Mr. Smith would subsequently blow his operation to the press at a most inopportune moment, and the clever new secretary of state would prove to be too cautious to want to cope with the consequences of covert action.

In March 1811, at the same time Ralph Isaacs was having his unpleasant talks with Folch, President Madison was finally getting around to saying something unpleasant to Robert Smith. He had his first interview with Smith on March 23 and wrote a long memorandum on what took place.

"I proceeded to state to him," Madison wrote, "that it had long been felt and had at length become notorious that the administration of the Executive department labored under a want of harmony and unity . . . that I did not refer to the evil as infecting our Cabinet consultations, where there had always been an apparent cordiality . . . but as showing itself in language and conduct out of doors . . ."

The out-of-doors language and conduct of Smith, his brother Samuel and their friends had become a scandal. They were bitterly opposed to Madison's major policy for dealing with the world war in Europe by embargoing trade with England and France. The Smiths were merchants and as badly hurt by these measures as were the New England traders. The Smiths and their friends were Jeffersonian Republicans but on this vital question they gladly joined with the New England Federalists. It is difficult to say which did Madison more harm—the press attacks they inspired or their intrigues in congressional cloakrooms. Perhaps worst of all were the intrigues of this cabal's Mister Inside, Robert Smith, who continually fostered bickering and actions at cross-purposes within the cabinet.

The situation was so bad that even John Randolph, certainly no friend of Madison's, abhorred it: "Our Cabinet presents a novel spectacle in the world; divided against itself and the most deadly animosity raging between its principal members, what can come of it but confusion, mischief and ruin?"

The major target of the coalition trying to undo the administration was Albert Gallatin. As secretary of the treasury he was the overseer of the commercial decisions putting into effect the trade-embargo policy. In their controlled press they slandered him for speculation, embezzlement and secret intrigues until he finally became fed up and on March 5, 1811, sent Madison his resignation. This forced Madison's hand because Gallatin, he realized, was the ablest member of his team. He refused the resignation and sent a letter off to Monroe asking him to come to Washington to take over the State Department.

Monroe at first was somewhat reluctant. He partially agreed with the Smiths' position that Madison, in making judgments between which power, Britain or France, should be more punished by our trade policy, almost always came down on the side of giving a break to the French and being tough with the British. He did not approve of the tactics of the Smiths and their friends, however, nor of the attacks on Gallatin.

He also wanted to be president.

Neither of them a slouch at political sleight-of-hand, Monroe and Madison reached a tacit agreement that it was all right for Monroe to come into the cabinet and try to tilt the administration toward a less hostile posture toward Britain—but of course always as a loyal subordinate, not an intriguing scoundrel like Smith. Which of the two was cleverer perhaps may be attested by the fact that a little more than a year after Monroe came into the cabinet the United States was at war with Great Britain.

Madison tried the traditional tactic for dumping unwanted subordinates who nevertheless are difficult to dispose of. He offered Smith the post of minister to St. Petersburg. Smith consulted his group. It was decided it would be better for their cause if he stayed near America's capital rather than go off to the czar of Russia's, even if he had no job. Smith resigned, threatening to appeal to the country. Madison dismissed the threat.

Three months later Smith issued an "Appeal to the People" through his friendly press contacts. He peppered it with references to confidential State Department documents, trying to make a clear case that Madison was pro-French because he was under secret pledges to Napoleon. Whatever the merits of the case or the maneuver, it threw Madison and his supporters into a frenzy and they filled their partisan paper, the *National Intelligencer*, with long diatribes on Smith's incompetence, and brought up the intrigue by which Smith had managed to become secretary of state through his brother's machination.

Smith had the last word on this one. He replied in the *Baltimore American*. "This advocate," replied Smith, referring to the writer in the *National Intelligencer*, "would have us believe that many persons both in and out of Congress thought that Mr. Smith from want of talents and integrity was quite unfit for the Department of State, and that his appointment was the effect of an intrigue. Were there any truth in this remark, it could not fail to convince every person of the utter unfitness of Mr. Madison for *his* office. It in plain English says that from the officious persuasion of a few intriguers he had appointed to the most important and highest station in the government a person without talents . . . "

Mr. Smith would be back the following year with charges of more secret strategies of the Madison administration. Meanwhile on April 1, 1811, James Monroe took over the job of secretary of state. When he looked over the reports which had come in from the president's men in Mississippi, he thought that further pursuit of negotiations on West Florida was as fruitless as Mathews thought it was.

On June 29 he dictated a letter to Mathews and McKee in which he complimented them for their services and terminated their mission to West Florida. A copy of this letter and an authorization to transfer their powers in this matter to Governor Claiborne at New Orleans were also prepared, as well as a brief letter to Mathews assuring him of his continued authorization to act in East Florida. But he never sent the letters. Perhaps the furor over Smith's charges caused him to lay them aside.

And so McKee stayed on in West Florida for the rest of the year and until mid-May of the following year continued his futile efforts. On May 14, 1812, the step the secretary of state had contemplated almost a year earlier was taken, and McKee was ordered to return to Washington.

During this time Vicente Folch in May 1811 had turned over his post to his son-in-law. By fall he was preparing himself for his court-martial. In January 1812, he was ordered to take the first available vessel to Spain, and while he was able to clear himself of charges of treason in the trial that took place later that year, his reputation had been forever tarnished.

Of the actors in the frustrating West Florida negotiations, two others, George Mathews and his scribe, Ralph Isaacs, turned their attention to another task. While McKee and Folch were having an unhappy time during the rest of the year 1811 and the year that followed, and while the fate of West Florida continued to remain unsettled, they tried to manipulate the future of the people who lived along the Saint Marys River.

CHAPTER IX
A RIVER OF SIN

When George Mathews and Ralph Isaacs returned to Saint Marys in the early summer of 1811 they found themselves in a boom town. It was one of two that had blossomed steadily over the past three years, one on each side of the river, one American, one Spanish. Although both Camden County, Georgia, and the Spanish province of East Florida in general remained sparsely populated, the ports on either side of the river flourished. This was because the broad peaceful river that lay between them had become an avenue for illicit adventure which few places anywhere in the world could rival in the teens of the nineteenth century.

The Indian word for the Saint Marys river was Thlathlothlaguphka, which meant "rotten fish." An even stronger odor was borne by breezes blowing over the river in 1811—the stench of slave ships. When the hatches were opened after a voyage of three thousand miles, decaying dead bodies were sometimes among the accumulated human waste to be emptied along with the cargo.

The hold of a slaving vessel was usually about five feet high. That seemed like waste space to the slave merchants, so they built a shelf in the middle of it extending six feet from each side of the ship.

When they had completely filled the bottom of the hold with their human merchandise, another row of slaves was packed on the platform. If the vessel was a little larger, having a hold of six instead of only five feet, a second platform was constructed above the first. Often the slaves had only twenty inches of headroom. They could not sit upright the entire voyage. In addition, the male slaves were shackled together in twos. In this way 200 to 250 slaves could be shipped in a 100-ton vessel.

Sanitary provisions consisted of three or four large buckets. Often the shackled slaves stumbled over each other trying to reach these buckets and fights broke out. After a while most abandoned the effort to reach the buckets.

To let some fresh air into these soiled quarters there were usually five or six air ports on each side of the ship, between decks. About six inches long and four inches wide, sometimes these holes were outfitted with canvas funnels to try to direct air currents into the hold. But whether of this first-class variety or not, they all were shut when the sea was rough and rain heavy. Many of the miserable passengers contracted amoebic or bacillary dysentery, known as the "bloody flux;" most of the rest suffered from high fevers. Under these circumstances it was not unheard of that nearly half the cargo died.

In 1807 the United States Congress passed a law forbidding the further importation of slaves. Such a law had been anticipated for years. Agitation to end the horror of slave trading was strong in England at the time the United States Constitution was written and had spilled over to this country. Article I Section 9 of the Constitution backed into the idea of possibly prohibiting further slave trade at some later date. "The Migration or Importation of such persons as any of the States now existing shall think proper to admit," the Constitution reads, "shall not be prohibited by Congress prior to the year one thousand eight hundred and eight." By 1807 Great Britain was about to abolish the trade and Congress acted too, forbidding the importation of slaves after January 1, 1808. Meanwhile the invention of the cotton gin had made the demand for slaves greater than ever because there was now more profit in cotton producing. The men prepared to break the law were in what may be called an American tradition—pursuit of the easy dollar. Anything in great demand means great profit and any laws that try to interfere are ignored, be the product traded human slaves, alcoholic beverages or drugs. In *Twenty Years of an African Slaver* Captain Theodore Canot gave the balance sheet of one voyage, complete with entries for hush money and bribes to officials. These latter amounted to $8 a slave paid to the officials in Havana. On a voyage transporting a cargo of 217 slaves his total expenses were $39,980. His total return was $81,419—a profit of over 100 percent.

Of course, smuggling slaves all the way from Havana into the United States cut into the profit, but it wasn't necessary to take the loss if an enterprising individual could set up business along the Saint Marys, basing the operation on the *Spanish* side. Many did this. Buckner Harris, for one, Governor David Mitchell of Georgia, for another.

But far and away the main man was Zephaniah Kingsley. Kingsley first appeared in Florida in 1803, obtaining a land grant of thirty-three hundred acres and swearing allegiance to Spain as so many others had done since 1790. By 1811 he was doing well. So well that he had acquired not only most of what is now Orange Park, a large suburban area of modern Jacksonville, San Jose and Beauclerc, two other sizable portions of Jacksonville south of the Saint Johns, but also Saint Johns Bluff, the high rise of land on the river first settled by Europeans, and Fort George Island lying between the Saint Johns River and Amelia Island. When he arrived in Florida he brought with him seventy-four slaves and a black wife, Anna Madgigene Jai, said to be the daughter of a chieftain on the Guinea coast and by contemporary accounts perhaps of some Arabian blood. The slave trade, after all, was founded on that combination—greedy African chiefs and Arab traders were the key to a steady supply of recruits. In some cases African chieftains started tribal wars solely for the purpose of capturing prisoners they could sell to the Arab merchants who in turn sold them to British, Dutch, French, Spanish and American sea captains and slave-trading entrepreneurs.

Exactly when and where Kingsley first entered the slave trade is not clear. Perhaps because his life-style was considered scandalous by many contemporaries, especially the longer he lived and the more southern society solidified on the subject of race, no full account of his life survives. As he lived on to the age of seventy-eight he shocked his neighbors by having not one black wife, but at least three others. He claimed to have married Anna, his African princess, in a native ceremony. He never claimed the others were anything but concubines. If his life-style differed from most people's who lived in East Florida and south Georgia in 1811, his background did not. He too came from a Scottish family which moved to America before the American Revolution and sided with King George III in that contest as had so many settlers in Florida and Camden County, Georgia. The South Carolina Assembly after the war confiscated the estate of his father, Zephaniah Kingsley, because he had been a "petitioner to the British commandant at Charlestown to be armed as a member of the loyal militia." Which was probably the event that propelled the young Kingsley into the slave trade. He plied that business in the West Indies and in Brazil before making his application for his land grant in Florida. Born in Scotland in 1765, he was only eighteen when the family was kicked out of Charleston. And almost as quickly as he settled into his new surroundings, he established a site for training new arrivals from Africa. He had a steady supply of these, most probably furnished by his wife Anna's father. To maintain his importation of his stock of Africans, he started a shipping company in 1811 and a chain of slave-trading posts running from the Saint Marys river into the upper country of rural Georgia.

How many slaves Kingsley sold is not known. No one ever keeps close account of contraband. But Kingsley's profits undoubtedly exceeded those of Captain Canot. A good field hand, Kingsley testified in a claims case after the Florida plot failed, was valued at between $500 and $600 ($1,625 to $1,950 in current dollars) and one trained in lumbering, $800 to $1,000. Kingsley's school, moreover, taught even greater skills than lumbering. He turned out carpenters and other craftsmen worth more than twice the sum a lumber-sawing slave brought. Contemporary accounts indicate that "Kingsley's niggers" were the prize product of the slave trade, selling at 50 percent above the market price. Kingsley defended his profession in a pamphlet published in 1829, *The Patriarchal Slave System*, that was well received throughout the South. He wrote, said Kingsley, to prove that "the slave or Patriarchal System of Society (so often communicated as a subject of deep regret) is better adapted for strength, durability and independence than any other state of society hitherto adopted." His opening lines were hardly flattering to southern society, but they applied to the lower class of whites and not to planters and so were forgiven. "Many suppose that the aversion to labor observable in the South, among the working classes of whites, proceeds from a natural indisposition," wrote Kingsley. "But a nearer view, and a better acquaintance with facts will show, that the radical cause is the want of health . . . " He gave as evidence the fact that "Northern mechanics" who migrated to the South, became "after a few years, weak and idle, and finally, falling a sacrifice to the abuse of ardent spirits." Some blame the hot climate, but Kingsley concluded that it was a matter of pigmentation. "Many years have elapsed since the first white people settled among the Southern swamps, and their descendents have not improved either in looks or longevity. It becomes evident that people of white complexions are unfitted by nature for that situation."

Not only were white laborers lazy, they consumed all they produced and still had to ask for charity for their families to survive. The blacks, on the other hand, used up little of the products of their labor, permitting a considerable profit to be gained by their owners, and thereby contributed to the general prosperity. "The labor of the negro, under the wholesome restraint of intelligent direction, is like a constant stream; that of the white man is economically measured out by his urgent necessities . . . Besides, climate enables the one to furnish articles of greater value; while the white man's labor is usually applied to raise cheap articles of food for the mere subsistence of himself and family."

Nowhere was the success of the patriarchal slave system more impressive than "the Empire of Brazil, perhaps the most extensive government in the world," said Kingsley. Here one million whites, another million free blacks and two million slaves enjoyed not only the economic blessings of the slave system but a monarchical government, a considerable improvement,in Kingsley's mind, over a free republic. At the time of writing, the Brazilian monarchy was getting the better of a war with the "free Republic of Buenos Aires," where not only was the dubious democratic form of government practiced but slavery outlawed. Brazil and Haiti, another place where slavery flourished, were destined to be leading world powers, in Kingsley's view.

At the end of this work, he turned aside from the larger argument of his treatise to justify his own personal way of life: "Health and bodily perfection are certainly before all other objects the most important. Improving the breed of domestic animals has occupied the attention of some of the most eminent and useful men in our country. How much more meritorious and laudable would the philanthropist be to whose energy and moral courage mankind were indebted for exposing and removing a prejudice that . . . completely neutralises the physical strength of the country, by placing one portion of the inhabitants in hostile array against the other. . . . The intermediate grade of color are not only healthy, but when condition is favorable, they are improved in shape, strength and beauty."

Thanks to Kingsley's energy, his black women bore him a large number of children of "intermediate grade of color." When he died, his will leaving his estate to them was bitterly contested by his collateral relatives. One of these was his grandniece, the mother of a famous painter. The sullen look James Whistler painted on his mother's face may not have been caused by her legal battles, but she fought doggedly for years to invalidate her uncle's last testament. Her argument was that it was against public policy to permit a man to give his wealth to progeny of miscegenation. Ultimately she lost and Kingsley's wife, Anna, and her children got what he had willed them. And when Anna finally died in 1870, their daughter Martha, her principal beneficiary, had even married a white man.

In 1811 another prominent man in East Florida who had a marital arrangement similar to Zephaniah Kingsley was given a big job to do by Governor Enrique White. George J.F. Clarke, surveyor general of the province, was ordered by the governor to lay out new streets and develop a new town plan for the port on Amelia Island. The governor complained that the bustling port was becoming disorderly.

George J.F. Clarke was not a newcomer like Kingsley. He had been born in Saint Augustine in 1774 during the time Great Britain ran the colony. But he too lived with a black woman, and like Kingsley he was determined their children not be denied their inheritance because of their "intermediate grade of color."

"I never have been married, but I have eight natural children by a free black woman named Flora, now dead," read Clarke's will, "all of whom I always acknowledged, freed, raised and educated. . . . I declare them to be equal, full, absolute, and general heirs. . . ."

George John Frederic Clarke had been apprenticed as a twelve-year-old boy to the powerful Panton Leslie trading company by his widowed mother. She bound him to keep inviolate the secrets of the company, to work always for its interests and obey its commands. In return young George was to get his "food, drink and clothing, a house, bed and clean clothes," and instruction in business and commerce.

The Spanish governor could not get along without the aid of Panton Leslie's credit and services, especially its excellent rapport with the Indians. And George Clarke learned how to make himself similarly indispensable. He also learned how to take advantage of whatever turned up.

By a deed of May 5, 1794, "John Leslie sold to George Clarke for 60 pesos a mullato slave named Philis, aged 18 months, who was born in Leslie's home of a slave named Flora." Three years later Clarke received a deed to Flora and in the same year he emancipated her "because of the fidelity and love with which she served him . . . " This little drama tells the story of the beginning of their long relationship. Little Philis was one of the children named as an heir in Clarke's will.

In 1808 Clarke and Flora moved to the port of Amelia and he went into trade for himself. He had earlier become surveyor general where his bilingual abilities served the official Spanish establishment well in properly recording the titles and dimensions of the land grants that had been given to foreign immigrants like Zephaniah Kingsley.

Clarke's general-trading company was only one of the many ventures that were prospering at the port. Slave trade was not the only business that thrived because of a change in American laws. The embargo of 1809 forbidding the lucrative carrying trade with the West Indies as well as the trade with the European powers then at war drove the enterprising shippers to Amelia Island, where they could continue their old business. Vessels crowded the island's harbor for miles and the town grew haphazardly. Governor White issued a decree on December 24, 1810, that from January 1, 1811, on, the port which had never had a name before would have one. "I have determined," he declared, "that it shall be called Fernandina, after our noble king, Ferdinand VII." Having named the town, he next decided Clarke should straighten it out.

Clarke drew up a symmetrical plan laid out in squares. He created broad streets running north and south and east and west. Each street had a width of seventeen *vara*, a *vara* being the Spanish equivalent of an English yard, less three inches. During the summer and fall of 1811 the sound of hammers and saws filled the air. Old houses were moved to new lots and new houses were built. And the governor kept tabs on the progress, sending instructions and receiving plans from Clarke.

More than five hundred persons made up the permanent population of Fernandina, which Clarke relocated "in an orderly fashion, with the changes necessary to provide greater usefulness, beauty, and harmony of the city." The careful documentation of the progress of what, for its day, was a massive project left in the records a detailed idea of what the town looked like when finished.

On Marine Street, facing the Amelia River, a narrow tributary of the broad Saint Marys and a sound safe harbor, stood George Clarke's warehouse as well as the warehouses and stores of other traders. On lot 5 of square 18 stood Zephaniah Kingsley's. The cosmopolitan population included a German doctor, Doctor Karl Sonntage and his son who operated the first nonmilitary hospital in Florida on two half lots on square 7 in the center of town. There was a French bakery, a Swiss carpenter, and even a Russian physician to supplement the services of the German doctors. Facing the river in the center of Marine Street was the fort, its flagpole being used as the center point from which Clarke's surveys were made. Off to the side of the southern edge of town were *casas de putas*, whorehouses for the entertainment of the sailors who swarmed the port. The prostitutes' clientele also included the auxiliary personnel from the slave trade, the adventurers who frequently passed the night in town after promoting the river crossing of the contraband human cargo. The practice was to move the slave ships upriver and offload them at camps on the south bank, the Spanish side. Then the slave runners would cross over to Georgia and create disturbances still further upstream on the Georgia side. The frontier guards would rush to protect the settlers, and the blacks were then moved across to Saint Marys.

Fernandina was also frequented by other questionable characters, poachers on timberland and cattle rustlers along the Saint Marys and its tributary streams. But the steady stream of merchantmen and their crews contributed most to the town's pleasure palaces. As many as thirty-eight ships were often in port or lying farther out. Bales of cotton, clandestinely shipped in from the United States, moved from the warehouses on Marine Street to the waiting ships. Lumber, masts and naval stores lay on the wharfs for loading. Provision merchants did a brisk business with sea captains supplying them with meat and flour for their crews.

Not all the men in town spent their leisure hours at the taverns or with the prostitutes. Amelia Island was also the site of prosperous plantations and an upper-class circle. On a hill above the town was the plantation of Domingo Fernandez. When writing *Notes on my Family*, Susan Fatio, whose Sicilian family had migrated from Switzerland years before and had become among the most aristocratic members of Saint Augustine society, recalled a Sunday she spent there as a girl:

> The commandant got permission from Mr. Fernandez to have a picnic there. . . . The principal families were invited and it was a great affair. . . . It was on Sunday, I am constrained to say, that this *fiesta* was given. There were a banquet and a ball, but the crowning pleasure of the day was a bull-fight. On withdrawing from dinner we were conducted to the arena. My father was one of the guests, and I was allowed to attend at the solicitation of some of my playmates, children of the "Contador". . . . Seats raised one above another encircled a large space. A young Spaniard, fantastically dressed in close-fitting garments with several little red flags in his hands, marched around a little while; then several dogs of various sizes, but not at all formidable looking, for they seemed bent on sport, were admitted. The matador played with the dogs, brandishing the flags in their faces and making them bark furiously. Then a hush, "the bull is coming," and a half-grown white bull was set loose in the arena. The dogs immediately made an attack on him, and the matador, shaking the flags in his face, incited the animal to turn on him instead of the dogs. With his stiletto he made agile thrusts and evaded attack on himself, darting up the steps of the amphitheater when pressed by the bull. All this vastly amused the company. Cries resounded of "Bravo el torete!" when the bull had the advantage, or "Bravo, Francesco! bravo el matador!" when the man prevailed. At last the little animal, which was declared to have made a good fight, was led off bleeding, but not badly hurt, they said. The company returned to the house; fruit was served—splendid watermelons, peaches and figs in abundance, and dancing, which had been indulged in during the morning and until dinner was announced was resumed. At the close of the evening we returned to the boats, the band playing all the while and the moonbeams dancing on the water.

Meanwhile, across the river in Georgia, another busy port was equally prosperous. And society in Georgia was equally varied. The mirror-image effect was enhanced by the fact that so many persons operated on both sides of the river.

West of the town of Saint Marys along the river were lumber mills and farms and villages such as Coleraine, Centerville, Traders Hill, where farmers traded. In the fall and winter, caravans came here from the interior of Georgia, and by oxcarts and horse carts farmers brought cotton, beeswax, honey, jerked beef and cowhides, all exchanged for flour, sugar, coffee, powder and shot. These markets products were constantly augmented by the produce: corn, beef and potatoes smuggled over the river from their relatives who had settled in East Florida. The Saint Marys River at many points was regularly the scene of such clandestine exchanges, as farmers, merchants and Seminole Indians traded with each other out of sight of any Spanish or American river patrols.

In their spare time, when trading had been done and they relaxed, these rural Georgians also enjoyed sport with animals, sport less refined than the tame bullfights in Fernandina. One of their favorite amusements was gander pulling. Gander pulling involved the excitement that went with the display of daring horsemanship and fast riding as well as the chance to bet on the results. The feathers were clipped from the gander's neck, which was then greased or soaped. The bird was suspended from a bar between two poles. The horseman dashed under the bar at full speed and, as he and the horse ran, caught the neck of the gander and tried to pull its head off. The spectators wagered on which rider would succeed. The one who managed to tear the head off the doomed bird was given the body as his reward.

Milder forms of amusement included horse racing and boxing. At every crossroads there was a quarter-mile race track for races between the horses from neighboring farms. The bets were generally small, a quart of whiskey or peach brandy. The boxing was closer in spirit to gander pulling. A fight customarily took place on every justice court day as the judges made their circuit. It took place in a ring, but rules were otherwise few and the fight was to the finish. One of the first laws passed by the Georgia legislature was to punish biting and gouging in the ring.

Nothing, though, surpassed drinking as the universal pastime in Georgia, as in all the rest of the country. President Madison had his well-stocked wine cellar and his laudanum. In Georgia the art of distilling corn liquor, the South's distinctive beverage, had not only already been invented but was flourishing as widely then as it would forevermore. Laudanum was medicine. Corn liquor was for opening eyes in the morning and closing them at night. Even the Methodists drank. As a chronicler of early Georgia put it, "to get drunk was mildly blameable, but to drink in moderation was temperance."

By 1811 Saint Marys had emerged from its earlier status as another of the rural villages where drinking, fighting and gander pulling filled men's days. It had become a cosmopolitan port rivaling Fernandina, where falsifying ships' documents to evade the Embargo Act, arranging the sale of smuggled goods from Florida and making smart deals were notable occupations. The first Presbyterian church, built in 1808, not only served as a religious meeting place, the boarded-up space between its elevated floor and the ground was used to store smuggled cigars and rum.

Saint Marys and Fernandina were almost equal in size as well as type of business enterprises. What distinguished them from each other was the large black population in the Georgia town. Of the 585 inhabitants of Saint Marys, only 349 were white. Also, within the age group of whites between sixteen and forty-five, 117 were men and only 65 were women. With few women, money in their pockets and time on their hands after the day's deals were done, the men of Saint Marys were available to accept the professional services of females such as those who occupied the houses on the south side of town in Fernandina. The imbalance between white and black population had its effect on prostitution as it did on society in general. It afforded slave girls a unique opportunity to hustle their way to freedom.

Records of prostitution by slaves are few, but in the summer of 1814 the Augusta *Herald* and the Augusta *Chronicle* both featured series on the activity in Saint Marys. The editor of the *Herald* condoned the practice, but the editor of the *Chronicle* condemned masters who received "$10 a month in rental from the wages of sin." Slave girls paid that amount to their masters for the time off from their regular duties to enable them to earn some cash. The nineteenth-century investigative reporter found out that these girls had heavy expenses for those days in addition to the $120 yearly cut they gave their masters. Housing, clothing and doctoring averaged

$320 a year. But their incomes so far outran their expenses that within a couple of years a girl could earn the nearly $1,000 she needed to buy her freedom.

It was to this lusty scene that George Mathews returned on June 9, 1811. He ignored the pimps and prostitutes, the smugglers and robbers, adventurers and sailors, and went directly to see James Seagrove and his circle. He wanted to get their reading on the situation before proceeding with his plans to organize the uprising in East Florida that his mission called for. Seagrove gathered together the leading citizens. He had forgotten his earlier feelings about the Ashleys. William and Lodowick Ashley, after all, were sons of Nathaniel Ashley, a fellow founder of the town, and so he invited them. He also invited John Floyd, the militia general, and the rich planter John Houstoun McIntosh. McIntosh was particularly important for Mathews's plans because by 1811 he had expanded his holdings in East Florida and even lived there from time to time.

They met at the home of William Clark, collector of the port. Clark had come to Saint Marys from Savannah nine years earlier and made his fortune. He had large lumber mills up the river and had built himself a large two-story house in town, one of the small number of homes in the elite three-thousand-dollars class. As collector of the port, the large legal and illegal fees he gathered for himself in his position augmented his income most comfortably. More important for Mathews, Clark's position was a good intelligence-collection post. From his numerous seagoing contacts who frequented both sides of the river, he was able to get a good idea of what was going on in Mathews's target area.

What Mathews heard was good news. Clark had picked up rumors which disturbed the group and which led them to take a keen interest in Mathews's plans. He hastened to have Isaacs write a letter for him in his name to Secretary of State James Monroe: "It is rumored that a regiment of Africans from Jamaica are destined for East Florida," the letter read, "and some of the inhabitants are in expectation of their arrival soon. From information I have collected, the best class of inhabitants there view it with just and dreadful apprehensions, and in the event would flock to the American standard, and acquit themselves in a manner becoming the legitimate defenders of our country's rights. . . ."

What he did not report in that letter was the skeptical view his Georgia friends took of the East Florida settlers' disposition toward rebellion. While agreeing that the specter of black troops should be enough to raise their racial feelings to the point of taking action, if that rumor were not true, they considered it doubtful whether Mathews could find the recruits willing to constitute the local authority his orders called for to hand over the province to the United States.

There was simply too much prosperity in East Florida. Prosperous people tend not to make revolutions. They gave him some examples. Long-staple, Sea Island cotton such as Kingsley grew could be sold for $0.75 a pound. Corn commanded a price of $1.25 a bushel in Saint Augustine. Lumber could be cut from the public domain and was, and cattle raising in East Florida had never been more profitable. All this had to be considered, not to mention the profits from contraband and slave smuggling which no one liked to mention out loud.

The prosperity of Florida, they told Mathews, had also affected life in Saint Marys. Prices were going up. No longer could a person buy fish for ten cents a dozen, or two fat hens for twenty-five cents and beef for three cents a pound.

This sort of talk only had the effect of making George Mathews's always florid complexion still redder. He decided to see for himself. He hired a boat and set out for a personal tour of the Spanish side of the Saint Marys. He sailed down the river past Point Petre, the post manned by the United States army's border command, into the Cumberland Sound and on into the Amelia River, landing just beyond the town of Fernandina. What he learned, he did not like.

CHAPTER X

A SECOND-BEST SOLUTION

George Mathews soon discovered that his friends in Saint Marys were right. Not only were big-time operators like Zephaniah Kingsley making money; worse, even small farmers were prosperous.

A modest-sized holding along the Saint Johns or on Amelia Island averaged twenty acres. On them were planted corn, potatoes, peas and pumpkins. Poultry and hogs were raised. And cattle were often the main money-maker. On twenty acres a man could raise and cow-pen six hundred head of cattle, sometimes seven hundred.

Stocks and droves of cattle were everywhere. The big landholders—the Sanchez family, Solana, Arredonodo, Atkinson, Craig, Kingsley—had large herds not only on their own lands but roaming the countryside. Stock cattle were worth $10 a head, so a man with a twenty-acre place and betwen six hundred and seven hundred cattle had between $19,500 and $22,650 worth of income in 1983 dollars from his cattle alone.

Corn was worth $6.50 a bushel in modern dollars, wheat flour $29.00 a hundred pounds, a dozen head of poultry slightly more than $20.00. Men selling their farm products at these prices saw no sense in rocking the boat. To gamble their fortunes on a revolutionary movement seemed to them foolish. Mathews's reconnoitering effort failed to produce men in place in East Florida willing to serve as the local authority he was looking for in order to conduct his mission according to the wording of his instructions.

He drove on, nonetheless, toward his goal. He simply turned to a second-best solution. He went back to Georgia and consulted with his friends once more. If he couldn't get together a group that was one hundred percent legitimately resident East Floridian, Mathews decided to settle for some who could just claim to be. In particular, he sought a leader who had the proper credentials. With the help of his good Georgia contacts, he found one—John Houstoun McIntosh.

McIntosh owned one of the largest plantations in Camden County, which he called The Refuge. As a highly respected large landholder he had served in the convention which wrote the Georgia constitution in 1798 and later as a justice of the county court with James Seagrove. When Mathews asked for help in putting together a group that could be made to appear to be East Florida residents, Seagrove had a candidate.

In 1803 McIntosh had purchased two large tracts of land in East Florida for twenty-eight thousand dollars. The land belonged to another American who had immigrated earlier to Florida. One was on Fort George Island, where he was a neighbor of Zephaniah Kingsley. The other was a two-thousand-acre property, the island of Ortega, which became in modern times a wealthy suburb of Jacksonville.

The Fort George Island property was particularly valuable as McIntosh developed it into a thriving lumber producer. By the time he met Mathews, he had a contract to ship three hundred thousand feet of lumber to England every month at a landed price of $10 per thousand foot. On the Ortega plantation he grew Sea Island cotton. These new roots gave McIntosh the same sort of stake in East Florida which caused the other transplanted Americans to shy away from Mathews's scheme. But his were older roots in Florida, which tugged him toward the adventure President Madison's agent had in mind. His grandfather, John Mohr McIntosh, had accompanied the founder of Georgia when James Oglethorpe in 1740 determined to make good his claim to the land where now his grandson grew cotton and cut lumber. The expedition was frustrated before the walls of Fort San Marco. John Mohr McIntosh was captured and hauled off in irons to the Moro Castle, the horror prison in Havana. He languished there for a dozen years and when finally released was a broken man. He swore a mighty oath, the kind his Highland ancestors were fond of swearing. McIntosh cursed the Spanish for all eternity and swore all future McIntosh males to avenge him. Some of that oath stuck to John Houstoun, his grandson. Of course, the oath had not prevented the old Scot's descendant from swearing allegiance to the Spanish Crown in order to gain his cotton and lumber land in Florida. But that was business. He had married a girl four years older than he was when only nineteen in order to add her family's fortune to his own.

So John Houstoun McIntosh had the Florida credentials Mathews was looking for in a leader for the rebellion he wanted to start, though he did not inherit as much of the McIntosh fighting spirit as a leader of such a cause could do with. He was not, unfortunately, a man in the mold of his older cousin John. His cousin was a swashbuckling duelist and a local revolutionary war hero in Georgia. At Sunbury, Georgia, Colonel John McIntosh had faced a force of five hundred British troops with less than half that number of men. The British demanded surrender of the small fort he was defending. "Come and take it," McIntosh challenged. They couldn't. As a reward the Georgia Assembly gave McIntosh a sword with his defiant words engraved on it.

John Houstoun McIntosh has been confused with his cousin by some early historians of the Florida Patriots War of 1811. They make him out to have been the revolutionary war soldier. This is a serious mistake. He was born on May 1, 1773, and was only a boy of ten when the revolutionary war in which his cousin distinguished himself broke out. How serious a mistake it is to confuse the two men will be seen as the story of George Mathews's operation unfolds.

Mathews appealed to McIntosh's keen business instincts. He

showed him his instructions, emphasizing the promise of United States military assistance once the revolt had started and the rebels requested it. With such backing, success was assured. Once East Florida was United States territory, Mathews suggested a land giveaway program better than the one the Spanish started in 1790. The leader of the rebel forces, naturally, would be the person best taken care of. Besides a large gift of land, the leader of the revolt would become territorial governor, with all that meant in power and prestige, not to mention opportunity to further augment his income.

McIntosh took some time to make up his mind. He wanted to be sure the plan would work. He sat down and wrote his friend William Craig about it. Craig was a fellow American resident of Florida. He was also the judge of the provincial court for Fort George and Amelia Island. McIntosh described the plan Mathews outlined. There is no record of Craig's reply, but McIntosh's letter certainly helped get the details of the operation into the wrong hands.

Mathews, of course, was not exactly a covert-action operator of the little-gray-man-in-the-shadows stripe. His reconnoitering in East Florida was not marked by much clandestine tradecraft. Also, he had made a curious contact. A man he had come to trust, Captain William Wyllys, was one of the transplanted Tories so easy to find in Florida. He had been a member of the Carolina Kings Rangers in 1783 at the end of the revolutionary war. Now he busied himself providing information to the governor of East Florida as well as to the British minister in Washington. There is no record to show whether he contacted Mathews or Mathews contacted him initially. But the contact was a good one for Wyllys in view of his double-agent activities.

Governor Enrique White, the man Mathews had earlier been warned would send him to Moro Castle if he tried the approach he had taken with Folch, died in June 1811, just as Mathews was sounding out people about his plan. White's death, a relief to Mathews, may also have made him careless. It certainly made him impatient to take advantage of the transition period. He yearned to get something going before White's permanent replacement arrived. He wrote in a progress report for Washington: "The present aggregate force at Saint Augustine consists of 150 men, 90 of whom are effective and fit for active duty, and even those could be easily subdued, as they are destitute of ammunition, and their fort (which in our hands might be rendered impregnable) at present is in a weak and decayed state."

But his eagerness and open operational style, McIntosh's letter, a report by Wyllys, or a combination of all three had blown his operation badly. The acting governor of East Florida wrote to Luis de Onís, the diplomatic representative of Ferdinand VII's loyal followers whom the United States government refused to recognize officially but wouldn't throw out of Washington.

He gave Onís all the details of Mathews's plot, including the generous land grants the old Georgian was offering. On September 5, 1811, Onís sent Monroe a sharp protest. He stated he had received an official letter from the governor of East Florida describing Mathews's activities.

"If that disturbed border be disturbed either directly or in-directly, through the conduct and intrigue of Governor Mathews, his agents or other citizens of the United States, or should its inhabitants be seduced to rebel against their lawful sovereign," Onís wrote, "His Majesty and the Spanish Nation at large will view this conduct with the utmost indignation, and cannot be accountable for the fatal consequences which must inevitably result therefrom."

The well-informed British minister to Washington also sat down and wrote Monroe, noting Mathews's activities "in corresponding with traitors, and in endeavouring by bribery and every act of seduction to infuse a spirit of rebellion into the subjects of the King of Spain. "I consider it therefore my duty, Sir," wrote Augustus J. Foster, "in consideration of the alliance subsisting between Spain and Great Britain, and the interests of his Majesty's subjects in the West Indian islands, so deeply involved in the security of East Florida, as well as in persuance of the orders of my government in case of any attempt against that country, to lose no time in calling upon you for an explanation of the alarming steps which Governor Mathews is stated to be taking for subverting the Spanish authority in that country, requesting to be informed by you upon what authority he can be acting and what measures have been taken to put a stop to his proceedings."

The request for information "upon what authority" Mathews was acting went straight to the heart of the matter. It is the question governments most dislike being asked about their covert activities. To it they must give a dishonest answer—the trouble is deciding which kind.

Mathews, of course, knew nothing of these diplomatic protests nor of the fact that the acting governor of Florida had blown the whistle on him a month before. In August, while Governor Estrada was putting the pieces together and planning his letter to Onís, Mathews was busily trying to pin down McIntosh's support and making further plans. McIntosh would go along if assurance of United States government assistance was firm. Mathews had Isaacs compose a careful letter to James Monroe in which he tried to establish that point while assuring his chief that the operation was going well.

"The inhabitants of the province are ripe for revolt," the letter sent off on August 3 said. "They are, however, incompetent to effect a thorough revolution without external aid. If two hundred stand of arms and fifty horsemen's swords were in their possession, I am confident they would commence the business, and with a fair prospect of success. These could be put into their hands by consigning them to the commanding officer at this post [Point Petre, outside Saint Marys], subject to my order. I shall use the most discreet management to prevent the United States being committed; and although I cannot vouch for the event, I think there would be but little danger."

Mathews went on to elaborate on problems he saw down the road for the operation. "This section of our Union is destitute of artillery. To me it appears that in the event of a revolution, and a consequent surrendering of the country to us, a corps will be indispensible."

Then in a way often characteristic of men charged with covert missions, he worried about security. Like some drinkers who think they are sober and everyone else at the party is drunk, and certain drivers who think everyone on the road but them is driving like a fool, certain covert operators fear someone else's slip will compromise their cover, never their own. Mathews said he hoped for an early reply and "that this will be confided to the proper departments only, for I can easily foresee that much injury to my operations would ensue from information given by clerks." He hastened to add, "This hint does not proceed from want of respect for your political sagacity, for I can with great truth assure you that it is not held in higher deference by any one than, sir, most respectfully, George Mathews."

So when James Monroe received the protests of the Spanish and British ministers in early September, he had on his desk a report from Mathews asking for important logistic support for the operation the diplomats were asking embarrassing questions about. Mathews need not have feared for James Monroe's political sagacity. He ignored the Spaniard's note and dissimulated to the British. He took almost two months, however, to mull over what he was going to say to the British minister, Augustus Foster.

He decided he simply would not say anything at all about Mathews or his activities. With disarming frankness he explained that the United States Congress in January 1811 had authorized the president to take possession of East Florida if ceded by local authority or in case of an attempt by Great Britain to occupy it. Since he had no facts to use to support this last case and did not want to mention the other, which, of course, was what Mathews's mission was all about, he looped a long throw in from left field.

First, he said that the United States had a right to take East Florida as indemnity for economic claims arising from spoilations caused by the closing of New Orleans in the last century. The United States had demonstrated great moderation in foregoing taking measures of self-redress long before, but at last such time had come.

He said that the United States simply knew that Great Britain had intentions of occupying East Florida. For commercial, geographic and strategic reasons the United States could not allow this to happen.

"Under these circumstances," wrote the secretary of state, "it would be equally unjust and dishonorable in the United States to suffer East Florida to pass into the possession of any other power. Unjust because they would thereby lose the only indemnity within their reach . . . dishonorable, because in permitting another power to wrest from them that indemnity, their inactivity and acquiescence could only be imputed to unworthy motives."

"Situated as East Florida is," the secretary continued, "cut off from the other possessions of Spain, and surrounded in a great measure by the territory of the United States; and having also an important bearing on their commerce, no other power could think of taking possession of it, with other than hostile views to them. Nor could any other power take possession of it without endangering their prosperity and interests."

The correspondence from Mathews evidently bothered him as much as the protests had. He could not get around to answering it. However, the press in the early nineteenth century was every bit as bent on fulfilling its role as the fourth branch of government as it is now. All diplomatic exchanges, such as the letters between Foster and Monroe, were regularly printed in a manner which the New York *Times* would applaud. The full text of this diplomatic exchange was published in the late fall of 1811.

Mathews had waited patiently and hoped each Friday the weekly mail from Savannah would bring him the word from Washington. No news, of course, was, in one sense, good news. His actions were not disavowed. So he continued to work, spreading promises about the land available for any volunteers from Georgia who might wish to go to Florida. The most lowly volunteers, men who would go as private soldiers, were promised fifty acres. When the papers printed the Monroe-Foster letters, he went into high gear. He thought that Monroe's answer was indirectly a signal to him. The secretary of state was taking the little warning about clerks and correspondence seriously. By his answer to the British minister, he was telling Mathews it was all right to go ahead without committing the matter to direct correspondence that could prove damaging.

Armed with the diplomatic correspondence, he was able to convince McIntosh to act, and together they began soliciting recruits. Mathews showed all who would listen his commission from the president and the newspaper accounts in which Monroe noted the act of Congress upon which authority his commission was based.

Mathews had earlier made big promises to Spanish residents of East Florida when he had unsuccessfully tried recruiting there, as the governor reported to Onís. He had assured them they could practice their religion freely once Catholic East Florida had become part of the Protestant United States—a literally cheap trick, since freedom of religion was guaranteed by the United States Constitution. He had figured the Spanish did not know that, since religious freedom had never been heard of in Spain. Security of their real and personal property, he had assured them, they could also count on. Then he had become expansive, promising to pay them all the indebtedness the Spanish government owed them, their back pay and allowances. To civil officials he had offered continuation of their jobs and salaries; soldiers he had offered a choice of serving in the American army or free transportation to a place they selected.

So what he was offering now in Georgia was nothing new for him. It is possible that the *media palabra* in which he had been told the true dimensions of his role back in January 1811 had included authority to promise land and positions in government such as he now dangled before the Georgians he met. Perhaps, however, he was simply a zealous recruiter. In any case, his pitch did not produce.

Not many men in Camden County had any stomach for fighting in the kind of conflict that might occur in Florida. They preferred horse racing and gander pulling. Not a single Spanish soldier sold himself for promises of steady American army wages. Spanish civilians had not bought Mathews's line, Americans in Florida preferred making money, and Georgia farmers preferred to wait and see.

Mathews did manage to interest some of the circle who gathered at Clark's house to take a more active role. Clark himself was interested as were the Ashleys and a few more. McIntosh was not an inspiring leader, but if he was willing to wager his sizable fortune, these men decided they would go along.

With this sort of general staff, Mathews next turned to another means of improvising "a patriot army." He had not heard anything about the two hundred stand of arms and fifty swords he wanted, but he still had his orders saying he could count on United States Army support. He decided to ask the commandant at Point Petre for the arms and men he needed.

CHAPTER XI

WHO'S IN CHARGE HERE?

To George Mathews his relationship with the American military forces in the area of his covert-action operation was perfectly clear. His orders spelled it out: "If in the execution of any part of these instructions, you should need the aid of a military force," they said, "the same will be afforded you upon your application to the commanding officer of the troops of the United States on that station. . . . "

The troops on station in the area were the several companies of dragoons encamped at Point Petre just outside the town of Saint Marys, a total of two hundred men. They were charged with the task of securing the border with Florida, not very arduous duty so far as any threat from the Spanish was concerned, but a nearly impossible task if the smugglers were considered.

In the early months of the new year, 1812, the president's special agent decided he could put them to better use than their assigned duties called for. After half a year of frustration in trying to recruit a patriot army for the Florida operation he was ready to abandon his nearly fruitless wooing of local farmers on both sides of the Saint Marys. There was a ready-made army at hand and he would use it.

He could either call on the Georgia militia, of which he was a general officer, or play the trump card his instructions gave him and order up men from the United States Army, or both. He decided first he would sound out the situation regarding the militia.

In February, 1812, he paid a call on Governor David Mitchell. The Georgia chief executive was on a visit to Jeffersonton, the county seat of Camden County. Whether the governor was on official bussiness or checking up on his slave-smuggling operations is not clear, but he listed carefully to Mathews's plea. Mitchell ordered General John Floyd, the commander of the Georgia militia, to hold his troops in readiness for possible action in the near future. General Floyd, who lived at Fairfield Plantation in Camden County and was one of the men with whom Mathews had consulted from the earliest days of his operational planning, was happy to comply.

But Mathews was not satisfied. The commitment did not have any solid numbers attached to it. Militias were volunteer forces. They could be mustered in for a specified period of time for a specific purpose, but it would be difficult to muster them officially to fight in Florida when so few men had been willing to give up gander pulling to go as individual volunteers to get fifty acres of good cattle-raising and corn-growing land. A hasty count showed Mathews he had perhaps 125 men he could rely on as a result of all his efforts at recruiting. Fort San Marcos, he knew, had never been taken by anyone, but he also knew that there were fewer than 100 effective troops there. He calculated that if he could confront them with a force more than double their strength, he had an excellent chance of doing what no one else had ever done. If he could get 140 men from Point Petre, he figured he could take the fort.

To get his operation going he was impelled by several pieces of information he acquired to move quickly as the new year got underway. He had learned that Sebastian Kindelan had been appointed as Enrique White's permanent replacement as governor of East Florida. He knew Kindelan from the time he had been governor of Georgia and the Spanish officer had been sent over from Cuba to work with him in quieting the boisterous Saint Marys border.

While he was governor of Georgia, George Mathews had taken a different view of raiding East Florida than he took now when armed with a presidential order to subvert the province. Miles's Law applied to early American government activity as well as it does to present-day bureaucracy: where you stand depends on where you sit. In 1794, when governor, he had feared the Spanish might retaliate to the incursions of Georgians by inciting the Indians and had issued a proclamation forbidding the assembly of troops and any other hostile acts against the friendly Spanish neighbors.

Despite this, Camden County rogues kept stealing slaves from Florida plantations and committing similar outrages. Together he and Kindelan developed a plan for strengthening border patrols. He respected the Spaniard as a tough regular-army officer and knew that once he arrived at Saint Augustine, it would not be easy to take the fort from him no matter how outnumbered. Now that he was the one who wanted to violate the border of East Florida, he did not relish trying to do it in defiance of his former collaborator in upholding law and order.

But Mathews had more on his mind by late February 1812 than this generalized concern with the possible consequences for his operation that the arrival of Kindelan might mean. He had received some intelligence from Captain Wyllys that convinced him he had to act swiftly. Wyllys sent a letter to McIntosh that alarmed Mathews and convinced him that there was no time to be lost if Saint Augustine were to be captured.

According to Wyllys, reinforcements were already on the high seas bound for Florida. The British were finally swinging into line behind their Spanish allies against Napoleon. As part of this decision they were sending troops to the garrison at Saint Augustine. These troops, based in the West Indies, were coming via Cuba. Wyllys counseled his conspiratorial contacts in Georgia to move "without delay" if they hoped to achieve their objective.

The Wyllys letter is the kind of unfathomable flotsam that collects around the remains of all old covert-action operations. In this case it triggered action by Mathews that proved to be precipitous and that had both fateful and unfortunate consequences. The information it contained was false, hardly unusual for information coming from a double agent. Who guided the hand of the letter's author at that particular moment cannot be determined at this late date. It could have been either the Spanish or the British principals to whom Wyllys regularly reported. Some historians even suggest that Mathews himself conspired with Wyllys to produce the report that set the operation in motion at that particular moment in March 1812, which ultimately proved to have been the wrong time. It is not difficult to think of a wily double agent like Wyllys as a triple agent. The idea that the British were coming added an element to the conspiracy that was useful to Mathews in prodding the United States Army into action. It also provided an essential element of information in support of the second condition under which Mathews's orders called for the takeover of East Florida. Mathews's instructions authorized him to act to take possession of the territory either when it was offered by local authority or, in the second place, if it were threatened with conquest by a foreign power. So the case can be made that what the letter said was not frightening to Mathews but precisely what he wanted to hear.

Whoever may have inspired the spurious story the letter related, it resulted in Mathews's calling on the wrong man for military assistance. Lt. Col. Thomas A. Smith, commander of the troops at Point Petre, was off on temporary duty in the Mississippi Territory. When Mathews made his request for 140 men on March 10, 1812, the man he had to ask for help was Major Jacint Laval.

Jacint Laval held himself in high esteem. He did not have an equally high opinion of the frontier general who approached him for assistance. Mathews and Laval had shared a little cottage near Point Petre for seven months by March 1812, but they seldom spoke to one another. Mathews had been busy with his recruitment schemes and had shut himself off in his bedroom with his fellow plotters most of the time. He never asked Laval to join in these sessions, but Laval had heard enough through the thin walls to know what was being planned. He did not like it.

Major Laval had certain fixed ideas about honor and patriotism that were bruised by the kind of covert plot he heard being hatched on the other side of the bedroom wall. Like General Lafayette he had left his native France to fight and be wounded in the American struggle for independence. After the war he had settled down in South Carolina as a planter and merchant. When the threat of war began growing larger and larger during the early years of the new century as both Napoleon's navy and the British fleet took turns capturing American vessels, he rejoined the army and rose to the rank of major in the Light Dragoons.

He had come to America full of ideals about fighting tyranny and defending liberty and the rights of man. In 1812 he saw the Spanish loyal to their deposed King Ferdinand fighting for the same things he had come to America to fight for. They were struggling to throw off the dictatorship of Napoleon as the American colonists in 1776 fought to overthrow the unjust British monarch, George III. To him what Mathews and his friends were planning was to steal from these patriotic Spaniards their fertile lands in Florida. He could not stomach such stuff. The uncouth old illiterate and his greedy companions might be able to claim American nativity but they did not represent the America he had chosen to fight for. When Mathews finally asked him for help, after all the attempts at secret plotting to recruit an army he had overheard had failed, Laval refused. Mathews was furious, of course. And the angry letters that both fired off to Washington (Mathews's being carefully edited by Ralph Isaacs) give such a graphic account of this encounter and ensuing events, their voices can still be heard shouting at each other down through more than a century and a half of time.

Their fight began when Mathews, as he was about to leave the cottage on the morning of March 10, turned to Laval and said, "Major, there's a bag of buckshot on my mantle. I'll need it made into cartridges."

The remark caught Laval off guard and he did not reply.

"I expect we're going to have a fight soon," Mathews continued. "Major, I want a ball put in each of the cartridges along with the buckshot."

"Who will account for these balls?" asked Laval. "Are they to be used at Point Petre or elsewhere?"

"Never mind about that," Mathews replied. "If they go out of your hand, you'll get a receipt."

Laval let the matter drop at that point. But the more he thought about it, the less he liked the idea. So by afternoon he ordered that no cartridges should be made. When Mathews heard about this, he stormed back.

"Major Laval," he asked, "will you order a detachment of one hundred and forty men to cross the Saint Marys?"

"No," Laval shouted back.

"Major," said the old general, "you have orders to occupy, hold and defend East Florida, or any part of it, which may be offered to the United States. Your orders are to obey my requisitions for men and materials. Do you dare defy the orders of the president of the United States?"

"I have unbounded respect for the president and his wishes," replied Laval, "but I have no orders to obey an unauthorized command. My orders are to hold and defend East Florida, as you say, when offered by the local authorities. These orders don't bind me to use troops to cause a revolution in East Florida."

"Major Laval, you fought for our freedoms in the Revolution, I did and so did Major James Seagrove of Saint Marys. We're all men of '76. The United States now has a chance to acquire East and West Florida. The opportunity may never come again in our lifetime. I talked with President Madison, with Robert Smith and the secretaries of war and navy. I know James Monroe is anxious for my success. You've seen my commission, you have your orders."

"General Mathews, I fought for your American freedom, but I didn't leave my native land so that avaricious men could grab land by debasing the ideals of '76."

"Are you saying that I, who lost twenty thousand dollars in fighting for my liberty, who never took a penny from my country, am—"

"No, general, not you," Laval interrupted, "but there are many associated with you who lack your patriotism. I see the advantage of acquiring Florida, but by negotiation, not by intrigue and theft."

"Then you refuse my order. You defy the wishes of the president of the United States?"

"I refuse, general, to do that which is unauthorized and illegal."

"I tell you that it is authorized by order of the president of the United States!"

"It is not! And you, sir, I order to leave my post. I am in command here. I do not want you to set foot here again!"

Mathews was astounded. He stomped off in a rage and sought out his friends in Saint Marys. He reviewed his orders and what he thought were the orders of the secretary of war he had seen before leaving Washington more than a year before.

On January 24, 1811, the secretary of war had sent confidential instructions to General Wade Hampton, the commanding general in the Mississippi Territory and to Colonel Cushing, the commanding officer at Fort Stoddert. He informed them that the United States Congress had passed a law authorizing the president to take possession of East Florida in case an arrangement was made "with the local authority" of said territory for ceding the whole or any portion of it to the United States or in case of an attempt by "any foreign government" to occupy that territory or any portion of it. The two officers were instructed to cooperate with Mathews in his efforts to execute the transfer of that territory to the United States.

"In the execution of the duty assigned him [General Mathews] and to fulfill the object of the law, he will in case of making such an arrangement, call upon you for such detachment of troops under your command as may be necessary to occupy and maintain certain military posts within the territory aforesaid. He will consult with you and you will be pleased to concert with him such measures, and make a disposition of the forces under your command as shall be best calculated to attain the objects in view."

Two days later, January 26, 1811, the secretary of war sent confidential instructions to Lt. Col. Thomas A. Smith, commanding officer of United States troops on the Georgia-Florida border.

"The President of the United States," these orders read, "having appointed General George Mathews and Colonel John McKee agents on the part of the United States to receive possession of the territory lying east of the River Perdido and south of the State of Georgia, and the Mississippi Territory, in the event of an arrangement being made for that purpose with the local authority of the same, and having taken possession of such military posts within the said territory, as by an arrangement with the local authority may be agreed to be surrendered, you are hereby authorized and directed, on the request of those gentlemen or either of them, stating that an arrangement has been made as aforesaid, to march with the troops, under your command, and to take possession of such posts within the territory aforesaid, as may be so agreed to be surrendered, and to hold and defend the same."

On the same day another set of instructions to Smith directed him to use the gunpowder and lead that had been forwarded to him to make enough cartridges for shooting practice by the troops under his command.

So at the same time Mathews had received his instructions signed by the secretary of state, instructions had gone out to the military commanders in the area of his planned covert operation which, as far as he could see, gave him the authority to command a coordinated action designed to carry out his plan.

Seagrove and the Saint Marys clique assured Mathews that Smith had understood these orders the same way Mathews did and that Smith was a man on whom they could rely. If Mathews hadn't rushed matters when he heard from Wyllys and had waited for Smith's return, things would have been different.

Thomas Adam Smith had been born in Virginia in 1781, but like Mathews himself, he and his family had migrated to Wilkes County, Georgia, after the Revolution and become owners of extensive properties. Brought up in Georgia, Smith understood the Georgians' point of view. He hated Spaniards and Indians. He agreed that taking Florida was a good idea. In addition to his right thinking, Thomas Adam Smith had the right connections. He was a close friend of Senator Crawford and Congressman Troup, both of whom had worked diligently to get congressional support for President Madison's Florida adventure. He named his two sons, William and George, for them. His brother-in-law, Peter Early, was also a congressman and later became a governor of Georgia. His father-in-law, James White, was the founder of Knoxville, Tennessee, and his wife's brother, Hugh Lawson White, was a prominent man in that bumptious frontier state. This was the kind of man, his friends in Saint Marys felt, Mathews should have dealt with, not a French immigrant with a high-flown sense of duty so difficult for a real American to understand.

Seagrove and his friends encouraged Mathews to go back and tackle Laval again. He agreed he would. But he did not take the chance of defying Laval's order to stay off the major's post. He sent Isaacs back with a letter.

The pressure Isaacs and Mathews continued to apply over the next several days wore Laval down. He finally agreed to let Mathews have fifty men. Wearily Laval later reported to the War Department that the old general and his tenacious assistant "almost tortured me to death to get me to coincide and coalesce with the troops of the United States then under my command to execute their infamous skeems [*sic*]." He issued orders to allow the men, soldiers and officers, to volunteer as a regular detachment of the United States Army and to serve as Mathews directed.

That was not exactly what Mathews had in mind. He could not very well have United States troops participating officially as a United States military unit in his planned attack. He wanted Laval to allow the men to volunteer as individuals and become part of the "patriot army" of the "local authority" which would request the United States to take them under its protective custody. When he tried to convey this thought to Laval through Isaacs, the major exploded again and countermanded his order. Nothing in his orders nor anything in his experience in the United States Army permitted, let along obligated, a commander to give his men leave to abandon their post and become volunteers bent on undermining the authority and seizing the territory of a friendly state.

Mathews then decided he would take a different and daring tack. He would subvert Laval's command. Putting his head together with Isaacs's, the two devised a scheme for wooing Laval's subordinate officers and winning them to their side in the quarrel. Laval's second-in-command, Captain Abraham Massias, and Lieutenant Daniel Appling were easy marks. Neither liked Laval and both found the old general and his smooth-talking secretary the kind of determined men they were glad to follow. The three of them came up with a plan of action they were sure would break the Frenchman.

Laval did not welcome Isaacs when, accompanied by Lieutenant Appling, he appeared at his door after midnight with a letter signed by Mathews. The letter was intended to bring matters to a head.

The local authorities in Florida, the letter stated, wished to surrender a part of their province, in point of fact, Rose's Bluff, a place four miles above Saint Marys and across the river on Amelia Island. In his official capacity as a commissioner of the American government, Mathews ordered Laval to march a detachment of fifty men to the bluff at ten o'clock the following morning to take peaceful possession and to hold and defend the land for the United States.

Isaacs and Appling found the major fully dressed despite the late hour with his sword buckled to his side. "Major Laval," said Isaacs, as he handed over the letter, "I have a requisition here from General Mathews for a detachment of troops."

Laval studied the letter. "Where is Rose's Bluff? Is it a military post?"

"Yes, it is, sir," answered Isaacs, "a military post in East Florida."

Laval seemed to study the hilt of his sword. He took some moments to reply. Looking up at last, he said, "I will not march any detachment from Point Petre. If I ever order a force into East Florida it will be my entire command, and then only after giving the contractor timely notice, so he can furnish provisions."

"You refuse, sir, either to allow volunteers to leave the Point or to order a detachment to take that part of Florida which is offered to the United States?"

"I most certainly do."

"Will you give me a written answer to General Mathews's letter?"

"No, at least not now. I need time to prepare an answer."

"I will be at your service, sir, until morning."

But morning came and Laval still had not prepared a written

answer. When Isaacs reported to Mathews, the general prepared to take step two. This was to inspire a mutiny by the major's men.

Under Isaacs direction, Captain Massias and the two lieutenants serving under Laval, Daniel Appling and Elias Stallings, drew up an indictment against their commanding officer. The document avoided as much as possible mentioning anything that would reveal too much about the real nature of the differences between these officers and their superior—their support of General Mathews in his quarrel with their chief.

Laval was cited on two charges—conduct unbecoming an officer and gentleman and neglect of duty. Listed under the first charge were sixteen specifications and under the second only three. Many of the specifications of unbecoming conduct were startling. The major was accused of encouraging soldiers to throw away beef supplied by the contractor, of using abusive language to Captain Massias and the contractor, of issuing orders through noncommissioned officers and soldiers, of treating commissioned officers with disrespect and contempt, of discharging prisoners illegally from the guardhouse, of giving his son William leave to fight a duel in Charleston, of borrowing money from private soldiers and not repaying it and of wasting public powder in firing salutes.

The shockers were the accusations of immorality. Specification 11 of charge 1 declared Laval allowed to pass "unnoticed and without investigation the complaint of Mrs. Gaddy the wife of a soldier against a soldier under his command for an attempt to commit rape upon an infant female aged between five and six years which attempt was attended with aggravated circumstances."

In specification 5 of charge 1, the major was condemned for "granting general permission during the months of November and December 1811 at Point Petre to a Sergeant under his command to sleep out of camp with the wife of a soldier . . . provided he would send the said soldier's wife to him occasionally, and that they might mutually enjoy the said soldier's wife which was duly complied with and which woman has lived in his kitchen from the 27th of January to this day the 27th of March 1812."

Only four of the specifications bore any relation to the real cause of the complaint. Specifications 6 through 9 of charge 1, levied by Lieutenant Appling, stated that Laval acted in an ungentlemanly manner on March 11 while in the quarters of Captain Massias, treating Generals Mathews and Floyd rudely. On the following day, with equal rudeness, he ordered a noncommissioned officer, in the presence of Massias, to double the guard, stating the regular officers could not be trusted. Finally, Laval was charged with ordering General Mathews, an agent of the president of the United States, off the Point on March 11 "in a most rude and ungentlemanly manner." He also had done so "with marked contempt and disrespect without any cause or provocation whatever, knowing at the same time that the General had powers and was treating with the Authorities of East Florida, which powers, he, Major Laval, had a copy of and knew the necessity of the General's presence at that critical moment."

Although the formal charges were not presented until March 27, by which time Colonel Smith had returned and assumed command, the statements of Massias, Isaacs, Appling and Stallings were made on March 12 and destroyed the little remaining confidence of the commissioned officers in their acting commandant. Captain Massias obviously was willing to do anything Mathews wished. So too were Appling and Stallings, and they were by then joined by the other captain on station, Joseph Woodruff. These officers offered to resign their commissions and volunteer to serve Mathews. The enlisted men were talking about going AWOL and joining the revolutionists. To prevent this, Laval doubled the guard. Eventually fifty men, one-fourth of his command, stood on guard and Laval himself remained on post during the four critical days from March 12 through March 16.

While all this was going on Mathews was also thinking about another string he felt he had to his bow, the gunboats of the United State Navy lying off the town of Saint Marys and patrolling the mouth of the river.

On February 28 he had written to the officer commanding these ships, Commodore Hugh G. Campbell. He told Campbell that the

United States government had decided to take possession of East Florida and that he had been commissioned to effect it. He asked him whether he had received instructions from the secretary of the navy to cooperate with United States troops at the request of General Mathews in taking possession of East Florida. When Campbell informed Mathews he had not received such instructions, Mathews told him "confidentially that circumstances justified the expectations of a speedy change in the political affairs of that country and suggested the expediency of holding the naval force on this station in readiness to act as occassion may require," according to the letter Campbell wrote Washington on February 29.

Further assurances from Mathews that he had orders from the president of the United States to take possession of Florida and that the War Department had already instructed the officer commanding the detachment of United States troops at Point Petre to cooperate in the affair convinced Commodore Campbell to attribute the failure of the Department of the Navy to send him similar instructions to an oversight, and he therefore expressed his decision to cooperate with the army in assisting the insurgents. But in his letter to Washington he wrote, "I should feel much more gratified in being honoured with instructions from you on this head."

Commodore Campbell had been in the waters off Amelia Island for more than a year before Mathews contacted him to ask for support. The reason officially given for his presence was that he was there to enforce the Embargo Act and the act prohibiting the importation of slaves. His presence made Lt. Justo Lopez, commandment of the Amelia Island outpost, nervous. He wrote Governor White in early 1811 that he didn't think the United States ships were hovering off the island solely for the purpose of preventing illegal shipping activities. White told him to remain vigilant.

On January 26, 1811, the same day General Mathews's instructions were issued by the State Department and the secretary of war was writing instructions regarding the Mathews mission, the secretary of the navy instructed Campbell to hasten the dispatch of five more gunboats from Charleston to Saint Marys. He said that although he had recently written on the subject of the illegal slave trade, he was so disturbed by the continued violations that he had to write again stressing the urgency and importance of the matter.

A week earlier he wrote to the officers commanding United States ships at the New Orleans station. "General Mathews," he said, "being charged by the President of the United States with important duties, in the execution of which, he may require your aid you are hereby ordered and directed, upon General Mathews showing you this order, and furnishing you with a copy thereof, to afford him every assistance in your power, in such manner and upon such service, as he may point out to you. . . . Copies of General Mathews Requisition upon you, you will without delay, transmit to Gov. Claiborne; to the commanding naval officer at New Orleans and to me."

No such order was sent to Commodore Campbell. If it had been, things along the Saint Marys River would have gone more smoothly for the old general. Having received such sweeping affirmation of his power to demand coordinated support from the navy for his operation as it related to West Florida, it seems unlikely that the failure to issue a similarly worded order to Campbell was an oversight. Since the cover of concern for the illegal slave trade was so natural and had been available for use since the days of Mathews's first mission to Florida, the omission must have been due to reluctance to blow such a fortuitous cover situation. Mathews had expected to find the navy in place when he first arrived on his second mission to Florida. In his initial illiterate report to Washington in February 1811 he complained he found no "armed Visil or gun bobt," and, hence, he decided the time was not ripe for his East Florida operation and went off to find Governor Folch.

The fact that Campbell had no clear order to provide support to Mathews and had to be persuaded by the general, relying on copies of his own instructions and those the secretary of the navy wrote to the officers at New Orleans, compounded the difficulties with Laval. When Campbell found out that Laval was not cooperating with Mathews as the general had assured him, he began to have doubts.

Although certainly not intended, the confusion about what Mathews's orders meant and exactly what the responsibilities of the United States armed forces were in supporting his covert action operation set a national style for such situations. At the Bay of Pigs and on the desert in Iran in 1980, it would be repeated.

On the day before the Bay of Pigs invasion, the order to deliver a second air strike against Castro's air force, an action all CIA operational personnel assumed was approved and vital to success, was cancelled by the White House. On the desert in Iran, Marine helicopters followed one set of instructions, army commandos followed another.

Faced with the situation, Mathews did what the bolder cold warriors did in the 1950s. He bashed on. His mutineers at Point Petre did their best to help him get on top of his troubles. During the night of March 14 and all the following day. Major Laval stood guard with fifty of his most trusted men to see that no officer or soldier slipped away to join Mathews's motley insurgent army. The harried major wrote two long letters to the secretary of war, one on March 16, the other on May 2, 1812. In them he gave complete details of what happened next, even the words he and the troublemakers used, thereby making it possible to recreate the scene. Just after the evening meal, Captain Massias, spotting the major pacing back and forth on the parade ground, could stand it no longer.

"Stop," he shouted at his superior, "I want to see you."

He ran up to the astounded major and said, "You've acted contrary to the wishes of our government. All the officers dissaprove of your arbitrary conduct. Why don't you leave the post?"

"Captain Massias," the major shouted back to the mutineer, "report to your quarters and hold yourself for further orders!"

"You bastard, you damned Frenchman," Massias shouted, doubling his fist and shaking it under Laval's nose, "if you leave this camp for fifteen minutes I'll march the troops to East Florida!" Laval did not allow him to say more. "You are under arrest," he yelled, and commanded his soldiers to take the captain to his quarters.

The major went immediately to his own quarters and drew up

charges against Massias. Then he buckled on his sword again and, with a pistol in each hand, returned to guard duty. Unexpectedly, late in the afternoon the next day Colonel Smith returned. He immediately assumed command, placed Major Laval under technical arrest and confined him to his cottage and the grounds of Point Petre. He ordered Massias back to duty, dimissing the charges against him. His grounds for such action were that he needed officers. He did.

As Mathews saw his Plan B, the recruitment of a sufficient force for his "patriot army" to enable it to take Saint Augustine, crumble because of Major Laval's refusal to cooperate, he fell back on yet another substitute for his original scheme of starting an uprising against Spanish authority by irate subjects. When he told Laval that a group at Rose's Bluff had offered that bit of land to the United States and that he needed United States troops to take possession of it, he was not faking. He had Plan C in operation.

Major Laval languished in his quarters and lamented. He poured out his feelings to the secretary of war in a letter on May 2. Laval appealed as an old soldier who had never failed to follow principles of honor and duty against the acts of young Colonel Smith, who suffered himself to be deluded by Mathews and "his confidential Jew, Col. Isaacs."

"Is it possible," he asked "that the government cannot be better furnished with officers than with Jews, rogues, traitors, conspirators? What age is this? What Prospect has an officer who would die at his post sooner than seeing his honor and that of the flag tarnished?" Laval's sense of honor unfortunately stopped short of viewing Jews as better than rogues, conspirators and other lowlife.

In concluding his letter Laval asked to be transferred from Point Petre and plaintively requested not to be left anywhere near Mathews. His request was granted. On June 13, 1812, Colonel Smith authorized him to wear his sword again and to go to Charleston to await further orders. At Charleston he received orders to proceed to a command at Sackett's Harbour on the eastern tip of Lake Ontario. The nation was now at war with England and this was an important front. The following year he was promoted to lieutenant colonel and shortly after to full colonel. In 1814 he received an honorable discharge. Two years later he decided to return to military life and requested active duty in Washington. After appealing to the president, he was made military storekeeper at Harpers Ferry, where he served until his death in 1822. He never was able to conceive that Mathews's action had been part of a legitimate plan approved by the president of the United States. To him it was impossible to believe that James Madison and James Monroe, two heroes of the American Revolution whom he had volunteered to serve, could countenance such activity. He was wrong in his faith in the noble character of the two men. In one sense, however, he was right about Mathews's scheme for accomplishing his mission. The idea of disguising United States soldiers as local patriots volunteering to oppose Spanish authorities went a bit beyond any instruction Mathews had *in writing*. Did it also go beyond anything *said* by the president when he gave Mathews what Richard Helms, more than a century later, called the "field marshal's baton"?

In the same testimony to the Senate Intelligence Committee investigating the operations the CIA undertook in 1970 to prevent the election of Salvador Allende as president of Chile in which Helms made the remark about the baton, he said something more. "The President came down very hard that he wanted something done and *he didn't much care how*. . . . " That was the "impression" he got, Helms said. Did George Mathews get the same kind of impression in President Madison's office in 1811 that Richard Helms got in President Nixon's in 1970?

That he did seems beyond any doubt. In March of 1812 when frustrated by the French major, the old general from Georgia acted like a man who had been given a job to do by "the highest authority," as CIA's official correspondence always guardedly referred to the president of the United States. He improvised in the face of his frustration until he got something going that bore at least some resemblance to the revolt of Florida citizens that he and the president had talked about.

CHAPTER XII

THE REPUBLIC OF ROSE'S BLUFF

Before he first confronted Major Laval, requesting cartridges, balls and buckshot on March 10, Mathews had set the stage for what he hoped would be a swift assault against Saint Augustine. The attack force had begun stealing across the Saint Mary's River and setting up an initial staging area on the Florida shore several days before.

The original plan, as Mathews outlined in a letter to James Monroe on March 14, called for a series of quick movements. First the insurgents would travel across the tributaries of the Saint Marys and across Amelia and Fort George islands to the Saint Johns, then down Pablo Creek and across the marshes to the outskirts of Saint Augustine. The town of Fernandina would be bypassed and the few Spanish posts on the Saint Johns outflanked by the overland route and cut off from escape by water. This last would be accomplished by the gunboats of Commodore Campbell. Mathews planned to order Campbell to anchor them at strategic points in the Saint Johns so that they would both block the Spanish and keep open the supply line to Georgia.

All this was contingent on the surprise attack Mathews had in mind for Saint Augustine. His plan was to reach Fort San Marcos at dawn on Monday morning, March 16. Since Sunday was more a day for riotous drinking than religious services on the part of the Spanish troops, he expected to find them in the same condition the Japanese found servicemen at Pearl Harbor after the traditional Saturday night partying of December 6, 1941. Guards would be napping, and the rest of the men still deeper in sleep.

The acting governor had not repaired the drawbridge. Kindelan had still not arrived to take charge of that and other necessary improvements that would once again make the fort the formidable bastion it had traditionally been and the Saint John's river a well-guarded place. Mathews calculated he'd take the old fort in a matter of a few hours at most.

The Spanish had fortifications at three places on the Saint Johns north of Saint Augustine. They had been surveyed by a Spanish army engineer in 1793 and were designed to command the river and prevent foreign vessels from sailing up toward Saint Augustine. By the time Mathews planned his invasion two of them, the Quesada Battery at the mouth of the river and the San Vincente Ferrer Battery a few miles up the river on the ridge running along the south bank, had been virtually abandoned. At one time the Quesada Battery had boasted two cannons, a two-story barracks and a large powder magazine. The fortification known as San Vincente Ferrer had two barracks buildings for permanently stationed troops and another building to house militia. In 1811 they were only served by transient troops.

San Nicolas, the third establishment, was the only one of consequence. It was located at the Cowford, a small settlement, now Jacksonville, where the King's Road crossed the river. The King's Road had been built early in the British period to connect their newly acquired Florida settlements with Georgia. The fort was more than a hundred feet in length on each side and its guns commanded both the river approach and the road. But Mathews planned to slip by it, following the creeks and paths to the east on the ocean side of the river. Once he had Saint Augustine and Commodore Campbell was in place on the Saint Johns, San Nicolas would be no worry.

When Laval refused to help him, not even answering his request sent by Isaacs to provide assistance for the crucial movement he had scheduled for March 12, Mathews began to improvise an entirely different approach. He decided he would take Fernandina first.

He knew that Lieutenant Lopez had only nine men besides himself in his total garrison. As far as he knew then, although the major had refused him, he could still count on Campbell. The fort that was located in the center of Marine Street, looking out over the marsh along the Amelia River, was as neglected as the two smaller batteries along the Saint Johns. Fort San Carlos was supposed to boast ten cannons, but half of them lay buried in the sand. And Mathews figured that, although some of the inhabitants were loyal Spanish subjects, Lopez had a problem with the majority of the population when trying to figure how he was going to put up a resistance more formidable than his few soldiers and nearly useless artillery afforded. Lopez might try to rally the citizens and ask them to defend the town, but many people in Fernandina were blacks. White men, Mathews knew, would not arm blacks. With Campbell's ships providing cover offshore, the force he had available should be able to take the place with ease.

Without help from Laval he had gathered a force of fewer than seventy men by March 10. Of them only nine were Florida residents. Not much of a "local authority" to hand over an entire province or even a town like Fernandina to. They were ready and waiting for action, however, on a ridge ten miles up the river from that town, a spot across the Saint Mary's from Lodowick Ashley's plantation. It was to Ashley's plantation that Ralph Isaacs returned with the news that Laval had not answered the letter Mathews had sent him to deliver.

The high command of conspirators gathered there, and soon Isaacs was at work on another writing assignment as well as another essential ingredient of the propaganda figleaf of the phony revolution—the flag the patriots would carry into battle. The writing assignment was to produce a document to explain what was happening and perhaps even justify it. Issuing such a document had become the style since Thomas Jefferson had written his in 1776. The French had Jefferson's product in mind in 1789 when they produced the Declaration of the Rights of Man. And similar manifestos were popping up all over Latin America by 1811. The manifesto of the East Florida Republic was hardly in a class with the Jeffersonian production—indeed, it should have been more modestly called the manifesto of the Republic of Rose's Bluff, the place where it was publicly proclaimed. It showed clear signs of the avarice that Laval complained to Mathews was the dominant trait of the men he had gotten together to run his operation. Lodowick Ashley and John Houstoun McIntosh obviously had a hand in it; they signed it. But if as a piece of instant ideology it may have suffered when compared with more well-known manifestos, it did make the points Mathews wanted made and satisfied the men who signed it.

Mathews explained to the men at Ashley's plantation on March 13 that a local authority for East Florida had to be formed immediately. This authority, then, could declare the independence of East Florida and cede it immediately to the United States. He indicated that only a skeletal local authority was needed since it would be a short-lived affair. He designated McIntosh the commissioner of the authority and Ashley the commander of the insurgent army.

The preamble of the agreement claimed that the inhabitants of East Florida were ceding the territory to the United States because they desired to free themselves from the oppression of Spanish rule and because they wanted to enjoy the advantages of a government based on the principles of liberty. Unlike Jefferson's declaration in 1776, the manifesto was vague about the specifics of the oppression that was being suffered and the principles of liberty to be enjoyed.

"Whereas the inhabitants of East Florida," the preamble began, "being called upon by a variety of the most interesting considerations to themselves and their posterity to emancipate themselves from the Spanish yoke and its galling effects and to take the management of their own affairs, into their own hand, and wishing to participate in the advantages of a government founded upon the principals [*sic*] of rational liberty, they offer unto the Government of the United States the Province of East Florida . . . "

Modest as were their military might and political resources, the reach of the new republic's leaders was vast:

> We cede unto the United States all of the lands belonging unto the said Province and bounded as designated by the Spanish Government, including all the islands, harbours, and inlets that belong to the said Province together with all the houses, arms, and ordinances, military stores and fortifications with everything there unto appertaining and every species of public property to which the Spanish Government had any claim when we took possession thereof.

Having gotten that key matter out of the way, the manifesto then went on to state what the United States was obliged to do in return for the gift it had received. The financial, physical and even spiritual needs of the insurgents were to be looked out for by the American government.

First, it was pointed out that the United States was pledging to help a political entity that had an "infirm and disabled status." The United States was pledged by the document to take care of all the soldiers and officers who participated in the rebellion by guaranteeing any "arrearages of pay due from their government." (The authors evidently were acutely aware that the Republic of East Florida had no treasury.) The next sentence either was intended to clarify that point or to make it appear that the insurgent army was comprised of officers and solidiers of the Spanish government who were in revolt and not, as in fact most were, adventurers from Georgia: "The United States will either by installments, as in their wisdom may seem proper, cause to be paid unto such officers and soldiers to amount of the pay they were entitled to receive from the Spanish Goverment, at the time they joined the Army of the United States." (The authors clearly understood for whom they were fighting.) "And further," the manifesto continued, "as their [*sic*] may be residents who aided and abetted in the cause of the revolution and who wish by residence to partake of its advantages, who have debts due from the Spanish Government of which they must be despared [*sic*] recovering by their adherance [*sic*] to the revolution—the United States doth agree to have such claims liquidated and paid by installments as may be convenient. . . .

This misspelled and somewhat muddied clause took care of the immediate needs of the participants in the operation, made provision for hoped-for growth of the group and did it all in what was to become the normal future American financial tradition—installment payments.

To provide for still more expansion of their band the United States government was pledged not only to recruit into the United States army Spanish officers and men who would join the movement but to provide pensions to those Spanish army members who helped but who were no longer fit for duty in the American army. Such pensions were to be equal to those given to officers and enlisted men in the United States army who became unfit for duty.

The important matter of land titles was generously handled. To those taking part in the rebellion the "United States guarantees their titles to their lands as well as their titles to all lands obtained by patents, warrents or in any other mode or manner from the Spanish Government as fully and amply as if they had been carried into complete effect by pursuing the method that the Spanish usages made necessary."

Not to leave out anybody, "The United States agrees to give, grant and confirm unto all those who have taken an active part in the revolution and who wish to become inhabitants of the province who have not heretofore had grants of lands in consequence of being subjects, to each and every one a tract equal in quantity and upon similar terms to those granted by the Spanish Government to the residents. . . . " Actually this was a particularly important stipulation; it made good on the promises Mathews had made to the Georgians who signed up for his operation. The next clause made this purpose perfectly clear: "And as the volunteers in the late revolution were promised a certain number of acres not exeeding"—here the document contains an erasure, but we know from the reports on

Mathews's recruiting efforts the number erased was five hundred—"warrants for this performance of said promise which is valid sacred and inviolate shall be granted."

The manifesto guaranteed freedom of religion, and took care of the Spanish priests in the province, assuring them their regular stipends and support received under Spanish rule.

Other clauses were devoted to maintaining some other aspects of the status quo that most residents of East Florida found desirable. The ports and harbors of East Florida were to remain open to the trade of all nations until May 1, 1813. Licenses to cut timber on the public land, which had been granted by the Spanish authorities, would continue to be honored as valid also until May 1, 1813, and all those inhabitants who wished to relocate in the United States could do so, also until that same date. They could take with them all their property, including their slaves. Reciprocally, United States citizens who wished to move to East Florida were free to do so. Another popular point was not overlooked; slave owners in East Florida who suffered any losses due to the insurrection were guaranteed their losses would be paid for.

The document looked down the road at some of the possible consequences of the rebellion: "Whereas the government at Pensacola and Mobile," it said, "will probably be excited to great agitation in consequence of this revolution and as they border upon tribes of Indians who might be engaged in acts of hostility, their reduction is rendered indispensible for the security of East Florida, and we inhabitants of East Florida having prior to this cession proceeded to raise an army and to appoint the officers for the reduction for such places, and having rendered ourselves incompetent to it by yielding up our funds to the United States, the United States doth agree to carry out the same into full effect unless in their wisdom it shall be deemed injurious to the province or the United States."

Mathews well knew how things were viewed in Pensacola and Mobile, and all of those involved feared Indian trouble.

The second contingency the document took into account was the fate of the fight going on in Europe between the Spanish loyal to their old king and the armies of Napoleon. In dealing with this matter, the document threw in the bait Mathews had dangled before Governor Folch.

In a long paragraph in which they again demonstrated their casual unconcern with punctuation and their characteristic disregard for the construction of readable sentences, the authors promised that, should the followers of Ferdinand best the Bonapartists, any inhabitants of East Florida who wished could then return to Spain. The cause of Ferdinand was popular with the Spanish-born inhabitants of Florida. Many were regularly contributing funds to support it. So the document ended by making the proper diplomatic noises Mathews had been told to make to Folch in West Florida. If, after the legitimate monarchy had been restored, the claims caused by the closure of the port of New Orleans in the previous century were paid, the rebels might even consider returning East Florida to Spain.

On the other hand, the inhabitants of East Florida were promised full rights as United States citizens and a seat in Congress once the total white population was sufficiently large to meet the requirements for such representation. In exchange for these privileges, the inhabitants were to swear allegiance to the United States and agree to live under all its laws.

The manifesto by the revolutionists of East Florida was a hybrid of an element essential to Mathews's plot to seize the province, namely, the formal cession of the territory by a local authority, and those things Mathews had promised his co-conspirators as rewards. Rather than being a Declaration of Independence from Spanish authority, it was a contract between a confidential agent of the president of the United States and locals he was hiring to help him do what the president wanted done. That is why it made strange reading. It wasn't up to Isaacs's customary standards because the men who were being hired tried so hard to get into it everything they wanted. Because he needed them so badly, Mathews had to allow Isaacs to put much of their language in—a not uncommon practice when a covert contract is written to secure the services of local agents.

This contract, of course, was not covert. It was designed for public consumption as well as private reassurance. Mathews had to buy his army, but on the other hand his propaganda effort required a public document because of what Thomas Jefferson liked to call "a decent respect for the opinions of mankind." By this Jefferson meant a selling job that would make people sympathetic to his cause. However, when Jefferson wrote the Declaration of Independence the cry came from a group determined to be free from British rule, a company of men who had no hidden sponsors. Mathews and Isaacs could not hide the fact that this time the shout was coming from mercenaries of Jefferson's handpicked successor, James Madison.

It is always difficult to hide the hand of the sponsor of covert manipulation of the affairs of another nation on the scale Mathews was attempting. And Mathews wasn't very good at any aspect of cover. Days before the manifesto was written people along the Florida side of the Saint Marys knew from friends over the river in Georgia that James Seagrove had been telling people George Mathews had a bunch of men who were coming to take the province. They were to look for signal lights on the shore. There would likely also be some troops from Point Petre coming too, the story went.

Lt. Justo Lopez, as alert to such rumors as he had always been for the previous two years, heard this news in Fernandina and took what he thought a logical step. He wrote a letter to the three justices of the peace in Saint Marys on March 10, the day Mathews first learned he was going to have trouble with Major Laval.

"Having learned with certainty," wrote Lopez, "that a number of citizens of the United States have entered our province, and who, united with some rebels to our government, commence to commit hostilities, by violating our territorial rights without the requisite of a protecting law, therefore, I hope you will have the goodness to inform me if the government of the United States have any part in or knowledge of a like nature, contrary to all the treaties of amity existing between the two nations."

Abraham Bessent, Stephen Moode and John Ross, to whom Lopez had addressed his letter, replied with a punt: "Sir," they wrote on March 15, "the undersigned have had the honor, this day, of receiving your favor addressed to them, and delivered by Mr. G. Atkinson. They have to regret that they are unable to say whether the proceedings alluded to in your letter are or are not authorized by the government of the United States; having no information, excepting that collected from vague report, similar in substance to that which the commandant appears to have received."

By the time they wrote this weasel-worded reply there was nothing vague about the rebels' presence in the commandant's territory. They had moved closer to Lopez's town, and their number had increased to 150. The appearance of the manifesto with its renewed promise of free land had stimulated recruitment. By March 15, as Atkinson crossed back over the Saint Marys River with the letter from the American officials, they had advanced from Rose's Bluff to another piece of high ground on Bell's River. They were now just four miles from Fernandina.

March 15 was the Sunday Mathews had hoped would find his men approaching Saint Augustine. Unable to do that, they were busy nevertheless. John McIntosh and Lodowick Ashley, in their capacities as commissioner and commandant, respectively, of the Republic of East Florida, proclaimed Rose's Bluff free of Spanish rule and formally offered it to the United States, and McIntosh sat down to write another letter to Justo Lopez, summoning him either to surrender the town or to join his garrison forces with those of the "patriot" rebels.

McIntosh's letter was as sweeping a bit of fatuous rhetoric unsupported by facts as the manifesto. The closest it came to reality was a passing reference to all the trouble Mathews had been having.

At the same time McIntosh made the wildly unfounded claim that the patriots had "already secured all the territory between the rivers of St Johns and St Marys." He added, "Had it not been for an unexpected circumstance we would have had possession of St. Augustine and the Fort on tomorrow night . . . "

Mathews was facing still another "unexpected circumstance" by the time McIntosh wrote this letter. Commodore Campbell had compared notes with Major Laval and learned that Laval was not cooperating as Mathews had sworn he was. Campbell promptly reneged on his promise to back up the operation with his boats.

Regardless of this new problem, by Monday morning the rebels were ready to try to take Fernandina, and Lopez called a meeting of leading citizens to decide how to reply to the letter from McIntosh. Meanwhile, Mathews had another go at the hesitant naval commander.

CHAPTER XIII
THE FALL OF FERNANDINA

By Monday, March 16, when he received McIntosh's letter, Lopez had already assessed the situation with George Clarke, who as surveyor general had measured and registered all the property in the town and surrounding countryside and knew better than anyone the allegiance of all the citizens who counted. He had also conferred with George Atkinson and Jose Arredondo, his two other most trusted friends. They all urged him to stand firm. Clarke, in particular, was convinced the town could be held against the rebel band.

There were only nine regular soldiers in Fernandina, but Clarke and Lopez went over the names of the men who were members of the Third Company of militia of Amelia Island, taking a nose count of those who could be trusted to fight. Atkinson, who was second-in-command of the company, assured Lopez that he and the company's captain, Santiago Cashen, could rally the men who were loyal. The five noncommissioned officers could be counted on, and out of a total of sixty-six men half were listed as loyal. Thirty-three were counted as rebel sympathizers, or possibly by then already with them. Clarke knew other men in Fernandina he was certain would fight, however, and told Lopez they could count on at least fifty loyal men.

He next suggested what Mathews had been certain no one would dream of suggesting. He recommended that the free blacks in town and some slaves be armed. Clarke lived with a black woman and all his children were what Zephaniah Kingsley called "of the intermediate grade of color." He didn't fear blacks. He told Lopez to count on fifty of them to join the loyal whites.

When Lopez put the plan to fight for their town to the meeting of citizens he summoned, it was enthusiastically supported. Monday afternoon and evening were filled with feverish activity. Half-buried cannons were dug up, cleaned and filled with powder, then loaded with nails and scrap iron. Cannonballs were in short supply. Additional cannons were borrowed from British and Spanish ships in port. Cotton bales were packed around the sides of the little fort and the guns facing the Amelia River.

Clarke, assisted by Joseph Hibberson, like himself a descendant of a family from the British period and a leading merchant, took charge of creating additional fortifications. Since the invaders would probably come along the ridge of land on the southeastern edge of town, Clarke and Hibberson directed black loyalists to dig entrenchments. Along the ridge these were also reinforced as the fort had been with more bales of cotton from Hibberson's, Clarke's and others' warehouses along Marine Street.

Altogether the town's defenders rounded up fifty muskets, a number of pistols, some swords and a total of nine assorted cannons. The magazine at Fort San Carlos had some powder, and this was augmented by powder borrowed from friendly sea captains' ships. The lack of a good supply of shot was corrected by distributing spike nails and langrade shot—long cylindrical missiles filled with nails, bolts, screws and iron scraps.

With the two easy approaches to Fernandina, the river and the ridge on the southeast edge of town, fortified, the defenders believed they could ward off the "rag-a-muffins from the fag end of Georgia."

Meanwhile Justo Lopez and his principal lieutenants were as busy with correspondence as were the leaders of the rebels. Negotiation, not battle, was the main business of nearly all the principal participants in the "patriots war" for most of the next forty-eight hours. McIntosh, Lodowick Ashley, Justo Lopez, George Clarke, George Atkinson, Joseph Hibberson, Jose Arredondo, Major Jacint Laval and Commodore Hugh Campbell conferred and wrote letters back and forth. Only George Mathews failed to put anything down in writing or have his scribe, Colonel Isaacs, do so. Mathews was on the receiving end of a lot of the hand-carried correspondence, however, and what he had to say was faithfully recorded. But he was too busy crossing back and forth over the St. Marys River and too exuberant to put anything down on paper. Isaacs was too busy putting the finishing touches on his design for the patriots' flag. All in all, when the exchange was over it is clear that the fight for Fernandina was a war of words not bullets. And again, as in the case of the accounts of the heated exchange between Mathews and Laval, the strong words traded face to face were written down for history to hear, not merely read them. (The dialogue that follows and the personal observations of the actors in the drama are quoted from either original correspondence or correspondence published in James Cooper's *Secret Acts, Resolutions, and Instructions under which Florida was Invaded by United States Troops*, published in Washington, D.C., in 1860. The documents accompanying the decision in *United States* Versus *Francis P. Ferreira*, Senate document 55, 1851, are from the official correspondence in *Letters to the Secretary of War*, National Archives.)

Early on the morning of March 16, Lodowick Ashley, commander in chief of the rebel army, followed up John McIntosh's demand that Lopez surrender with another demand of his own. Actually, it was a limp kind of ultimatum. It contained all the sweeteners that the manifesto of the Republic of East Florida had listed to try to convince the loyal Spanish subjects that they weren't being conquered but were being offered a good deal:

"The patriots of the district situated between the rivers St. John's and St Mary's invite you to unite with them in their patriotic undertaking," Ashley wrote, "which is to place themselves under the protection of the government of the United States, which guarantees to every man his religion, his liberty, and his property, and that she will pay to every soldier and every individual the amount that may be due them by the Spanish government, &c., &c . . . "

He stipulated that the garrison should "march from the lines with their arms up," but quickly added, "they shall receive their parole as soon as their arms are given up."

The property of the citizens of the town "shall be considered sacred without being examined into or touched." And its owners were assured they not only could keep it but continue to use it "in the same manner that it was previous to the capitulation."

However, Ashley made it clear that the island was going to be immediately ceded to the United States "within twenty-four hours." Then he added what the patriots were sure the citizens of the smuggling capital of the south Atlantic coast would be happy to hear: "The island shall be ceded . . . " said Ashley, "under the express conditions that Fernandina shall not be subjected to the restrictions on her commerce that exist in ports of the United States, and shall be free to British vessels and produce, and to other nations paying the usual tonnage and import duty; and, in the event of the United States and Great Britain going to war, the port of Fernandina shall remain open to British merchants and goods, and shall be considered a free port . . . from this time to the 1st of May, 1813, if Great Britain will permit it."

Next he gave the timber cutters assurance they could continue chopping down the public forest, also until May 1, 1813.

Ashley asked that Lopez appoint commissioners to "negotiate with the patriots at Low's plantation . . . for the purpose of effecting a treaty founded upon the foregoing principles."

The letter sounds as though either the patriots were not very anxious to engage in any actual combat to achieve their ends, or that they wanted to be able to allow General Mathews to claim with better semblance of truth that all the people of northeast Florida were united in their desire to become part of the American union. Perhaps both.

At the very end, however, there were a few harsh words. They had nothing directly to do with the deal, if it could be quickly and quietly arranged. They were prompted by what George Clarke had done about the defense of the town—his decision to arm blacks, an action that made slaveholders shiver with anger and fear.

"We are informed, sir," Ashley growled in writing, "that you have armed the negros on the island against us; we hope it may not be true; for if we find it to be so, you will recollect that we solemnly declare to give the town of Fernandina no quarter."

His final sentence contained another threat, though not so fierce a one. "The United States gun-boats will cooperate for the purpose of preventing British vessels, &c., from acting hostilely against us."

Lopez ignored the remark about the blacks. He appointed George Clarke, George Atkinson, Jose Arredondo, Joseph Hibberson and Philip Yonge commissioners and began drawing up instructions for them. Before sending them off to talk to the patriots he sent a quick note to Commodore Campbell.

"I have the honor of informing you," he wrote, "that a number of men who call themselves patriots have taken up arms and demanded the surrender of this post to them, saying that the United States had determined to take possession of this province by force of arms. I have to request of you, therefore, to say if you are in possession of such orders."

To Ashley's letter he merely replied, "I refer you to Messrs. Joseph Arredondo and Joseph Hibberson for the answer to your letter of this morning."

At three o'clock on the afternoon of March 16 George Clarke and George Atkinson were rowed to the mouth of the harbor with the note for Campbell, whose flagship lay at anchor there. They subsequently reported Campbell's answer to Lopez. Campbell dodged. He explained to Clarke and Atkinson that he had just sent a note off to General Mathews. He said he wanted Mathews to clear up one point, and until Mathews did he couldn't possibly give an answer to the Spanish commandant.

Clarke and Atkinson were not about to be put off. They said they would wait on board until Mathews's answer was received. By evening, when still no answer had come, they returned and reported to Lopez.

Unknown to them the reason for Campbell's hesitancy was not simply a matter of a single question. He was having very grave doubts about his earlier decision to do what Mathews wanted. He had asked Major Laval whether it was true that the army was in full support of the operation. When Laval informed him the answer was decidely no, he refused Mathews's request to move his gunboats.

Mathews, acting on what he had thought was his understanding with Campbell after he and the commodore had gone over Mathews's orders from the president and Mathews's copy of the orders sent by the secretary of the navy to the naval commanders at New Orleans, ordered Campbell on March 15 to send one gunboat to Rose's Bluff, station two more at Bell's River above the town of Fernandina and have his other boats stand ready off the town. Instead of complying, Campbell had contacted Laval. Now he had his ships lying some distance from the harbor and had asked Mathews to clarify Laval's statement. While he stewed over his problem and Clarke and Atkinson returned disappointed, Jose Arredondo and Joseph Hibberson were having trouble with an angry and impatient Colonel Ashley.

Justo Lopez was feeling relieved, having received a strong reassuring letter from Major Laval.

"You desire to know of me, sir, if the United States are to be considered as principals or auxiliaries?" Laval wrote. "I have the greatest satisfaction in informing you that the United States are neither principals or auxiliaries, and I am not authorized to make any attack upon East Florida; and I have taken the firm resolution of not marching the troops of the United States, having no instructions to that effect."

Almost immediately on top of this good news, Lopez heard the bad. Arredondo and Hibberson had been shouted at by Ashley? "I've only delayed marching my men because I had expected your commandant to accept my generous offer. I don't want to shed blood, but now you're asking whether the United States is a party to our offer? Stop stalling!" Ashley demanded. "The negotiations are over! Go back to the island and tell everyone I'm going to land today. Get out of here before I have you shot!"

Then Ashley calmed down. He obviously had no stomach for a fight, despite his bluster. "Look," he added, "I'll not fire a single shot if you don't fire on me. If you surrender, I'll comply with everything I said in my letter to Lopez."

Since he had the hapless commissioners in his power, he dismissed them with one final blast. "But, by God, if we're fired on, we'll show no quarter and we'll confiscate all your property!"

The commissioners were not impressed. They were determined and resourceful men. Someone had let slip the news that Mathews had left Rose's Bluff, where he earlier had been for the ceremonial reception of the local plantation there as the territory of East Florida they were ceding to the United States. So before they went to see Ashley, they had gone across the Saint Marys to Point Petre.

There they were met by a captain of the United States forces and escorted as though a war had been declared and they were enemy negotiators. They had a letter for Major Laval, but they asked the captain coyly whether they ought to present the letter to him or to General Mathews. The captain fell for their ploy and admitted Mathews was there. He said while Laval was the commandant (something Colonel Smith would make sure was changed the next day), if they were coming on public business, they should talk to General Mathews. He escorted them to meet the general.

When they showed him their letter, it was Mathews's turn to be coy. He told them Laval was the commandant; however, since he was commissioned by the president of the United States to take possession of the province of East Florida, he would be happy to answer any questions they had. At that point Laval walked into the room. It was a tense moment.

"Gentlemen," said Laval, "I would be happy to confer with you in my quarters. I cannot speak here." He gestured for them to leave with him, glowering at Mathews.

As soon as they had entered his quarters, the major let fly. "That old man has made my life a nightmare! I've had to stand sentinel in my own camp! He and some disloyal officers have done everything they could think of to seduce my men into joining those outlaws in their revolutionary escapade! I've mounted guard myself to keep them in camp!" He continue to pour out his feelings.

"They have used every strategem they could think of, this old general and his Jewish lackey, to engage United States troops in this nefarious enterprise. I have refused. I've told them that the troops of the United States under my command would never march into the territory of a nation with which the United States was at peace. Believe me, gentlemen, when I say to you that I assure you the conduct of General Mathews, no matter what he may say, could never be condoned by the government of a great and honorable nation such as the one to whom I have sworn allegiance."

The commissioners were impressed by Laval's candid statement about what had been happening and how he felt about it. They made a point of praising him in their report to Lopez.

However, they still felt they ought to talk to Mathews himself. They found him later in company of his friend, John Floyd, the brigadier general of the Georgia militia. He was brimming with confidence and fielded their questions firmly and calmly.

He assured the commissioners he had instructions from his government to receive East Florida or any part of it from local authorities and, in case he had any indication that any foreign power intended to take it, he was authorized to act immediately to seize the province before the foreign power could manage to do so.

When they asked him if he considered the individuals who were at Rose's Bluff to be the local authorities, he replied, "Of course."

He read them the terms of the treaty he had signed with McIntosh at the ceremony ceding Rose's Bluff. They recognized it as essentially the same document the patriots had sent to Lopez. It contained the same articles that had been suggested as terms of capitulation that the Spanish commandant was to agree to in surrendering Fernandina.

He then added he had also received positive information that the British contemplated landing two regiments of blacks at Saint Augustine. The commissioners were astounded at this news. When they asked him where he had gotten that information, he replied, "From a reliable person who was a half-pay British officer." They shook their heads in disbelief.

Mathews's bold embellishment of Captain Wyllys's letter to add a dash more justification to what was happening raises some suspicion. The possibility that he had a hand in the fabrication of this bit of fraudulent information from the double agent looms larger at this point in the affair than at any other.

Arredondo and Hibberson were not impressed. They told Mathews that most of the men gathered on the ridge across the river in their province were not Florida citizens but Georgians who had only become part of the plot because he had promised them five hundred acres of free land.

"We have a proposition, general," said Hibberson. "If you will withdraw your support from these people for one week, we obligate ourselves to surrender Amelia Island to you if before the end of the week we have not driven these insurgents from our territory."

Mathews would not dignify this proposal with a reply. The commissioners had no choice but to leave.

It was from this meeting that they made their way to Low's plantation on Rose's Bluff, where they encountered the irate and impatient Colonel Ashley. It was when they told him Lopez would never surrender the island to them but might to General Mathews if he would take forthright responsibility for what was going on that Ashley exploded. Neither his tone nor his words ruffled them. When they wrote their report to Justo Lopez, they described the incident this way:

> After much uninteresting conversation, we agreed that if General Mathews wished to treat on the part of the United States, that you could then treat with him with honor. They assured us that General Mathews would be at Low's house at ten o'clock this morning. . . . All of which we reported to you verbally last night.

Long before ten o'clock that Tuesday morning, March 17, a lot of things had begun to happen. At seven o'clock Commodore

Campbell had made up his mind, even though he had not received from Mathews the reply to his question he had told Clarke and Atkinson he was awaiting. He sent a note to Lopez:

> Sir: I have been waiting until this hour for General Mathews' answer, which I have not yet received, and I hope that this will be a sufficient excuse for not having replied to your letter from Mr. Atkinson. I take the liberty of informing you that the naval forces of America, near Amelia, do not act in the name of the United States, but do it in aiding and assisting a large portion of your inhabitants, who have thought proper to declare themselves independent, and are now in the act of supplicating you to unite with them in their cause. You can readily, sir, form a conception of the task which has been imposed upon me, but I hope that it will be accomplished without the effusion of human blood.

Lopez could not have had a conception of the task which had been imposed upon the worried United States naval officer. Campbell simply did not have the guts to defy the old general, veteran of the Revolution of 1776, a man so senior to him in years and rank. He reported the torturous process by which he made up his mind to do what he did on the morning of March 17 in two letters he wrote weeks later to the secretary of the navy.

In his letter of April 11, 1812, by which he submitted a copy of his early morning note to Laval, he explained: "I wrote it in haste. . . . That letter was written in answer to one from the commandant demanding the reason for the naval force appearing so near Fernandina, if they were not to act against that place by the authority of the United States." He then stated the problem as he saw it. "To acknowledge the first, would have implicated the Government. To have said they had no intention against the place, would have been to no avail." Campbell went on to say that he was convinced that Lopez was fully aware of the official reply Mathews had given earlier to Atkinson's query on the subject. When Atkinson had presented Lopez's query to the three Saint Marys magistrates, Campbell explained, the magistrates, although their devious reply to the Spanish commandant disclaimed any knowledge of

United States involvement, actually had referred him to Mathews, Laval and Campbell.

"Mr. Atkinson called on me at my lodgings," Campbell wrote, "where, and while in the act of explaining his errand, which was written in Spanish, General Mathews with Colonel Isaacs entered my apartment, took a seat, and observed he had just left the camp of the patriots, where they had about 200 fine fellows in arms. I immediately introduced Mr. Atkinson to the General, who made known his errand as heretofore stated. General Mathews immediately unveiled himself, threw no disguise upon his actions, and took a bold part, instead of appearing in the background. He assured Mr. Atkinson that the patriots would descend Belle [*sic*] River, and demand the surrender of Amelia Island in the morning; *that he had demanded of me five gun-boats to aid and assist the patriots; that in case* a surrender of the town of Fernandina was refused to the patriots, *the gun-boats would knock it down about their ears.* . . . [italics, Cooper, *Secret Acts*]"

Campbell might have made a better chief of covert operations than Mathews. He was obviously disturbed that the general blew his cover so blatantly. Mostly, however, he was disturbed by the position the incident put him in. In his next letter to the secretary he complained that Mathews had put him in a position he called "unofficer-like." He said he had told Mathews the day after their meeting with Atkinson "that the public manner in which the patriots were to be assisted by the gun-boats will be sufficient cause for England, as the ally of Spain, to join with that nation and retaliate."

Campbell was shocked by Mathews reply, but it would have been applauded by the war hawks in Congress who were pushing the country into war. Mathews replied he thought that was splendid, that if the attack on Fernandina brought on war with England, it would have answered "a very good purpose."

Campbell told the secretary he was amazed at the change that had come over Mathews since "the 12th or 13th of March. From one of the most grave, silent, and prudent of men, he is now more gay and unreserved than any man on the station." The commodore summed up in these wordy words: "Taking into view the power he must be invested with to enable him to act thus unreserved," he wrote, "with that of his authority to demand naval assistance whenever he may think proper, likewise his public declaration to Mr. Atkinson, messenger from the commandant, that so completely drew him from behind the car, and placed him in the most conspicuous point of view, that dissimulation became no longer requisite to his purposes, consequently placed me in the most unpleasant of circumstances."

Having decided that he would stick by the general officer with whom he had to deal face to face, even though the old man had blown the whole operation, he added, "These remarks . . . do not proceed from dislike or any unfavorable cause . . . they are merely to show the outlines of his conduct." He resolved his dilemma by deciding he would support the senior officer on the ground with a twist of logic worthy of a 1950s cold warrior: "My declaration to assist the patriots," he told the secretary of the navy, "I consider an individual responsibility, that cannot by any means implicate the Government."

At the same hour he sent his note off to Justo Lopez he ordered the gunboats to sail down the Amelia River.

On Bell's River that morning the patriot encampment was the scene of great activity. Some of the men were busy assembling flatboats. Some were at work changing the wording on the flag that Ralph Isaacs had designed for them—a white banner with the silhouette of a soldier in blue charging with fixed bayonet, and the legend *Salus Populi, Lex Suprema*.

When it had been proudly unfurled for the earlier cession ceremony Mathews had attended, some of the men laughed. Although in 1811 many of the men in northeast Florida and southeast Georgia signed their property deeds by making a mark, those who had any education at all could read Latin. *Salus* meant "salvation," "safety" or "refuge." To those who were not illiterate it seemed ironic to claim what they were doing was for anybody's safety or salvation, so before sailing for Fernandina, they insisted on changing their slogan. They substituted *vox* for *salus*. The idea that anyone with a cause could claim his was the voice of the people had already taken root in America. The Voice of the People Is the Supreme Law sounded just fine.

Getting the patriots' act together after all the negotiation and talk was a slow process. They did not start off until nearly mid-morning and did not arrive at Fernandina until late afternoon. By then the action was over.

Colonel Ashley and patriot commissioner John McIntosh had been too busy on another matter that morning to bother with either the gathering of the boats or the changing of the flag's legend. True to the agreement of the day before, Lopez had sent two representatives to meet General Mathews at Low's plantation. Ashley had promised the general would be there.

Philip Yonge and George Atkinson made their way up Bell's River at mid-morning, looking anxiously back over their shoulders at the United States gunboats tacking into the port of Fernandina. When they arrived at the plantation McIntosh and Ashley met them with a guard, had them blindfolded and took them to a shed some fifty yards from shore. Yonge and Atkinson asked for General Mathews. McIntosh and Ashley told them he had not come and they did not think he would. They suggested Lopez's representatives deal with them. Yonge and Atkinson said they would wait for an hour to see whether or not Mathews came.

Ashley again went into a rage. He shouted they were treating him with contempt. Again he threatened to march immediately to Amelia Island and show no quarter to the inhabitants of Fernandina. Suddenly, however, Mathews and Isaacs arrived, and Ashley and McIntosh withdrew to let the representatives of the Spanish side confer with the man who mattered.

"Are you authorized, general, to take possession of this province by force of arms in the name of the government of the United States?" Lopez's representatives asked.

Mathews was not as bold as he was when trying to impress the naval commander. He said no, he was not, but he was allowed to take possession of it from the hands of local authorities, which is what he had done.

"You then, general, consider the land we are now on as part of the United States?"

"Yes, from Rose's Bluff."

"Are the naval forces of the United States authorized to cooperate with the party that are now preparing the attack upon Amelia Island?"

Mathews again demurred. He answered the navy would not assist.

"If we repel the rebels, you consider yourself authorized by your government to take possession of Amelia Island by force of arms?"

Mathews answered, "I have orders from my government to take possession of it, in case there should be any appearance of the British attempting to send a force to take it; and I now have positive information that they are going to send their black troops for this purpose."

Yonge and Atkinson ignored this repetition of the fictional British threat so evidently a favorite of the old general.

"If the United States naval forces fire a gun upon Amelia," said Yonge, "we can then surrender with honor to superior forces; but we will never surrender to those men whom we can repel."

Mathews answered, "This is an affair between yourselves, because United States gun-boats will not fire a gun, nor will they interfere with you, unless some British vessel should aid you, and in this case they have orders to fire upon you. And I am informed," he added, "that you have been supplied with arms and ammunition by some vessels that are now in port."

"We have a right sir," Yonge replied, "to ask the British who are in our ports as allies, their assistance, and even to take from them arms and ammunition, which we have done."

"They had no right to interfere in this business," Mathews insisted, "and if they did, as I have understood they intend doing, the gun-boats have orders to fire upon you."

The two men from Fernandina told the general they considered the United States had already committed hostilities toward their province by sending the gunboats into their port with the obvious intention of supporting the rebel patriots' attack if only by scaring the citizens and deterring them from resisting.

"You may think what you please," Mathews replied, adding a non sequitur, "because this is an affair of my government."

"We are charged to inform you, general," George Atkinson said, "that there are a number of citizens of the United States, who have joined the party that is going now to the attack of Amelia, and they are there now"—Atkinson pointed toward the men preparing to enter the flatboats at Low's plantation's landing—"and we demand that you detain them."

"I have no knowledge of them, I have no command over them," Mathews lied. "You ought to appeal to the authorities of Georgia."

Yonge and Atkinson tried to shake the general's story. He refused to change it. At last they had to admit to themselves their mission had failed, and they returned to Fernandina.

They were appalled by what they saw there. Four gunboats were at anchor before the town, three of them within pistol-shot range of the beach, their matches lit, their cannons ready to fire.

Mathews had lied about his relationship with the men getting into the boats at Low's plantation, but not when he said the gunboats would not fire unless fired upon. He had not heard what Campbell's final decision had been. In fact, Campbell made two final decisions.

By seven o'clock in the morning he had decided he would let his boats be used to support the patriot attack. As they sailed for the harbor he gave orders that the boats' guns were to cover the debarkation of the patriot forces and assist them until the Spanish flag was down. Two hours later he changed his mind and made his final decision. He began signaling from his flagship that the boats were to hold their fire. By this time the first of the flatboat flotilla of patriots was clearly in view approaching the town. Young Lieutenant Winslow Foster, commander of gunboat 62, consulted with Lieutenant Grayson, the young officer who commanded the other boat, which like Foster's lay directly opposite the batteries of little Fort San Carlos. Foster told Grayson he could obey the order if he liked, but he, Foster, was going to fire on the batteries if they fired on the patriots' flatboats. Grayson decided he would obey orders. Foster's decision sealed the fate of Fernandina.

When Campbell saw that Foster was not obeying him, he ordered a skiff lowered from the flagship and sent an officer with instructions to demand compliance with the order to put out the guns' matches and to withdraw his vessel from in front of the fort.

The defenders of the town observed this but didn't know what to think. They saw the skiff approaching Winslow's boat, but they also saw the flatboats approaching.

On shore a man yelled to the gunboat crew, "Keep off or remain neutral until we decide the contest!"

"If you fire on them, we'll fire on you," Winslow shouted back.

The townspeople began deserting their positions. Although Clarke, Atkinson and the other officers of the loyal militia tried to keep them at their posts they flocked to Commandant Lopez's house across the plaza from the fort. They called out, "We must surrender!" Lopez stood in front of his house, gazing out toward Winslow's boat. It was almost three o'clock. People kept shouting, "Resistance is impossible, Save our lives and property . . . " Lopez looked upstream toward the approaching patriots' boats. "Who will take the flag of surrender?" he asked. No one moved. Then George Clarke stepped forward. "I will."

The citizens shouted their approval. The free blacks and slaves who had formed part of the defending forces quickly gave their weapons to the white men. They did not want the Georgians to find them bearing arms.

Clarke got into a rowboat with a white flag flying from it. Out in the river in front of Fernandina he met Ashley and offered him the town.

A force of sixty patriots landed at Fernandina Bluff, a mile below town and marched north to the center of Fernandina. They reached Lopez's house at four o'clock. Lopez came out with tears running down his cheeks and offered his sword to Ashley. The patriot leader buckled it around his waist, then ordered the Spanish flag struck.

The patriots' banner with its new device, *Vox Populi, Lex Suprema,* was run up the flagpole.

As the Spanish flag came down, Winslow weighed anchor. The gunboats slowly sailed north into Cumberland Sound, where Commodore Campbell already had arrived. When the boats rested anchor Campbell called his officers to the flagship. He requested they give him their copies of the orders he had issued that morning. He told them he wanted to make copies of them. Years later Winslow stated that the boats' commanders surrendered the orders to Campbell. Neither the originals nor any copies of them were ever seen again.

On March 21 Commodore Campbell wrote one more letter to the secretary of the navy giving his version of what happened. "The boats proceeded on the morning of the 17th instant, took their station near Fernandina town, in a quiet and friendly manner, the commander of those boats having orders not to fire a shot unless first fired upon, and previous to the approach of the patriots I gave a positive order not to fire a shot on any pretext whatever. The measure had the desired effect of preventing blood, which inevitably would have been the cause with the loss of the town."

That was one way of putting it. Actually the fall of Fernandina appears to have occurred thanks to the whim of Lieutenant Winslow Foster, who decided he would ignore his ambivalent chief. But then nothing in George Mathews's operation thus far had gone according to the script. Which is often true of covert operations. So is the tendency to report them in a way that best serves the interests of the participants, as Commodore Hugh Campbell did.

As the patriots' boats kept unloading, the inhabitants of Fernandinas weren't sure what the script called for. Not surprisingly, many wondered if it included an end to their lives.

CHAPTER XIV

ON TO SAINT AUGUSTINE

The townspeople had not read the notes Ashley had sent to Commandant Lopez and were not familiar with the inducements they contained and the assurances they gave. Although Ashley might talk tough when excited, he clearly never spoiled for a fight. The way Fernandina fell suited him just fine. He was greatly relieved he did not have to try to make good on his bloodthirsty boasts. People did not need to fear for their lives from him.

Eventually as twilight fell 180 weary patriots found their way from Fernandina Bluff into the town plaza. They were tired and hungry, but they were willing to follow Ashley's leadership. They had been promised land and dreamed of the day their produce would fill the warehouses along Marine Street. They were in no mood to loot them and burn them down, upsetting the merchants with whom they planned to deal and destroying the depositories which would store the products they hoped to sell free of United States embargo restrictions. They knew the terms proposed to Lopez promised exemption from United States law for another year.

Ashley and McIntosh closeted themselves with Lopez, Clarke,

Atkinson and the other loyal supporters of the Spanish commandant. They drew up terms of capitulation, and Lopez signed them.

The terms were those that had been promised. Lopez and his troops, all nine of them, were allowed the honors of war. Upon delivering their arms and promising never to fight the patriots again, they were to be paroled within the limits of the town. All real and personal property remained to their owners. The patriots promised not to examine, touch or destroy any of it. Amelia Island was to be ceded to the United States within twenty-four hours. After the cession, the port of Fernandina would be exempted from United States customs laws and remain open to British ships as well as to trading vessels of all other countries until May 1, 1813. Even in case war between the United States and England broke out, the same would apply. Everyone who remained on Amelia Island was guaranteed all his civil and property rights and those who chose to leave were free to go. Those deciding to leave would have one year's grace during which they could sell their property without penalty or tax. Even if the United States were to fight a war with Spain, those persons electing to remain loyal to Spain could leave and have their property sold by agents.

The terms were as painless as the battle had been. After Lopez signed, George Clarke, his brother Charles, and George Atkinson signed on behalf of the townspeople. John McIntosh signed for the Republic of East Florida.

George Mathews had not remained with Ashley and McIntosh after Atkinson and Yonge left the patriots' camp following their futile conference that morning. Their pressing questions about the direct involvement of the United States in the operation weighed heavier on his mind than he had admitted to them. He went back across the Saint Marys so no one could say he was directing the patriots' attack. He did not, however, have to stay at Ashley's plantation this time. Thomas Adam Smith was now in command at Point Petre and Laval confined to quarters. The general could take refuge with the sympathetic Colonel Smith. There he waited until the returning gunboats brought the news that Fernandina had surrendered without a shot.

Ashley and McIntosh lost no time in sending for him. At least one part of the script was followed to the letter. On the morning of March 18 their messengers brought their greetings to General Mathews with the request that he accept cession of the town of Fernandina and all the territory between the Saint Marys and the Saint Johns rivers from the "constituted authorities of East Florida."

The general immediately called on Colonel Smith for a detachment of troops. Lieutenant Appling and two companies of fifty men were ordered to cross the Saint Marys River and accompany him to Fernandina.

They sailed from Point Petre in the afternoon. When they reached shore Mathews went across the plaza to Justo Lopez's house, and Appling drew his men up in formation before the flagpole. The general met McIntosh at Lopez's and they went through the formality of McIntosh's presenting to Mathews the articles of surrender signed by the Spanish commandant and the patriots. Then they strode out of the house, which faced the plaza and the flagpole, where by now the United States Army troops were drawn up for review.

After reviewing the troops McIntosh, on behalf of the patriots, delivered the province to Mathews, who accepted it in the name of the president of the United States. The patriots' voice-of-the-people banner came down the pole, and the flag of the United States went up. A rifle volley was fired, and the patriots, safely massed behind the troops, cheered loudly. A few of the townspeople joined in.

The celebration of the victory was not a boisterous affair. The day following the cession of the territory to the United States, the American troops began the task of monitoring the affairs of the town. The patriots continued to behave themselves. There was no looting, no disturbance of the public order. Mathews was in a jubilant mood. He was also very busy. He had an operation still to bring to conclusion. He somehow had to secure the entire province by either a successful military operation against Saint Augustine or by cowing the Spanish commander there into surrendering as he had done at Fernandina. And he also had an occupied town to govern.

Turning to the second task immediately, he appointed a friend from Saint Marys deputy and himself assumed the role of customs collector. To help govern the town, he requested that a company of marines come down from Cumberland Island. Captain John Williams and his marines arrived by the end of the week.

With the government in hand, he encouraged the patriots to move south, establishing Sunday, March 22, as the formal date for departure.

Now that they had won the town, some of the locally important men, who earlier would have nothing to do with Mathews's plot, joined what they thought was the winning side. William Craig, the man whom Governor White had named judge of northeast Florida and to whom John Houstoun McIntosh had unburdened himself earlier about the operation, now became a patriot. So did Daniel Delaney, one of the immigrant oath takers who had secured a large grant of land from the Spanish and was one of the wealthiest men in the province. The patriot army was divided into two commands to accommodate the acquisition of a man as important as Craig. Ashley continued as head of the first command. Craig was named commander of the second. Delaney became a co-commissioner along with McIntosh.

But despite their reorganization the patriots continued to be an undisciplined group. Some left on their way south as early as March 19, as soon as they found boats. Others followed over the course of the next couple of days. How many, in all, made their way down the Saint Johns River is hard to say. Colonel Smith, in later reports, estimated their number as 100. Justo Lopez, in the count he made for Sebastian Kindelan when the latter arrived in June, listed 106 men of the three militia companies in northeast Florida as rebels.

On Saturday, March 21, Mathews sat down with Isaacs and sent a progress report to James Monroe. He proudly sent as an enclosure the document of cession he had obtained from the patriots on March 17, which he described as "a letter, No. 1, from the constituted authorities of East Florida, requesting me, as commissioner of the United States, to take possession of all that tract of country lying between the rivers St. Marys and St. Johns, including all the islands between the same. . . ."

He informed the secretary of state that he had requested and was receiving military assistance from Colonel Smith, and bitterly complained about Major Laval's frustration of his initial plan. "I have little reason to doubt," he wrote, "had Major Laval not defeated my first plan, by refusing me aid, I would, by this time been able to have informed you of the cession of the whole of East Florida to the United States." He was not dismayed, however, and quickly added, "I hope, in a few days, to give you that agreeable intelligence, for the patriots have crossed the St. Johns and are in rapid march for St. Augustine, and, I think, with a sufficient force to reduce it effectually, if properly supported by Commodore Campbell."

Campbell had already been given the word by the old general and was once more acquiescing in the wishes of that authority figure. Campbell, by the time Mathews wrote Monroe, had ordered three gunboats to proceed toward Saint Augustine and anchor within the bar "as near to the fort as prudence may direct." He added that the boats were not to fire "unless an insult should be offered to the flag of the United States; in such case you will repel that insult by every means in your power."

It can only be surmised that by sending his ships under the guns of the Spanish fort, Campbell was in fact looking for such an insult, an incident he had to be certain would greatly please General Mathews and help the cause along. For in the same order, he made clear to his officers that their activities were part of a coordinated military effort. "The United States troops near St. Augustine," the order stated, "may require some assistance from you; in that case you will communicate with them through the North River. Should this be objected to by the governor [at St. Augustine], it will be your duty to resist such objection by demanding the privilege of that navigation as part of the province ceded to the United States. Be on the alert. Guard against surprise. Moor your boats in the most advantageous situation to support each other in case of necessity. You will likewise render such services as General Mathews may require. . . . "

Campbell not only was back on the team, he was trying to be one of its most valuable players.

On March 23 the patriots arrived at Picolata, an undefended Spanish post on the east bank of the Saint Johns, fourteen miles from Saint Augustine. En route they had taken the surrender of the three Spanish soldiers who were at Fort San Nicolas, at the Cowford. After a brief rest they moved on, and on March 25 they were near enough to Saint Augustine to see Fort San Marcos and the houses of the town.

They made a recruiting and foraging expedition out of their unopposed march. Acting governor Juan Estrada had sent out an order that on the approach of the rebels all loyal men should burn their buildings, destroy their livestock and other property and make a run for Saint Augustine. The order was not obeyed. The patriots found full barns and fat cattle awaiting them, and helped themselves. They also persuaded some important landowners to sign up. Zephaniah Kingsley was at his large, prosperous Laurel Plantation, west of Cowford, on the outskirts of what is now Jacksonville when the patriots passed by. He would always insist that he had been forced to join on pain of having his place plundered. Whatever happened, his property was not seized and he remained with the patriot forces for as long as they appeared to have any chance of success and, like Craig and Delaney, became one of the leadership group.

On March 26, the day after they arrived two miles from Saint Augustine, the patriots' leader, John McIntosh, reverted to the use of his favorite weapon—rhetoric. He sent Juan Estrada a letter, more florid even than the one he had used to try to seduce Justo Lopez into surrender:

> The people of East Florida having long suffered under the Tyranny of an arbitrary government and being threatened that a body of merciless savages would be thrown into their country, have unanimously with the exception of St. Augustine declared themselves as independent people. They have organized themselves as a military body and have taken possession of all the country round St. Augus-

> tine . . . they have . . . offered to the commissioner of the United States to cede to the United States the province of East Florida under certain beneficial term.

He then listed all the same sweeteners that had been tried on Justo Lopez. "We now demand the surrender of the town and citidel of St. Augustine in order that the people therein may participate in the beneficial consequences that must result from an annexation to the United States."

Following the same pattern he and Ashley had used previously, in conclusion, he made some threats. American gunboats, said McIntosh, were sailing for Saint Augustine and American troops were marching behind the patriot forces. And in case the Spanish commandant planned on any help from his Seminole Indian allies, he could forget it. The patriots had talked to the Seminole chief, King Payne, at Picolata, and he had assured them he would remain neutral.

Juan Estrada may have been somewhat upset by the news that he was facing a full-scale attack by all the American forces in the neighborhood and the news he could not count on his Indian friends. If so, he didn't show it. In reply to McIntosh he curtly disdained surrender and bluntly refused to confer further with the patriot chief.

McIntosh and Delaney scurried north to consult their chief of operations. They had hoped to find General Mathews on his way down the Saint Johns with Smith's men and expected to meet him at Cowford. But a heavy northeaster was blowing offshore and the winds and rain had prevented the troops' departure. The two patriot leaders continued on to Fernandina. Because of the storm they didn't reach the town until March 31, and so on that day they and he signed the papers ceding East Florida "to the walls of St Augustine" to the United States.

In his letter to the secretary of state written ten days earlier, Mathews had told Monroe he was holding the already prepared articles of cession in his hands "until the entire province is CONQUERED, CEDED and SURRENDERED to the United States, which event is near at hand . . . . " The articles of cession, in fact, were almost identical to the manifesto the patriots had addressed to Justo Lopez when they tried to get him to surrender and join their cause. He tried to explain to the secretary what he thought the articles were intended to accomplish in addition to the bare rape of the frail province. And he asked for comments.

The article which left Fernandina a free port until May 1, 1813, he said he had put in because he felt it made "the British government less likely to take umbrage or complain of our taking the province." Also it would help his Georgian and other Southern constituents. "In addition," he added, "through that medium, the people of the Southern States would be able to get clothing for their negroes, and the Government, through the house of Panton and Forbes, their supplies for the Indians." Still another thought occurred to him on this point. "Besides, it will afford considerable revenue [from the collection of shipping duties] to the Government, if we engage in war with Great Britain; and suggest the query whether it will not be best to extend it to May, 1814."

He also felt he had to explain two other articles. The fifth and sixth dealt with matters with which the secretary of state might well have concern. The fifth article called for the taking of Pensacola and Mobile as "indispensible for the security of East Florida," and the sixth article suggested the idea of returning East Florida to Spain might be entertained if the Spanish faction loyal to Ferdinand VII prevailed against Napoleon and if they would pay for the damage to cargoes caused by the closing of New Orleans.

Mathews said he had worded the fifth article so as not to commit the United States Government directly to the conquest of West Florida. The article suggested it would be done by the armed forces of East Florida. He couldn't resisted adding, however, "I think it is impolitic for us to permit them [Pensacola and Mobile] to remain in the possession of the Spaniards."

Regarding the sixth article's incursion into international diplomacy, Mathews remembered the newspaper accounts he had read concerning Secretary Monroe's reply to the British minister's protest about United States activities in Florida. "The 6th article," he wrote, "is with a view to cover and support your letter to Mr. Foster." The secretary of state had chosen to backstop United States covert operations in Florida with a bold lie to the British representative, and Mathews wanted to reassure his chief that he was aware of this.

Mathews took the opportunity to send his compliments to the president, and, as all operators tend to do when reporting what they think their chiefs want to hear, he also took the opportunity to ask for more help from home. Not satisfied with what Smith and Campbell were doing in the way of military support, he wrote, "Pray, send two or three armed vessels to lay off St. Augustine."

The storm's delaying the departure of Smith's troops made him impatient. He asked Smith to give him a corporal's guard and took off for the patriot camp in front of Saint Augustine on April 4 ahead of the main body of men. Commodore Campbell commented that Mathews was even more elated than he had been on the verge of the capture of Fernandina. The old general was so carried away by the smell of success, Campbell wrote, that when he left Fernandina, he made a speech to the people of the town bragging that after Saint Augustine, he would not stop. He would go on to Pensacola, on to Mobile and see that all Florida was turned over to the United States. After that he said he would go still farther. He would go on to Mexico, revolutionize the country, then continue southward. He intended, he said, to settle down finally in Peru.

Three days after Mathews left Fernandina, Smith's troops were on the move. A parade had begun. Up the Saint Johns river, ever deeper into the Spanish province, went three parties. First, the patriots, then Mathews and his four-man guard, and then Smith with the United States Army. As they proceeded, they enacted a similar ceremony in each place they halted for a night's encampment.

First a patriot orator would make what one witness described as "a handsome speech," offering the place where they found themselves and its environs to the United States. George Mathews would reply in the same grand style of his oration when he left Fernandina. He accepted the territory in the name of President Madison. Then he turned to Colonel Smith, who in another speech would pledge to keep and defend it against all enemies. The speakers knew what they were doing. The purpose of the parade was to breathe life into the fiction that Smith's army was not invading the territory of a friendly nation with whom the United States was at peace. When the patriot speaker and Mathews had finished, Smith's troops were marching across the United States.

By April 11 the whole road show was in sight of Saint Augustine. They stopped at the remains of an old fort, and once more gave their speeches. They were taking possession of a place that was a symbol of what their operation was finally to become—a racial conflict.

The place called Moosa Old Fort had been settled originally in 1739 as a result of a Spanish decision to add yet another burden to the lives of their English neighbors to the north. For some years before that date fugitive slaves from the Carolinas and Georgia had fled to Florida. In 1733 a Spanish royal decree declared such fugitives were to be henceforth free. In 1739 the Spanish govenor in Saint Augustine established a settlement for thirty-eight families of freed blacks, assigned priests to them and ordered the place have simple fortifications. He called the settlement Gracia Real de Santa Teresa de Mose. Over the years this was shortened and corrupted to Moosa. It was the first free black community in America.

Word of what was happening spread, and more blacks from the British colonies sought refuge there. When James Oglethorpe invaded Florida the following year a major battle took place at Moosa. On June 15, 1740, a force of three hundred blacks and Indians nearly wiped out his army. They killed fifty of his men and took twenty prisoners. The siege of Saint Augustine went on, however, the blacks withdrew into the town for protection, and they never returned to live at the Moosa village.

The fort was retaken by the British, but Oglethorpe could not take Fort San Marcos, and he abandoned his siege and went back to Georgia in July. The fort fell into disuse. Then in the mid-1750s it was rebuilt and a strong stockade constructed.

In 1756 a black militia company was organized at Moosa and became an integral part of the colony's defense force. Moosa was the northern bastion of the colony's outer-defense ring. A drawing of the fort made in 1763 as Florida was about to be handed over to the British shows a village of thatched huts, a large chapel, two small bastions with two three-pounder cannons and a moat. The British continued to use the fort until 1775 when they dismantled it.

When the Spanish returned, the army engineer who supervised the rebuilding of defenses including the fortification of the Saint Johns River suggested rebuilding Moosa. One large house that still remained was fortified and given two embrasures from which cannons could be fired on any boats that might penetrate Saint Augustine inlet. But again the place fell into disrepair. In December 1811, aware of Mathews's plotting, the council of war of acting governor Juan Estrada decided to repair it. Before repairs could be made, the patriots and Colonel Smith appeared and took over the house as their headquarters.

On the following morning after their arrival at Moosa, the American army saw a Spanish gunboat coming up Robinson Creek, the small tributary of Saint Augustine's North River on which their camp was pitched. The gunboat fired. One cannonball hit a sandbank near which one of the soldiers was sleeping and buried him in the sand. Two more shots were fired, passing over the tents of Smith's troops. Hastily they assembled in fighting formation and raised the American flag. When the gunboat's commander saw this, he turned back.

Smith, Mathews and the patriot leaders held a council of war. What they decided to do next was entirely in keeping with what had become their usual modus operandi. They decided to try a fusillade of bold words once again to overwhelm the Spanish. They would send Captain Massias with a message to Juan Estrada demanding the surrender of Saint Augustine.

Captain Massias was rowed down Robinson Creek on the morning of April 14 carrying a white flag of truce. Disembarking from the boat, he and his soldiers approached Fort San Marcos across the salt marsh. As they neared the walls they were commanded to halt. Representatives of the Spanish commandant came to meet them. Massias, through a translator, tried to make his mission clear. He was interrupted. The defenders of Saint Augustine told him to go back to his camp. If he did not do so immediately, he would be shot.

This unpromising turn of events didn't unduly upset George Mathews. He was still bubbling with confidence. He sat down to write another progress report, this time to President Madison. The report reflected his expansive mood. He told the president that the United States was getting a large and valuable land with live oak, cedar and pine sufficient to build all the navy the nation could ever need. And, as he was talking about all of Florida, since the articles of cession of East Florida contained the clever device for taking West Florida in the name of the security of East Florida, he suggested Tampa Bay on the Gulf coast would be a perfect place to anchor such a navy.

Having conquered Florida, he proceeded to suggest how the territory should be administered, in particular what men should do the administering. John McIntosh, he suggested, would make a fine territorial governor, unless Madison preferred General Floyd, who was also quite acceptable to Mathews. James Seagrove would make an excellent surveyor general and Charles Harris of Savannah, a good district judge. Ralph Isaacs was just the man to be the territory's attorney general.

Despite his glow, Mathews felt called upon to give his version of what had happened between him and Major Laval. According to the general, Laval had double-crossed him, "refusing to obey my requisitions after having pledged himself to do so." After "the persons engaged in the revolution . . . had passed the St Marys which in relation to them may be called the Rubicon, he without giving me the least previous notice in a clandestine manner sent word to them that he would neither support them or obey my requisitions. . . . "

Then, in a passage which seems foreboding, he told the president of Laval's arrest. The premonitory part of this explanation is the way he tried to protect himself against any possible charges that he had not carefully concealed the hand of the man to whom he was writing in Washington who had ordered him to launch the operation.

"He is now under arrest," Mathews wrote of Laval, "the charges I think will break him." Then he added, "The conduct of his however reprehensible respecting his deceiving me does not constitute any part of the charges exhibited as it would be the only means whereby the government could be implicated in all this business . . . . "

He must have thought a bit at this point, or perhaps his capable secretary, whom he was recommending to be attorney general, suggested he cover still further the part of his anatomy his flamboyant operational style had exposed: "I have not in any instance committed the honor of the Government or my own reputation by any act—nor have I pursued any clandestine means to accomplish the objects of my mission with any subject of E. Florida." That last clause was laughably disingenuous. He went on to make clear that what he meant by it was that the "applications" for admission of Florida to the United States had been the spontaneous product of the "patriots."

George Mathews had done his best while in Saint Marys the previous fall to keep up with the news. The Savannah newspapers came weekly to the little town and so he had learned about the exchange of notes between James Monroe and the British minister. He had been very busy in March 1812 and so had Ralph Isaacs. They most probably had no idea of what the press coverage of their operation had been, nor of what was the biggest news story in the nation's press that month. Mathews certainly had no idea when he started for Saint Augustine on April 4. Another letter was written that day. It was addressed to him and written by the secretary of state. The letter had grown out of the press play about a matter that had occupied much of James Monroe's time.

CHAPTER XV
A HIGHER PRIORITY

A newspaper which regularly reached Saint Marys, Georgia, and was read with interest by the men with whom George Mathews planned his Florida operation, was the Savannah *Republican*. Published every Tuesday, Thursday and Saturday by John H. Evans, it was a sturdy Jeffersonian-party paper. It had printed the Monroe-Foster correspondence. It always published official correspondence and news from Washington, particularly that which showed the Madison administration in a favorable light. The paper also stayed on top of state and local news, and included bread-and-butter items such as arrivals and departures at the port of Savannah, notices of runaway slaves and other matters of personal importance to its readers.

Advertising income was as important then as now, and the paper ran a number of personal classified ads, such as announcements of new dressmaking establishments. More important were the advertisments paid for by patent-medicine purveyors. Americans, like most mortals, have always liked to be sold easy solutions for life's pains and problems. The front page of the Savannah *Republican* carried ads for Dr. Daniel Coit's Family Pills, which cured "yellow fever, bilious fevers, ague, cholic pains, flatulencies, indigestion, hypocondriacal and hysterical complaints." It was "composed of vegetable germs and roots." Other often advertised medicines were Lee's Worm Destroying Lozenges and Dr. Rogers Vegetable Pulmonic Detergent. Dr. Rogers' cure for all respiratory illnesses filled the back page of every issue in March 1812. Each ad carried fifteen lengthy testimonials.

On Thursday evening, March 19, two days after the fall of Fernandina, the story of George Mathews's triumph intruded into the medicine ads. It was not a particularly supportive story. First, the note began by saying there had been rumors "for some days past that Amelia Island has been surrendered to a body of men who made their appearance in that quarter for the purpose of taking possession of it by force. . . . " The rumors had contained inconsistencies which had led the paper not to print any of them. "A letter in the last southern mail from a gentleman of respectability" convinced the editor, who wrote: "We have news that the revolutionists have planted the standard of liberty and independence on Rose's Bluff opposite St. Marys in East Florida. A long way this from St. Augustine, where they are apprized of the scheme and are prepared to give their revolutionizing a warm reception."

The paper might not have meant to sound hostile; it may have only meant to give the news the minor attention it deserved in view of the big news from Washington, where President Madison had sent Congress a report of the uncovering of a plot to subvert the nation. The paper printed his entire message.

President Madison had sent his sensational message to the Senate ten days before, and the Savannah *Republican* could at last tell all. According to the nation's chief executive, the British government was trying to divide and destroy the country. It had employed an American citizen, named John Henry, to foment disloyalty throughout the New England states, encouraging them to go to the brink and beyond. In case war were declared by the United States against Great Britain, the New England states would declare themselves seceded from the Union and would receive the protection of

Great Britian through the medium of its remaining colony in America, Canada.

The news was a bombshell. Harriet Otis of Boston, daughter of the secretary of the United States Senate, was so upset by the news she poured out her feelings in her diary in a flutter of mixed metaphors. "Monday, March 9th. The Senate were detained until a late hour reading the base and unexpected disclosures of John Henry!!!" She had known him in Boston and had thought him "noble minded."

> This man who has so lowered his proud spirit as to become the base agent of the British government in spying out the dissentions of the country to which he had sworn allegiance on being dissappointed of a reward equal to his expectations has had the shameless effrontery to betray the transactions of his employers to our government . . . how astonishing does it seem to me that this rolling stone who fluttered about without any other apparent aim than his own amusement should have been harbouring in his breast such views. . . .

Madison thought he had given Congress a spy-scare story of greater shock value than the Burr conspiracy, and one with even greater benefit for him than the Burr story had been for Jefferson. The man who had ordered the covert subversion of Florida was intrigued by what this tale could do for him. For one thing, it would dissipate the cloud of complaint about what happened in West Florida—a cloud that had buried his proposal to make West Florida part of the United States when he had suggested it in his last State of the Union message in December 1811.

More important was the spy story's value to him in an election year. During the course of the year, presidential electors would be chosen to meet in December 1812, and he wanted to be reelected. But he was having party problems. The "war hawks" of his party had been clamoring for war with England since Congress had opened. They complained he was dragging his feet. He had been, of course, because support for such a war was not strong in other than the western and some southern states. In New England, there was almost none. Yet a year earlier his party had pulled a major upset in the key state of Massachusetts. Elbridge Gerry had been elected governor in that Federalist stronghold and the Jeffersonian party controlled the legislature by a slim margin. Massachusetts would hold elections again in April. The Henry spy story might successfully pin the label of traitor on the Federalists and assure Madison the electoral votes of that important state. It would certainly please the war hawks, and he could sweep the country as the champion of patriotism.

In the first days after he sent the message to Congress, everything seemed to go smoothly. The Senate called for an investigation. Senator Giles asked for the names of Henry's co-conspirators, confident that a number of prominent Massachusetts Federalists would be revealed. A Senate committee waited on Secretary Monroe, expecting him to come forth with the list. He did not reply promptly. Meanwhile, Jeffersonian newspapers the length of the land followed the same course as the Savannah *Republican*, running columns of the president's spy-scare message and supporting editorials suggesting this was the worst calamity that had yet befallen the young nation. This pleased the president and rewarded the months of effort he and James Monroe had put into the project.

All during the months of January and February, while George Mathews was trying to get his Florida plot off the ground, they had been working on a plot which they considered a matter of much higher priority. Given the fact that for more than a year Mathews had been working on the Florida mission they had assigned him in January 1811 he perhaps should be awarded the credit for putting in a greater total effort, but neither plot deserved any prize for thoughtful preparation or execution. The Henry letters spy plot and the plot to steal Florida taken together raise not only serious questions about the political morality of Madison and Monroe, but serious doubts about their sagacity. In the case of Florida they had been perfectly comfortable supporting phony rebellions and lying about them to inquiring British and Spanish diplomats. In the Henry case they were not only equally at ease with their consciences spending public funds for party purposes, they bought letters from a self-styled spy which proved to be as worthless as the East Florida Republic's manifesto. No other president and secretary of state ever fell so completely for the scams of con men.

On Christmas Eve, 1811, two men landed in Boston. One had been there before, was an American citizen and had a wide circle of friends from his earlier visit. His name was John Henry. The other man called himself Comte Edouard de Crillon. He said he was a French nobleman, an anti-Bonapartist. Henry remained most of the time at the Exchange Coffee House on State Street getting drunk. Comte Crillon busied himself making the right contacts. One of the most important was Governor Elbridge Gerry, Madison's friend who was facing a reelection fight in April. Gerry gave him letters of introduction to the president and the secretary of state.

Armed with them, Crillon went on to Washington in early January 1812 and presented to Madison the letter from Gerry which described him as one "who for his professional, literary and polite accomplishments had been much respected by all his acquaintance." Crillon also had with him an equally glowing letter from the bishop of Boston to the bishop of Baltimore, introducing him as "the very respectable Count de Crillon Knight of Malta with whom I have had the honor and happiness of getting acquainted during his too short residence in Boston."

Crillon knew how to make the most of a short residence. He charmed Madison, praising the president's fine wines and basking appropriately in the presence of the Father of the Constitution. He dined so often at the president's house, the French minister commented in a dispatch to Paris, "that I thought I ought to receive him myself." The French minister, however, was suspicious of Crillon's credentials. The two politicians from Virginia were in no way wary of the worldly Frenchman. When after a quick, dazzling softening up he told Madison he had a friend who held documents proving an English-Federalist plot to dissolve the United States, Crillon soon discovered he had made his mark. Madison told him to see Monroe and work out a way to get the evidence safely into State Department channels.

Monroe proved no more resistant than Madison. And Crillon

could enjoy the pleasure all professional confidence men share. He played with his too eager marks for a bit and let them work themselves up into feverish excitment. Confidence men claim they commit no crime, they merely let their victims do it. The true artists, like Crillon, simply discover something the mark wants so badly he loses whatever ethical sense he has in his eagerness to get it. Victims of confidence men frequently don't have an abundance of ethical principles to lose. In Madison and Monroe, Crillon, it would seem, found a pair of rather typical targets.

On February 1 Crillon told Monroe, yes, he could get the incriminating letters but the price was twenty-five thousand pounds sterling. The next day Monroe wrote Crillon. As is typical in such cases, Crillon had put the price higher than he knew Monroe could afford to go. That always clinches the deal. The con man knows that if he asks more than the mark can afford, the mark will pay every cent he does have to make the buy. And, also, the confidence-game operator can delight in the sycophantish tone of the mark pleading to be taken.

"I have the utmost confidence in your honor as a soldier and gentlemen," Monroe wrote, "and in your generous and sincere zeal to make known to our government the full extent of the intrigues which have been carried out in this country by means of a certain secret mission." Unfortunately said the secretary of state, he only had fifty thousand dollars he could spend on the deal. This was the total amount left in the intelligence budget.

Crillon played with his catch. After a suitable delay, he replied that when he had mentioned this to the man who had the letters, this person had flown into a rage. John Henry refused to be insulted that way! Indeed, Henry, Crillon slyly reported, threatened to burn the letters rather than accept such an offer!

Then again following the script of classic confidence games, Crillon said that following a strenous effort he had persuaded his friend to accept the paltry sum, the equivalent of only eighteen thousand pounds, if he, Crillon, could somehow find a way to supply the missing seven thousand pounds to make up the total twenty-five thousand which Henry insisted was his last price.

More dramatic letters passed between Monroe and Crillon. Finally, at five o'clock in the morning of February 5, after arguing all night with Henry, Crillon said, he had at last gotten Henry to agree. He had had to offer to deed his ancestral estate in France to Henry to make up the difference.

He had great fun with this one. The estate in France was, of course, a fiction, but Crillon told Monroe that Henry had cried, "my name will be rescued from oblivion living near Crillon, the habitation of your ancestors, and of a man who has been my friend." To frost the cake, Crillon also made use of his phony claim to be a Knight of Malta and made Henry his squire and allowed him to assume one of Crillon's several other bogus names, Adrien.

The final agreement was written on February 7. Henry was to hand over his letters to Monroe for fifty thousand dollars and a deed to Crillon's estate, which Crillon would give to the secretary of state. Monroe further promised free passage to France for Henry and his two daughters on a United States naval vessel, and agreed not to publish the papers until after Henry had sailed. Crillon then had to have more fun. The following morning he wrote to Monroe from Albert Gallatin's house. The confidant of the president was, at that point, a guest of the president's most trusted cabinet member. Henry wouldn't sign! He had been trailed by two British secret agents, and he was afraid for his life!

By Monday morning, February 10, Crillon and Henry had enjoyed themselves enough. The agreement was made. Amazingly, this whole story was told to the French government in dispatches from the French minister in Washington. Crillon's own papers in the archives in Washington corroborate it. It is regrettable that Monroe could not have thought it wise to spend some of his intelligence funds on rudimentary information gathering, such as checking the credentials of foreigners who sought him out to sell him documents.

The man who called himself Comte Edouard de Crillon was actually a man named Soubiran, son of a goldsmith, who traveled all over France pretending to be all sorts of people before finding the con-game opportunity of a lifetime. He had said he was a French army colonel, an ambassador and the knight of various other orders in addition to Malta. Evidently he had had some military experience. French records show he was once a member of the staff of one of Napoleon's key generals but was court-martialed for misappropriating funds. When he met John Henry he was a fugitive in England, the only place in Europe where he was safe from Napoleon's police.

Henry, when Crillon met him, was in England trying to collect from the British government for services he claimed to have rendered the Crown. He claimed to have performed a valuable political-intelligence mission for England three years earlier. In 1808 and 1809 Henry had submitted to the governor of Canada a number of reports about the reaction of New Englanders to Jefferson's embargo. The men in Whitehall in 1811 refused to pay him anything for them. The letters contained nothing the British minister in Washington had not reported from reading the American newspapers.

When he told his tale to the French con artist, the bogus count conceived the plan which succeeded so brilliantly in Washington. They agreed to sell the letters to the Americans, share the profits and return to France in triumph, having gotten France's enemy England into a lot of trouble with America, perhaps even a bothersome war that would divert British armed forces from their main objective of defeating Napoleon. They shook hands and sailed for Boston.

John Henry's bona fides would have been easier to check than those of the phony French count had James Monroe been disposed to spend his intelligence funds on matters of routine importance rather than manipulating the American press with misinformation.

An immigrant, born in Ireland in 1777, John Henry came to the United States in 1798 and through the help of a rich uncle in New York obtained a captain's commission in the United States Army, which was being expanded at that time in anticipation of a possible war with France. Always on the lookout to improve himself, the following year he married the daughter of a prominent Philadelphia clergyman, a marriage which gave him excellent entrée into some of the leading families of that city as well as of Baltimore. The year after marrying Sophia Duche he resigned his commission and moved to Cambridge, Massachusetts, following a trail of contacts his wife's family's connections marked out for him to the homes and businesses of important people there.

Two years later, he moved again. This time to Windsor, Vermont, where he read law and wrote strongly pro-Federalist articles for the local newspaper. One New Englander, Sidney Willard, noted in his *Memoirs* that he dined with Henry and his wife in 1804 in the company of the governor of Vermont. He described Henry as handsome, entertaining, devoted to his wife and daughters and a man who had seen much of the world.

Henry was determined to see still more. In 1805 he went to Canada and tried to get appointed a judge. He was turned down by the Canadian lieutenant governor on the grounds he was an American citizen and not a lawyer. Lieutenant Governor Gore pointed out that Henry had not even been admitted to the bar in Vermont, let alone Canada.

Henry's venture into espionage began in 1808 when, on a visit from Canada to Boston, he wrote a letter to Herman W. Ryland, secretary of Lower Canada. He obviously hoped the letter, which talked about the strong anti-Jefferson and antiembargo feelings of his important friends in Boston, would come to the attention of James Craig, the governor of Canada. It did. Craig asked Henry to come to see him. Craig wanted to know whether, in case of war between the United States and England, the irate merchants of New England might be counted on to keep their states neutral or even possibly be willing to try to detach them from the Union. In January 1809 Henry returned to Boston with credentials from Craig which he was authorized to present to any political or business leaders he deemed willing to promote neutrality or secession.

There is no question that Henry's main activity while in Boston in 1809 was espionage. He not only had a clearly stated spying and political-action assignment, he had a "cut-out" for correspondence, Canadian Secretary Ryland, and even a code. In a letter to Ryland on February 10, 1809, Henry complained that the code Governor

Craig had proposed he use was too complicated. He suggested simply using the index of code the governor proposed. "In the index," he wrote, "there is a number for every letter of the alphabet so when I do not find in the index the particular word I want, I can spell it with the figures which stand opposite to the letters." He went on to give an example. "If I want to say the troops are at Albany, I find under the letter "t" that "16" stand for "troops" and the number "125" for "Albany." The intervening words "are at" I supply by figures corresponding with the letters in these words." He went on to promise he would never identify Craig in the correspondence nor sign his own name. "They will merely be designated by the initials AB."

This amateur spooking was as close to real espionage as the letters ever came. Within days Monroe was forced to admit to the Senate that they contained no names of any Federalist leaders nor anyone else of importance in the affairs of the New England states. The Federalists and their papers swung into action. They did a job that twentieth-century investigative reporters would be proud of. All the Henry letters were printed. And all the facts in his opportunistic biography were printed too. The Charleston *Courier*, an antiadministration paper, was typical. For example, it printed the schoolboy cipher letter quoted above to show it up for what it was. And on the same date, it went directly to the point in its editorial comments:

> It has somehow leaked out, that several letters have been received from certain members of Congress announcing the administration are waiting to see the results of the Eastern Elections before they finally decide on war with England. . . . The general election in the State of Massachusetts takes place on the first Monday of April. . . . so Madison sends Congress the March 9th message appraising them of a horrible conspiracy. His calculation is that the message will just have time to reach the interior parts of that state on the day of the election . . . We trust Massachusetts will disappoint him. We believe they will not allow their feelings to be triffled with for such nefarious purposes.

The press of the president's party which had gleefully begun the fray continued to try to hold up the sagging story as best it could. But as more and more was revealed about the letters' contents and the way in which they had been acquired, their task became more and more difficult. On April 4, 1812, the *National Intelligencer*, the official party paper Thomas Jefferson had established years earlier and the Madison administration's main advocate, printed an editorial which shows the trouble the president's supporters were having with his propaganda ploy. "A futile attempt is being made to stiffle the force of Henry's evidence, to screen from the public the damning facts he exposes to view," the *Intellingencer* said, "by magnifying the amount of the compensation said to have been made by our government to him for his disclosure. . . . When a man is convicted of housebreaking or murder, is his conviction less important to society because a reward was paid for his detection or apprehension?"

When the tale of the payment to Henry was uncovered and printed in full detail, including the tracing of the bank drafts on the United States Treasury, the boomerang impact on the administration was staggering. It was, of course, Madison and Monroe who had magnified the matter, not anything the opposition press had done. The man who had changed the date on the letter transmitting the West Florida Declaration of Independence so that Secretary of State Robert Smith could lie to the British minister about it, also allowed Secretary of State James Monroe to arrange to have John Henry transmit the tell-tale letters with a covering note, dated February 20, 1812, which indicated Henry was offering them to the United States gratuitously out of the goodness of his patriotic heart.

The Baltimore *Federal Republican* on March 25 printed a notarized statement from an employee of the Mechanics Bank of New York that "Mr. Henry had in mid-month offered a check from the Bank of Columbia in Washington for $48,000." The Bank of Columbia was the principal bank through which the disbursements of the federal government were made. Subsequently the fact that it had indeed been a check signed by the treasurer of the United States was revealed. "If this is the way secret service money is to be employed," said the *Federal Republican*, "we trust the American people will raise their indignant voices."

Some further digging by the opposition produced all the sordid facts about the payment. As revealed by the Baltimore *Federal Republican* and the Virginia *Patriot* on February 10, Albert Gallatin, the secretary of the treasury, gave a warrant to Thomas T. Tucker, treasurer of the United States. By this instrument Tucker was to pay John Graham, clerk of the State Department, an order for forty-seven thousand dollars, "on account of the contingent expenses of foreign intercourse." The warrant was countersigned by Richard Rush, comptroller of the United States.

The editor of the Virginia *Patriot* wrote: "I have also before me a copy of a warrant for the other $1,000 drawn from the contingent expenses of the Secretary of State's office, the $49,000 being all that was left of the secret service money unexpended. And so to make up the $50,000, another $1,000 was drawn from another source."

The Baltimore *Federal Republican* then traced the transaction to its conclusion. Henry drew a check from the Bank of Columbia for $48,000 and presented it to the Mechanics Bank in New York and "changed it as follows: two checks, one for $17,337 and one for $20,000 and $10,162 paid Mr. Henry in cash."

A chorus or complaint did go up as the *Federal Republican* asked it to. The Charleston *Courier* wrote on March 28, "Mr. Madison must stand condemned for giving fifty thousand dollars of the public treasure for what can answer no purpose whatever save a miserable attempt to serve his reelection to the presidency."

"Paying too dearly for the Whistle," was the title of the editorial in the Baltimore *Whig* of the same day. "Henry only proves what was never doubted, that the English ministry employs agents to foment disaffection in the United States. . . . If our executive gave fifty thousand dollars for this superfluous proof, it was, we think, lavishing too much of the people's money on a spy for a whistle."

The Charleston *Courier* returned to the attack in its next issue: "At the very time the Congress are borrowing eleven million dollars and are imposing direct taxes, excise laws, a stamp tax and other heavy burdens upon the people to defray the expenses of the government . . . the administration lavishes upon a traitor and foreigner thousand of dollars with the patriotic hope their reelection to office may be secured."

On March 28, 1812, the New York *Morning Post* summed up the matter (getting the figures a little off): "Henry's gone to France with *forty five thousand dollars*—Craig lies quiet in his grave—the Old Dominion has nominated Mr. Madison as president for the ensuing term, and—*that's all.*"

When the Henry letters are examined it is clear that the opposition press had the better of the president. Leaving aside his characteristic deviousness in initially trying to hide the fact he had paid for the letters, they were duds. Henry had tried to make them look incriminating by erasing some passages and replacing them with asterisks. These erasures can be read even today, however, as they must have been by Monroe. And they are not incriminating. Not only were no Federalists named, the letters did not even show strong evidence that New England might secede. Henry seemed to acknowledge this when on March 6, 1809, he told Craig that he had not seen fit to use the credentials provided him, "nor is it probable," he wrote, "that I shall be compelled for the sake of gaining more knowledge of the arrangements of the federal party in these States, to avow myself a regular authorized agent of the British government. . . . I have sufficient means of information to enable me to judge of the proper period for offering the cooperation of Great Britain."

This appears to have been fudging. And among the spate of press revelations that were made in March 1812, there appeared one piece of evidence Henry knew he was feeding the Canadian governor what the intelligence trade calls "snow." Henry wrote a letter to his cousin, Edward J. Coale, of Baltimore on February 27, 1812, in which he stated that should these letters be published he "repels with indignation that the letters contain a single line that should expose any human being in the U.S. to censure."

The debate in Congress in its investigation of the letters soon went from bad to worse for the administration. By March 14, five days after the president's message set off the controversy, Monroe had admitted there were no Federalists' names. Josiah Quincy, one of the ablest Federalist members of Congress, skillfully wrung everything he could from the embarrassment of the ensuing revelations—the false note from Henry supposedly transmitting the letters free of charge, written ten days after they had been bought from him by Monroe, the details of the treasury transaction, and the fact that while the letters did show the British had designs on the Federalists, the Federalists had no equivalent desire to succumb to British advances. One member of Madison's own party, perhaps its most erudite ideologist, fellow-Virginian John Taylor of Caroline, exclaimed that in laying the papers before Congress the president had either been wise or mad. Wise if to prevent war as John Adams had used the XYZ papers in the previous century to wind down hostility at the height of earlier difficulties with France and England, or mad "if to wind up the mob to make the war plunge." Realizing exactly what the president had been up to, Taylor said that Madison had been "in my eyes, mad."

The episode turned out to be a field day for some opponents of the president within has own party, especially one who held a heavy grudge, Robert Smith, the secretary of state whom Madison had fired. The line Smith took had fateful consequences for the old general attempting to do the president's bidding in Florida. Smith blasted the president on March 11. It was indeed a black day for George Mathews. Major Laval had just refused to help him. What Smith said did him even greater harm.

Smith denounced the whole Florida operation in strong language and, at the same time, in injured tone. He declared Madison was determined to possess Florida by intrigue and "pecuniary bribes." He, on the other hand, had advised Florida's occupancy by a military force provided the claim to the territory was a lawful one. Smith obviously did not want to go too far out on a limb. He realized some of Madison's other most effective critics within their party were "war hawks" and expansionists. Madison's intrigue resembled "those set up in similar circumstances by Bonaparte."

The Charleston *Courier* editorialized on Smith's speech. "It is some time since we learned that the American government intended to posess themselves of West Florida under pretenses resembling Bonaparte's," the paper said, "but $100,000 and other secret means . . . employed by Congress to war over or purchase Governor Folch . . . what will be these States at a more advanced age if at so early a period they have already fallen into corruption and decrepitude? The want of talent . . . may be lamented, ignorance may be pitied, but no apology can be made for treachery and corruption."

A week later the paper was printing the Henry letters and noting the news from Fernandina: "The farce of receiving the Province from a handful of insurgents assuming to themselves the glorious name of Spanish patriots in the mother country is disgraceful in the extreme. If Florida must be ours, let the arms of the United States take it, and not receive it second hand."

Papers friendly to the administration tried to play down the news of the fall of Fernandina or explain away the involvement of the United States navy. The *National Intellingencer* back-paged the news. Niles Weekly Register, a forerunner of United States News and World Report, at first reported rather glowingly the "formidable appearance of the revolutionists." Later it said "it appears as though the part the officers of the United States have acted in regard to this island was on their own personal responsibility—but in some of the papers the contrary is strongly insinuated. The general conduct of the government is completely at variance with this supposition—but it is possible it may have been found expedient to root up and destroy this nest of smugglers and therefore to give an indirect countenance to the seizure of the island . . . "

By the time Niles Register tried to put the best face on Mathews's mission on April 7, the president and his secretary of state had decided they couldn't take any more comparison between the Henry and the Mathews missions. Compounding their fiasco with the Federalists with Florida was too much. They decided to cut their losses.

Monroe had on his desk an accumulation of letters from Mathews, all of them unanswered for months. The presence of the

British minister in Washington had forced him to get around to the questions Augustus John Foster had raised about Florida. But Mathews was conveniently far away and could be ignored. Of course, in the first two months of the new year, 1812, Monroe had been too busy to write. He had been almost fully occupied in negotiating with Crillon and developing what he and the president thought was going to be a more significant bit of covert action than that in Florida. In the midst of the misery both were suffering from the Henry-letter operation going sour, Mathews's letter of March 14 arrived.

That letter was frightening when read in the midst of the revelations of the trickery and stupidity he and the president had shown in their bid to score a preelection play against the Federalists. The March 14 letter was the one in which Mathews complained about his being double-crossed by Major Laval. It had also transmitted the prepackaged East Florida Manifesto and Declaration of Independence with the incriminating assurance that "the contents generally are real." It also transmitted the letter the double (triple) agent William A. Wyllys had addressed to McIntosh claiming black troops were en route to Saint Augustine and urging immediate action. With uncharacteristic concern for the clandestine, Mathews had erased the name "Wylley." He lapsed back into his freer style immediately and in the next sentence explained he had held further conversation on the subject with the agent "but the delicate situation he is placed in (being a half-pay British officer) prevented him from committing himself on paper." He put that in because he was seeking to make clear to Monroe that in addition to the "real" declaration and manifesto from his synthetic Florida rebels, his actions were justified by the part of his instructions that authorized him to preoccupy, defend and hold Florida against any threatened intervention by a foreign power.

Even worse reading while the Federalists in Congress were flaying the administration and the opposition press was printing the details of their payment for alleged proof that the British were intervening in American affairs, was Mathews's praise for the way the United States naval commander in the area was cheerfully supporting intervention in Florida and his request for still more military aid.

Not only was it clear that further discussion of Florida in the press, making the unfortunate comparison between the administration's activities there and the purported crime of John Henry, was too much to bear, but any leak of this Mathews letter would be catastrophic. And since Albert Gallatin's confidential warrant, and all the other confidential money transactions had found daylight, what Mathews had written might obviously be next. There was no question about what had to be done.

James Monroe sat down on April 4 and composed a long letter. It contained the same large dose of dissimulation he and Madison had made their style in dealing with national affairs.

CHAPTER XVI

THERE MUST HAVE BEEN SOME MISTAKE

Dept of State
April 4, 1812

Genl George Matthews [sic]

Sir

I have had the honor to receive your letter of the 14th of March, and have now to communicate to you the sentiments of the President on the very interesting subject to which it relates. I am sorry to have to state that the measures which you appear to have adopted for obtaining possession of Amelia Island and other parts of East Florida, are not authorized by the law of the United States under which you have acted.

That was certainly straight to the point. From there on the letter displayed the secretary of state's often demonstrated skill at doctoring the facts. It is difficult to recognize the act passed by Congress authorizing Mathews's mission, or the instructions he received on January 26, 1811, or the events which actually had taken place in West Florida (not to mention the mission Governor Claiborne gave William Wycoff in writing) from the version of United States policy toward Florida that flowed from James Monroe's pen.

You were authorized by the law, a copy of which was communicated, and by your instructions which are strictly conformable to it, to take possession of East Florida only in case one of the following contingencies should happen, either that the Governor, or other existing local authority should be disposed to place it amicably in the hands of the United States, or that an attempt should be made to take possession of it by a foreign power. Should the first contingency happen, it would follow that the arrangement being amicable would require no force on the part of the United States to carry it into effect. It was only in case of an attempt to take it by a foreign power that force could be necessary, in which event only, were you authorized to avail yourself of it.

In neither of these contingencies, was it the policy of the law, or purpose of the Executive, to wrest the province forcibly from Spain, but only to occupy it, with a view to prevent its falling into the hands of any foreign power, and to hold that pledge under the existing peculiarity of the circumstances of the Spanish Monarchy, for a just result in a amicable negotiation with Spain.

The views of the Executive respecting East Florida are further illustrated by your instructions as to West Florida. Although the United States have thought they have a good title to the latter Province, to which they thought they were justly entitled, it could not be presumed that they should intend to act differently, in respect to one, to which they had not such a claim. I may add that altho' due sensibility has been always felt for the injuries which were received from the Spanish Government in the last war, the present situation of Spain has been a motive for moderate and pacific policy towards her.

Then he fired Mathews, in the way such things are usually done.

In communicating to you these sentiments of the executive, on the measures you have lately adopted, for taking possession of East Florida, I add with pleasure, that the utmost confidence is reposed in your integrity and zeal to promote the welfare of your country. To that zeal, the error into which you have fallen, is imputed. But in consideration of the part which you have taken, which differs so essentially from that contemplated and authorized by the government, and contradicts so entirely the principles on which it has uni-

> formly and sincerely acted, you will be sensible of the necessity of discontinuing the service in which you have been employed. You will, therefore, consider your powers as revoked on the receipt of this letter.

By the time Monroe wrote that letter, not only had the administration been flailed by the Federalist press, he was inundated by the pressure of negotiating with both the British and the French as the nation drew daily nearer to involvement in the Great Powers' War. Monroe's discomfort is understandable. His misrepresentations are understandable, too, to all practitioners of realpolitik, less so to people who like plain talk.

Monroe evidently thought so too. He wrote another private letter to Mathews. He told Mathews that it had been painful to disagree with the way he had acted, and he again assured the general "the utmost confidence is reposed in your patriotism." To reemphasize this point, Monroe said, was the reason he was writing the second letter.

He could not resist, however, adding something he hoped would convince the soldier to keep quiet. He suggested that, in fact, Mathews had broken the law. A law passed in 1794, Monroe said, forbade any activity such as Mathews had engaged in which contemplated taking possession of any part of a foreign country, under penalty of severe punishment.

The act of June 5, 1794, made it unlawful for any person "to provide or prepare the means for any military expedition or enterprise to be carried on from thence against the territory or dominions of any foreign prince or state." Persons guilty of such action could be fined three thousand dollars and sentenced to prison for three years.

Monroe had reason to be concerned that Mathews might explode when he heard the news that the administration was putting the full blame for the phony war in Florida on him. He knew Mathews was a hotheaded Scots-Irishman. Also before taking the step, he and Madison had conferred with trusted members of Congress, Representative George Troup of Georgia and the man who picked Mathews to do the Florida job for the president, Senator William Crawford. Both urged that the matter be given some sober second thought. Troup suggested that the United States should insist the patriots were a legitimate group of revolutionaries. Monroe reminded him that eight United States gunboats had taken part in the capture of Fernandina and the details of what had happened had already been put on his desk by Ońis, who had received a report from Saint Augustine. Justo Lopez had explained the events of mid-March to acting-Governor Estrada who had immediately asked the representative of Ferdinand VII in the United States to make a formal protest to the State Department. It was decided the best that could be done for Mathews was to send the private letter along with the official one relieving Mathews of his duties.

The perfect person to take the bad news to Florida was fortuitously at hand. Mathews had sent Ralph Isaacs to Washington with the follow-up reports he had written after March 14. These described what was happening on Amelia Island and what plans were for marching on to Saint Augustine, transmitted the articles of cession and the other documents of the revolution and, again, asked for more military assistance. Monroe knew how close the two men were, and while it was unfortunate for Isaacs that he would have to be the bearer of bad tidings, it was fortunate for Monroe. Isaacs was stung to find what he and his chief had thought was going to be a cheerful review of a progress report turned into a cheerless discussion of dismissal. It was Isaacs who wrote more than two years later the only account of what transpired.

Monroe told Isaacs that the Florida situation was the most distressing he had faced in all his years of service to the nation. Isaacs clearly resented this and defended Mathews. He reminded Monroe that the president had made it quite plain to the general and to him what he wanted to see happen in Florida and that they had considerable latitude to act as they saw fit to accomplish their mission.

To pretend, as the letters to Mathews did, that what had happened was the result of some sort of undisciplined zeal on Mathews's part was unfair, to say the least. Isaacs pointed out that they had kept the State Department fully informed. He was thinking of the letters written the summer before, which the secretary had never answered, as well as the more recent correspondence.

Most tellingly, he reminded the secretary that Mathews's request for 250 muskets, made just before the action took place at Fernandina, had been honored in Washington. The secretary of war had ordered the military agent at Savannah, Major Thomas Burke, to send these arms to Point Petre. Such arms had, in fact, arrived there by the time Isaacs left for Washington.

Such argument affected Monroe, even softened him, but it had no affect on the decision to dismiss Mathews. It possibly did affect the next decision Monroe made. He had said in his official letter to Mathews that he was turning Mathews's responsibilities regarding Florida over to Governor Mitchell. Monroe now asked Isaacs to be the liaison officer between Mitchell and Colonel Smith. As for Mathews, Monroe told Isaacs to be gentle with the general and assure him that he and the president were certain he had acted from the best of motives and that they were hurt by having to do "violence to his feelings." He told Isaacs to tell the general it was the secretary's belief the general "would soon be reinstated." Monroe didn't make clear what the general would be reinstated as. He vaguely declared, instead, that "the government had not lost their confidence in him and he would soon have proof they had not."

Monroe also asked Isaacs to assure Colonel Smith that he was not being held responsible nor condemned for obeying General Mathews's request for military assistance. Monroe further wanted Isaacs to reassure the patriots that "not a hair on the head of any person concerned in the revolution in E[ast] F[lorida] should be hurt . . . that they should not suffer, in person or property, for their efforts. . . ."

Isaacs was reluctant to take his new assignment, but Monroe's show of some heart and his affection for the man whose letters he had been writing for two years convinced him that he should. No one else could possibly soften the blow as he could. And he was glad to hear that the patriots would not be abandoned. When Monroe showed him a copy of the orders that were going to Governor

Mitchell, outlining his new responsibilities, he felt he saw where he could do some good in a liaison role.

Monroe wrote instructions for Governor Mitchell on April 10. The first part of them were not to Isaacs's liking. The instructions repeated the fiction that Mathews had exceeded his orders and reiterated the administration's innocence. But at their conclusion the pledge to protect the patriots was specifically made. That was at least something.

"It will be improper to expose these people to the resentment of the Spanish authorities," Monroe wrote. "You will come to a full understanding with the Spanish Governor on this subject, and not fail to obtain from him the most explicit and satisfactory assurances respecting it."

Isaacs agreed to head back south to talk to both Mitchell and Mathews.

The Mitchell instructions were only part of the official communications sent out from Washington in April 1812 as Madison and Monroe sought to extricate themselves from the covert action operation in Florida. After Mathews was disavowed, the secretary of war sent orders to Smith directing him to receive and obey orders respecting the future disposition of his troops only from the governor of Georgia. On April 8 the secretary of the navy wrote Commodore Campbell. He had gotten Campbell's correspondence describing the tortuous thinking by which finally the commodore came to allow his boats to back up the patriots' move on Fernandina. The secretary said he appreciated Campbell's conviction that he had done what was right, but hastened to explain the new official line about Mathews. He ordered Campbell to get his boats out of Florida waters and to be sure not to cooperate any further with Mathews.

The news about the disavowal of Mathews hit the press before Isaacs had a chance to return with the official copies of Monroe's two letters. The opposition papers saw it for what it was, while the proadministration press, as to be expected, put the best face possible on the development. Mathews himself was off to Picolata negotiating with the Indians. He was rightly worried that if the situation of the patriots and the troops dragged on into a prolonged stalemate, the Spanish would try to bring the Indians into the conflict to tip the balance. He became the classic cuckold, the last one to know.

The other principals—McIntosh, Ashley, Campbell and Smith—reacted to the news in ways that were predictable.

McIntosh and Ashley were stunned and frantically reassessed their situation. Ashley decided to resign as commander of the patriot army. McIntosh was equally scared but counseled hanging on. "God only knows, what will be the consequence with the unfortunate characters involved in this transaction," he wrote to Governor Mitchell, "I think the government can never abandon them to inevitable ruin, after being in some degree *invited* to *this revolution* [italics his] and formally ceding the Whole Province to the United States except the Garrison and town of St. Augustine."

McIntosh convinced his colleagues to put a bold face on affairs. The thing to do was strengthen their forces. He called for a regiment of volunteers to be comprised of eight companies. Each company would have a captain, two lieutenants, and an ensign and sixty-five enlisted men. He also suggested the patriot army's new regiment have a new colonel, a lieutenant colonel and two majors. The new military organization revived George Mathews's old recruitment lure, liberal land grants for volunteers. The new colonel was promised a grant of three thousand acres, with the rest of the officer corps likewise liberally provided for down to one thousand acres for the lowly ensign. Each enlisted man was promised five hundred acres. To further spur recruiting, each person who brought in a recruit was promised an additional twenty-five acres per man.

The Savannah *Republican* and other papers in Georgia and elsewhere in the South not only published this appeal put out by the patriots but other propaganda the men at Fort Moosa prepared. They made the usual exaggerated case those in their position always do. They explained they had rebelled because of the long suffering they had endured from the corrupt and tyranical Spanish rulers of the province. Now they feared if the United States would not accept them, they might be sold by Spain to its ally England. This would have the direst consequences not only for them but also for the

United States. They appealed to all Americans to heed this point well. They then bragged about their military exploits. Without artillery, they said, they had seized the armed port of Fernandina. They had been forced to ask for help from the American naval commander in the area because of this lack of the necessary armament. Without any American aid, they had then marched boldly across the province, taking it all in the name of their East Florida Republic and had gone all the way to the walls of the formidable Fort San Marcos at Saint Augustine. They would never surrender. If fail they must, they would leave East Florida and abandon all their property. They would never bow to the Spanish yoke and trudge meekly off to the dungeons and scaffold the Spanish traditionally prepared for rebels.

Next they undertook to answer Monroe's official account of United States policy which he had invented for his dismissal notice to Mathews. Wicked men, they said, claimed the United States would abandon them, but an act of Congress had authorized President Madison to accept part or parts of East Florida from the local authority. An officially authorized agent of the president had given proof of this. They quoted from Mathews's original orders and said that he had received oral instructions as well. Some people said, they noted, that the law and the instructions meant that the local authority had to be one having jurisdiction over all of East Florida. This could not have been the intention, otherwise the words "part or parts" would not have been used. The United States government could not desert the patriots.

If the patriots put the news of Mathews's disavowal in terms that suited their cause and personalities best, so did Commodore Campbell. The nervous navy officer's answer to the word he received, ordering him to get out of the tight spot he had gotten himself into, was equally typical.

"By this day's mail I am honored with your instructions of the 8th instant," he wrote to the secretary of the navy, "which renders me the happiest of mortals and relieved me from a state of anxiety that no language can express. I shall immediately with pride and pleasure carry into effect the orders of our much beloved President by withdrawing myself from General Mathews and ordering the gunboats from Spanish waters."

Colonel Smith waited patiently for his instructions after he heard that he was to henceforth take his orders from Governor Mitchell. He had confidence the governor would conduct himself as a frontier Georgian should be expected to. . . .

David Mitchell was another Scot. He had been born there and had moved to Georgia as a boy of seventeen when he inherited the property of an uncle who had died aboard a British prison ship during the Revolution. He prospered in Savannah as a young lawyer and became an active participant in politics as a loyal supporter of Thomas Jefferson. In fact, he was such an ardent supporter that he fought a duel in 1802 with a local merchant who did not share his zeal for Jefferson. It was not a simple matter of upholding injured honor after an argument with an exchange of shots in the air. Mitchell's opponent fired first and his bullet struck Mitchell in the side. Mitchell missed. The second shot cut through Mitchell's trousers. Mitchell took better aim and shot the man dead.

The exhibition of marksmanship and legal murder was a great help to Mitchell in his career. A year later he was made a major general in the Georgia militia and seven years later he was chosen governor of the state. Whether overcome by conscience once in this important post or worried he might not be so lucky another time, one of the first acts he signed as governor was a bill outlawing dueling.

He was, of course, quite well acquainted with the Florida border and had listened attentively to Mathews's appeal for the use of his Georgia militia. He may already have had some personal stake in the success of the illegal trade in the area. (Later after his stint as governor and his role in the Florida affair he would be appointed an Indian agent in 1817 when James Monroe became president, thereafter for the next four years supplementing his two-thousand-dollar-a-year salary by being an illegal slave trader, which made him the subject of a federal investigation. Testimony amassed as evidence by the United States attorney general revealed that Mitchell frequently moved groups of over fifty Africans from above Fernandina to the area under his control as Indian agent and harbored them as laborers until they could be sold.)

As a bold improviser, Mitchell was certainly equal to George Mathews, and Smith hoped that with the Georgia militia at his command Mitchell would make certain the United States troops were not stranded.

When first hearing a report of what had happened at Fernandina, a sketchy account of which he received on March 28, Mitchell had not liked the news. The quarrel between Mathews and Laval angered him. He couldn't understand why the American government had not issued explicit orders to its military officers making support for Mathews perfectly clear. On the other hand, without such explicit orders, he felt Mathews had acted without proper authority. He hoped, he said, for the honor of the United States that the government was not responsible for the patriots' revolt. And as the governor of Georgia he was reluctant to mobilize the state's militia with all the expense that meant for his nearly empty treasury. On the other hand, if as a consequence of what had taken place the Spanish made any move to retaliate on Georgia, he would immediately call out his troops to defend his state. All this he told in a letter to John Floyd, the militia's commanding officer.

After he had received a more complete report from Senator Crawford of the incidents that had occurred in Florida he was convinced he had no power to send his militia into that province. In a second letter to Floyd on April 16 he said he thought it was evident that the patriots had been misled by promises of American aid in the form of both United States troops and Georgia militia. He regretted that such an able officer as Thomas Smith had been placed in the situation in which he now found himself, but he could not order the militia beyond the state line. He did order Floyd, however, to hold his forces in readiness for marching.

At this point he received his instructions from James Monroe, and on April 24 set out for Saint Marys to get a look at the situation at close hand. His orders, he quickly saw, created a dilemma for him. Monroe characteristically had placed water buckets on both his shoulders. He was ordered to turn his attention and direct his efforts to "the restoration of the state of things in the province which existed before the late transactions." He was told to restore Amelia to the Spanish governor together with "such other parts" and to make sure that he communicated "*directly* with the Governor [italics, Monroe's] or principal officer of Spain in that Province, and act in harmony with him . . . " On his other shoulder he had to balance an order to make certain no harm came to the patriots at the hands of a possibly vengeful Spanish official.

Ralph Isaacs arrived at Saint Marys during the first week in May and conferred with Mitchell. George Mathews arrived too, and Isaacs had at last to confront him with the bad news.

Mitchell's first actions as the man in charge reassured the patriots. He sent word to Smith to hold his position. Since Commodore Campbell had definite orders to move out, he appealed to him rather than ordered him to keep his gunboats on the Saint Johns River to protect the rear of Smith's troops. Forgetting how elated he was, Campbell once again, as he had at Fernandina, decided to defer to the senior man on the spot. He not only kept his boats in Florida waters, he added an additional one to the two already on the Saint Johns River.

Mitchell then began negotiations with the acting governor, Juan Estrada, sending his personal military aide with a note informing Estrada of Mathews's dismissal and of the American government's desire for peace and harmony in the area. But it was an ambiguous letter. It did not directly suggest any terms under which the American troops would be withdrawn.

The letter angered Estrada, who replied in a curt note of his own that he had read about Mathews's dismissal in the newspapers but was amazed, in view of this, that the American troops continued to occupy Spanish territory. He said he could not possibly negotiate until these troops were withdrawn, and although he didn't anticipate any immediate conflict he recognized no other authority except his own south of the Saint Marys and any military action that might occur would be the fault of the United States.

Mitchell and Estrada were sparring, and less than frank. Mitchell had deliberately not been explicit on the subject of troop withdrawal because he had sent off a query to Monroe which he wanted answered before he did anything further. It was a clever query, giving the secretary three contingencies to consider. What should he do, Mitchell asked, if the British were to introduce troops to support the Spanish? Second, he pointed out the discrepancy in coordination of United States forces in the area that arose from his having been granted the authority to decide what Smith's army troops should do while Washington had directly commanded Campbell to leave. He pointed out he would have to have naval support to carry out his mission and requested appropriate orders be sent to the commodore. Finally he wanted to know what he was supposed to do in case the patriots refuse to give up, "in which case the Spanish authorities would not be able to repossess those parts occupied by United States troops."

Estrada, for his part, had been less than frank with Mitchell's messenger. He was planning an attack. On the morning of May 16 Colonel Smith was called by his guard to observe a Spanish schooner and four launches moving up the North River from Saint Augustine. They drew up to the creek on which Moosa Fort was located, and anchored. At ten o'clock the Spanish opened fire with the schooner's two 24-pounders. The schooner and launches were filled with soldiers. Smith realized he could not hold Moosa against such force. He ordered most of his men to retire in such a way as to leave the impression of complete withdrawal; meanwhile he stationed fifteen sharpshooters behind the ruins of the old fort. He gave orders for them to fire when the Spanish came within sixty yards, and to try to kill as many of the enemy as possible before withdrawing too.

As planned, the main body of Americans beat a hasty and obvious retreat. The Spanish ships came on faster when they saw this. The American sharpshooters waited. The Spanish advanced still faster. Somehow the sergeant in charge of the sharpshooters misjudged the distance. He ordered his men to fire when the Spanish were still four hundred yards away. The American musket balls fell harmlessly in the water of the creek. The Spanish shells smashed into what remained of Fort Moosa. The bombardment, which went on until four in the afternoon, was the one real battle of the Patriots War, and it was bloodless. Not a man fell dead or wounded, but by the time the Spanish withdrew, some important points had been settled. Smith was determined to get revenge, and when Mitchell heard of the attack he decided he had felt one water bucket drop from his shoulders. He now had an excuse to delay any withdrawal of American troops. He would henceforth devote his efforts to protecting the patriots rather than trying to see to it that the territory they claimed was returned to Spanish rule. Isaacs in his new role as liaison officer sent Mitchell's order to hold his ground to Smith, and if fired on by the Spanish again to assault and take Saint Augustine.

While Mitchell, the new man in charge, was wrestling with Washington and the Spanish, the chief of operations who had been fired was alternatingly fretting and fuming. Isaacs showed Mathews the two letters from Monroe on May 9. By then he had heard others refer to them but he refused to believe or accept his fate. He read and reread the official dismissal letter, then turned to the personal note and studied its every word with Isaacs's help. It took some time for the news to sink in. And then he blew up.

He told Isaacs he would expose everything that had been told him privately by the president. He would write the newspapers and give a complete account. He would show up the perfidy of the president and his pliant helper, James Monroe. He asked Isaacs to help him pull together all the documents—his instructions of January 1811 as well as instructions for his first mission the year before that, all the letters that had been sent to Washington advising step-by-step what he was doing. He would reveal his conversations with the president, "much of what is called 'back stairs' instruction," as Isaacs put it, when he wrote Monroe about Mathews's reaction. He would tell how he was supposed to use the one hundred thousand dollars that Congress had appropriated to bribe Governor Folch.

His anger rose still higher. Finally he declared he'd go to Washington and "blow them all up." He'd personally thrash Madison, perhaps even kill him.

Such anger and bitterness is often felt by men who work night and day on covert operations until their nerves are frayed; they lose control of themselves in the frustration of defeat, especially defeat that as in Mathews's case they have good reason to feel is flavored with more than just a dash of betrayal. Among the many versions that differ from the official account of what occurred in Dallas, Texas, on November 22, 1963, one rather well-developed case has been made that President Kennedy was killed by a conspiracy among the covert operators who felt betrayed by the Bay of Pigs. The British author Anthony Summers in his book *Conspiracy* examines this thesis in some detail. He indicates that key members of the staff of the congressional committee that reexamined the assassination in the late 1970s, as well as members of the committee itself, believed Cuban exiles who were part of the CIA's failed attempt to overthrow Castro in 1961, combined with Mafia figures who were feeling too much heat from President Kennedy and his brother Robert, arranged the president's assassination and hired Oswald. One Cuban even strongly implicated a CIA officer, a man associated with the CIA's anti-Castro operations. This man, the Cuban claimed, shared the Cubans' sense of betrayal when Kennedy, like Madison, decided to abandon his covert operators. Kennedy left them on the beach rather than give them full United States military support—thereby avoiding the embarrassment of explaining that they were not a group of Cuban patriots who had spontaneously started out to capture their country but a covertly trained brigade paid by the CIA. Madison, 150 years earlier, had set the tone: he could not face criticism of his covert plot to steal Florida while at the same time trying to show that his political opponents had consorted with British covert-intelligence collectors.

George Mathews was calmed down before he went to the extreme of his threats for revenge. A familiar technique was used. Isaacs assured him that Monroe meant what he said when he promised the general would soon see that the administration would show appreciation for his services. Senator Crawford relayed the message. When the dust settled, Mathews was assured he would be named governor of East Florida. . . .

By the end of May Monroe had gotten back to Mitchell and

answered his questions in a way that sounded as though there could be some substance to that promise, in spite of the dubious record that had been established in previous promises made to Mathews.

To Mitchell's query as to what he should do in case of any British move to reinforce the Spanish, the answer was, Attack the British. Regarding the confusion about who was to control the activities of Commodore Campbell's squadron of ships, Mitchell was told new orders would soon be forthcoming putting him in charge of the navy's actions as well as the army's. In response to his third question about what to do about the patriots, he was told the matter was up to him. He could either withdraw the United States troops or not if the patriots chose to stay and fight, but it was rather obvious what Washington *hoped* his decision would be. He was told not to withdraw, *if* that was ultimately what he decided to do, until he was assured by the Spanish authorities that the withdrawal of American troops would in no way jeopardize the safety and well-being of the patriots or their property. In short, he was to insist on total amnesty for the rebels before he left them to the mercy of the Spanish governor. In addition, he was ordered not to induce the patriots to give up their efforts to overthrow Spanish authority. The United States government, Monroe told him, while not responsible in any way for what the patriots had done, considered itself responsible for their well-being since they had been assured by an agent of the United States government that their revolt had been approved. Although Madison and Monroe had been forced, because of their blunder in the Henry affair, to, as it were, throw George Mathews to the lions, they weren't ready to quit the coliseum. They intended to stay at the game of getting Florida. The administration, of course, did not expect the Spanish authorities would be willing to grant total amnesty to the rebels, so making the grant of such amnesty a condition for withdrawal of United States troops was a safe ploy, especially in conjunction with assuming responsibility for the safety and welfare of the patriots.

Mitchell accepted the challenge willingly. The attack on Moosa had changed his mind completely about what his course would be and with this reinforcing set of instructions from Washington in hand, he set to work. He sent his aide, Colonel Cuthbert, to Savannah to raise one hundred volunteers for reinforcement. He intended to back up his order to Smith. Once adequate forces were gathered, he would find some excuse to draw out the Spanish and then attack Saint Augustine.

June 1812 was a time of action and decision in Florida, in Georgia and in Washington. On June 11 Sebastian Kindelan arrived to take charge of his new post, governor general of East Florida and commander in chief of its armed forces. The very day he arrived he sent emissaries to Colonel Smith and to Governor Mitchell. Captain Francisco Rivera went to Smith's camp carrying a curt note demanding Smith immediately withdraw his forces beyond the Saint Johns River. Jose Arredondo of Fernandina was sent off to cross the Saint Marys and give the word to Mitchell.

The continued presence of United States troops in Florida could not be tolerated, Kindelan's letter to Mitchell said. Unless the governor of Georgia ordered their removal, it would result in conflict and universal condemnation of the United States for invading the territory of a friendly nation with which it was at peace. In the name of Ferdinand VII and the Spanish nation, Mitchell was invited to get the American army out of Florida within the next eleven days.

Mitchell replied to this with a long letter reviewing past events and condemning the Spanish officials for everything that had happened, in particular for the attack on Fort Moosa. If Kindelan attacked after eleven days he would find the hitherto forebearing forces of the United States, who had failed to initiate any action to date out of respect for a friendly neighbor, no longer able or willing to show restraint.

While these notes were passing back and forth, Colonel Daniel Newnan of the Georgia militia was traveling through the Georgia piedmont rounding up recruits and the militia of General John Floyd was mustering to await word from the governor in Saint Marys.

A now pacified George Mathews penned a note to Washington. He was still hurt and bitter, but he was not going to cause any trouble. "If I thought myself justifiable in exposing to public view confidential informations and conversations I have no doubt I could justify my conduct to an impartial public and make it very evident that I have not in any instance exceeded my powers," Mathews wrote. " . . . the good of the country forbids it; for I think it highly improper at the present crisis to do any act that would lessen or injure the President in the opinion of his fellow citizens, or in the approaching election. The good of our country may require all his influence aided by the best of our citizens."

What Mathews was referring to was what was now the nation's and the president's major concern, a concern which forced Florida from the chief-executive's mind. Four days before Mathews wrote his letter Congress had acceded to the president's request and, on June 18, declared war on Great Britain. James Madison now confronted the gravest crisis of his career. That he needed the aid of the best citizens, no one doubted. Many people, in fact, were not convinced even that could help him, and many were not inclined to wish him as well as his former agent George Mathews did.

CHAPTER XVII

FRONT BURNER BACK BURNER

1812 was a leap year. That meant it was a true anniversary year of the birth of Payne Todd, James Madison's troublesome stepson. And whether for that reason or not, it was a year that began with Dolley Madison having one of her most brilliant and busiest seasons since the Madisons took over the president's house. The house was full of young relatives, and Payne Todd came over regularly on weekends from his school in Baltimore, the tough priest who was in charge leniently permitting this. Nephews Alfred and Robert Madison, Dolley's younger brother, John C. Payne, her cousin Edward Coles, and Dolley's widowed sister Lucy Payne Washington all lived there. As if this were not enough, Dolley also invited twenty-year-old Phoebe Morris, daughter of a longtime Philadelphia friend, to stay for several months.

Dolley, getting pudgy, still presided over splendid soirees. Betsy Patterson Bonaparte was a dazzling presence at many. Phoebe Morris wrote her father, "How I wish you could see Madame Bonaparte in all her splendor of dress and all the attractions of beauty. I think I never beheld a human form so faultless . . . She is truly celestial, and it is impossible to look on anyone else when she is present."

Perhaps one reason Madame Bonaparte could look so well was that she was being paid off handsomely by her husband's brother. Jérôme had been forced back to France, but Napoleon paid Betsy fifty thousand sterling a year to keep her and Jérôme's child, Napoleon's nephew. People, especially Federalists who accused Madison of being pro-French, mumbled about a possible heir to the French emperor's throne living a princely life with his mother in the United States.

Washington Irving described a typical Wednesday afternoon at the president's mansion as a crowd "of great and little men, of ugly old women and beautiful young ones." Dolley dipped snuff from a cloisonné box and used a bandanna for "the dirty work," as she swept around the room in silks, feathers and jewels.

But whatever the gaiety, the reality was that the nation had been hovering on the brink of war with Great Britain, or France, for months. As winter turned to spring the scales tipped in favor of war with Great Britain—a war that might be labeled a leap-year event. For whatever the total facts in the case were, it was a war that was declared one day after any reason for its happening ceased to exist. Leap years, of course, have one day too many. On June 17 the British Parliament revoked the Orders in Council under which the British navy had been seizing United States ships and impressing seamen as a means of enforcing its blockade against France and the supplying of Britain's enemy by enterprising American merchants. The next day, June 18, Congress declared war on England. The cause of war, the declaration said, was the inequitous orders in council. June 18, 1812, was altogether one day too many.

James Madison's tenure as secretary of state and his first term as president had both been haunted by the great war in Europe.

It seemed to William Preston, another favorite young son of a friend of Dolley's who spent a good deal of time with the young people who crowded the president's house, that Madison was ready to sink under the burden of his office. He found the president "pallid and hard," his manner "cold and stiff." He was "often at his desk by candlelight in the morning." He kept asking "What has Congress done?" Altogether, Preston found him "exceedingly harrassed and manifestly defective in that vigour of character demanded. . . . He wanted a talent for affairs, was deficient in tact, and in persistence of purpose. The opposition . . . was a source of daily annoyance . . . exciting him to petulance and querulousness. . . . Admidst the perplexity of his public affairs he did not see clearly and therefore did not step firmly. . . . His judgement was not clear about the war or the mode of conducting it, nor had he about him friends whose pertinacity and firmness might supply his defects in these qualities." And although the words came from a bitter Madison opponent rather than from a young friend of the family, the Philadelphia *Aurora* aptly summed up what Preston wrote about the president, saying that if Madison had any war fever, "it must be a species of *intermittent,* which is vulgarly called *the shaking ague.*"

The only surety in June 1812 was that the United States was badly divided and about to begin a war for which it was not prepared, and in which disaster soon followed disaster.

In the midst of dissension and many difficulties, Madison had little time to think about the mess in Florida. The war was more popular in the South, however, and Florida was not totally forgotten, particularly by the citizens of Georgia, whose governor was now the man in charge there. Even before war had been declared, the citizens of Milledgeville, the state capital, had passed resolutions and sent petitions to Washington calling for a fight with England. They were well aware that such a war would also mean that Florida, property of England's ally Spain, should be fair game. In a mass meeting on June 3 the citizens of Savannah passed resolutions in favor of immediate war with England and immediate occupation of Florida. The editor of the Augusta *Chronicle* at the same time, pointed out that seizing Florida was a necessary defense measure once war with England was underway.

The day after war was declared, George Troup of Georgia introduced a resolution in the House of Representatives requesting the Special Committee on the Spanish American Colonies consider the expediency of authorizing the immediate occupation of East and West Florida. Three days later a bill empowering the president "to take possession of a tract of country lying south of the Mississippi Territory and of the State of Georgia" went before the House. And on June 25, it passed.

The bill looked like the old act of January 1811 under which George Mathews started on his mission. It even included the same sum, one hundred thousand dollars, as operational money to run the occupation. And, as customary on delicate matters, both the House and Senate considered the new Florida bill in secret session.

Things didn't go well in the Senate. Smith's friends combined with the Federalists in what they saw as another chance to embarrass the president and leave him stuck with the anomalous situation he had created in Florida. The American army was already there, thanks to what his agent Mathews had done. The bill was defeated in the Senate by a vote of sixteen to fourteen.

Meanwhile, back at the swamp Kindelan and Mitchell had reached a standoff. Smith's troops had pulled back a mile and a half from the ruins of Fort Moosa, but there they and the patriots sat. When Mitchell answered Kindelan's letter refusing the Spanish governor's ultimatum to get the troops out in eleven days, he noted with special umbrage that the new governor had brought a company of black troops with him from Cuba and was reported to be arming all the blacks in Saint Augustine. Kindelan did not answer Mitchell's letter for six months. He realized negotiation was futile and began to plan other means of defending his province.

The story about the black troops was used with good effect, meanwhile, in the recruiting effort that was going on in Georgia. The Republican Blues and Savannah Volunteer Guards gathered in that port town, eager to go south to deal with the situation. On June 12 they struck their tents and marched to the docks, where gunboats waited to take them to Fernandina. In Milledgeville the recruits gathered at the capital to hear their orders. On July 1 they marched toward Dublin for a general muster of troops from central Georgia. The local paper loved the farewell scene as the troops prepared to leave the state capital. "Tears . . . the pearly ethereal drops, which gild and adorn the generous cheek of Patriotism, were seen to steal from the eyes of many. Parents separating from their sons, wives from their husbands and connections, unfolded a scene affecting and sublime." By the last week in June more than five hundred troops were reported en route to Colonel Smith's camp to fight the Spanish. They had enlisted for two months' duty.

Kindelan, for his part, had made contact with the traditional allies of the Spanish—the Seminole chiefs.

While Mr. Madison's larger war was going from bad to worse in the summer and fall of 1812, his little war in Florida was also taking a new and ugly turn.

CHAPTER XVIII

BLACK AND WHITE AND RED ALL OVER

Life in the salt marshes outside Saint Augustine was not the kind of duty that appealed to either the officers or men of the United States Army. As the summer of 1812 dragged dragged slowly on, they had more and more to complain about in the letters they wrote: "Lately my health has been bad in this climate," Captain Fielder Ridgeway wrote to his brother in Maryland. "I have a wound in my right leg I am afraid will not get well in this climate." He hoped he'd feel better if he could only get something good to eat for a change, and he wrote to a sergeant stationed at the army's backup post on the Saint Johns seeking help on that score. "I have not had one pound of butter for many days (I am sick) I have requested Lieut Stallings and Mr. Ruddle to procure me some. I suppose its scarce and they have not taken pains that I hope you will to procure me 4, 5 or 10 pounds. Also chickings, ducks, I prefer the Mascovey Duck if they can be had. I will be glad if you can Send me a Small Roast Pigg . . . "

A company medic, William Kinnear, told his mother and brother his low opinion of the place where "fortune has at length directed me. . . . it is in fact but a fit receptacle for savages and wild beasts the scenery of the country exhibiting nothing except a desart—pine barren and vast regions of untrackless swamps where nothing can be heard by the lonely traveller save the screeching of the owl or howling of the wolf, his fears anticipating an attack from the more dreadful Indian . . ."

By the time Kinnear wrote that letter Indian attacks had become more than a fear of a lonely traveler in the marshes of northeast Florida. Blunders by the patriots and persistent activity by Governor Kindelan had managed to turn the conflict into a race war.

The patriot leaders, after Mathews was relieved of his command, decided they would create a more formal political structure and, thereby, perhaps gain the attention of the American government to their claims for recognition. On July 10, 1812, they elected fifteen delegates and empowered them to write a constitution. Never at a loss for words, they produced a four-thousand-word constitution in two weeks time, and on Saturday, July 25, John Houston McIntosh, Lodowick Ashley, William Craig, Buckner Harris and the rest of the familiar cast met at Zephaniah Kingsley's plantation. On Monday, July 27, as the legislative council called for by the new document, they elected John McIntosh "director of the Territory of East Florida."

In addition to this chief-executive post, the constitution called for a unicameral legislative council and an elaborate system of courts. All free white males could vote, but only those who held property valued at one thousand dollars could be members of the legislature, and to be eligible for the director's job a man had to have at least one thousand five hundred dollars in other property in addition to a minimum of five hundred acres of land.

The document made perfectly clear what the purpose of this exercise in civics was all about. The fifteen constitutional-convention members stated that "it is expressly and unequivocally and unanimously declared by them that it (the new government they had created) is intended to exist and be in operation only until the United States shall acknowledge this territory as a part of the United States."

Three days after being installed in his new most high-sounding post, McIntosh sat down and wrote James Monroe. He had earlier appealed to Commodore Campbell to send a boat to Saint Augustine and had been ignored. To Monroe he complained about the way the United States Army was administering Fernandina, the one prize jewel McIntosh liked to believe was the patriots' possession. The people in the town loyal to the Spanish governor were being protected by the army, he said. These people were regularly in contact with Kindelan, and they were plotting to confiscate estates and property of his faithful followers. He threatened to burn down the houses of the pro-Spanish faction. Monroe ignored him too.

The administration of Fernandina, in fact, was going quite smoothly. Captain Abraham Massias, after a brief period in which the marine captain John Williams ruled the town, took over in early July and proved to be a brilliant occupation governor. Williams was called back to the line to use his marine company to protect Smith's supply route from Saint Augustine to Fernandina. He had also allowed the leaders of the Spanish citizens, Jose Arrendondo, Philip Yonge, and James Cashen, to form a committee of public safety, an act that set off the protests of McIntosh. Massias allowed this arrangement to continue, but instituted a series of tough rules and regulations that enabled him to run the town firmly but fairly.

Massias's troops were assembled each morning and night, under arms, showing that they, not the citizen committee, were the ones really in charge of maintaining law and order. Soldiers and noncoms patrolled the streets in groups of three, reporting to sentries every half hour during the day and every fifteen minutes at night.

Massias was particularly careful to keep tight control over his countrymen's favorite pastime—drinking. No tavern keeper could sell liquor to an enlisted man at any time, and sailors from naval or merchant vessels were required to leave town before nine in the evening. All grog shops were ordered closed at that hour. No late brawls had an opportunity to get started to disturb the night's tranquility.

On the side of fairness, all property-owners' rights were respected, and George J.F. Clarke was kept at his old job of adjudicating all disputes over titles and boundaries of real estate. Town beautification was encouraged. Rules were even established governing the distance trees could be set out from the front of property lot lines. Massias also insisted on standards of public health that were unusual in America in those days—every resident was held personally responsible for keeping the street in front of his house clean; garbage was to be collected every day and dumped into the Amelia River. No one began talking about any more progressive method of handling garbage disposal in America for over a hundred years. Abraham Massias was ahead of his time in one further sanitary measure: owners of mules, horses and hogs were ordered to keep their animals outside city limits.

He also kept the same tax, twelve dollars a year, on store and shopkeepers that the Spanish had maintained. This and his strict collection of duties from ships led to quarrels with the patriots, who wanted the money paid to them, and with the town's preponderant population—serious practicing smugglers. Such tough measures made them remember that Massias was a Jew. Following familiar anti-Semitic fashion they complained the Jew was putting the money collected into his own pocket. An investigation was ordered. Colonel Smith, who was put in charge, cleared Massias of the ridiculous accusation with a pointed notation that what the smugglers really desired was less vigilant conduct of the town's affairs.

While patriot chiefs were busy either creating elaborate governmental structures or trying to get their hands on the custom receipts at Fernandina, their disavowed case officer, George Mathews, was still trying to help their cause by concerning himself with what he knew was a more important matter. He knew Sebastian Kindelan and he had not dealt with him about border problems while governor of Georgia in vain. What the Indians were likely to do was the key to turning the standoff at Saint Augustine into a victory for one side or the other.

Even before Ralph Isaacs found him to deliver the bad news from Washington, Mathews had turned his attention to the task of jawboning with the Indians. His first journey to meet with the chiefs of the Seminoles at Picolata in late April and early May was what spared him hearing about his dismissal as early as patriot leaders and Spanish commanders did. He talked with King Payne, ancient Seminole chieftan, and thought he had gained an understanding the Indians would remain neutral. Also, an agreement was made to hold a more general conference.

In June Mathews and McIntosh met with the old chief, the chief's son, known as Chief Payne to distinguish him from his more illustrious father, and Chief Payne's half brother, known as Bowlegs. Bowlegs offered to be an ally of the Americans. Whereupon Mathews and McIntosh made a fatal error—they refused the offer. They wanted no Indian allies. Why they did not does not explicitly show in the records, but a look at the principal underlying characteristics of the Indian society that the Georgian plantation owners confronted gives a reasonably good explanation.

Mathews told the twenty-seven chiefs gathered at Forbes's store in Picolata that this was a white man's war and that Indian interference would not be tolerated. If the Indians got involved, retribution would be swift. He distributed gifts and told them to go home and stay there. McIntosh explained that the Great White Father in Washington had sent men into Florida against the Spanish, not the Indians. "We are not here to harm you," he told them, and added that when the patriots needed beef they would be glad to buy it from the large stocks of cattle the Indians had. Bowlegs was furious and felt he had been treated with disdain and disrespect, but he submitted to the decision of the old chief, his father, and neutrality appeared assured. McIntosh was so pleased he issued a proclamation declaring permanent peace had been arranged with the Indians in the "Territory of East Florida," where he ruled as director.

The Spanish had been busy too. Before Kindelan arrived, as early as March, acting Governor Estrada had sent emissaries to Indian councils. They were blacks who had regularly handled liaison and translation duties for the Spanish. He reminded the Indians about the land hunger of the Americans and the traditional friendliness between Spanish governors and Seminoles. Kindelan renewed this line as soon as he got into position and had surveyed the situation. He sent agents to tell the Indians that the July constitutional convention of the patriots had been held for the purpose of devising a plan to seize and distribute their lands.

Rumors of these moves disturbed Mathews, and he decided another meeting was needed to confirm the promise of neutrality. Taking McIntosh with him, he once more journeyed in mid-July to Alachua some forty miles west of the Saint Johns River to talk with King Payne again. He was not in a diplomatic mood. He had been brooding about his personal situation and since Congress was not in session and he learned that Senator Crawford was at home in Georgia, he decided he would leave Florida and talk things over with his friend Crawford.

This time Mathews was even blunter with the Indians than he had been a month before. He told the ninety-year-old chief that the Americans must have peace. He vowed to King Payne that if there was any trouble the Indians would be driven from their land, their homes burned and their villages destroyed. McIntosh chimed in, sending word to Bowlegs, who wasn't present at the meeting, that he would be made a vassal.

The meeting was Mathews's last effort for the patriot cause. It proved to be as fateful for them as his earlier headstrong acts. He returned from the meeting to Saint Marys and from there traveled north and west to Lexington, Georgia Crawford's home. They talked about the recent session of Congress and the failure of the passage of the bill to authorize the now wartime army to move in and take over all of Florida. Mathews described his actions from the moment the patriots moved into Florida and outlined the most recent developments, including the new constitution.

On the subject of his dismissal, Crawford was most sympathetic and, for the first time, Mathews heard in detail the story of the Henry letters. Crawford told him that by playing politics with these letters, Madison and Monroe had worked themselves into a corner so far as Mathews's activities were concerned. They had to disavow him. Crawford and Mathews decided that the best course now was for them to do what they could to get the administration to recognize the patriots and accept East Florida as a gift as the patriot constitution of July prescribed. Mathews would go on to Washington to lobby for this and Crawford would write Monroe telling him Mathews was coming for that purpose.

"Upon the subject of the disavowal the genl. will not speak, when with you or the president, unless you mention it," Crawford wrote Monroe, "and in that event you must prepare yourself for some harshness of expression." However, the senator said he believed Mathews was more concerned now with the fate of the patriots than his own problem. If the patriots were recognized and their territory taken into the United States, then, said Crawford, "I believe he would be reconciled to the mortifying position in which he had been placed by the disavowal of his conduct."

Mathews left Lexington and together with his faithful secretary Ralph Isaacs headed for Augusta. He took one detour, in spite of the fact that he was suffering from a fever and found the journey on horseback extremely enervating. He still had Indians on his mind. He stopped to see Benjamin Hawkins, agent to the Creeks, and asked him to try to get the Creeks to urge neutrality and restraint on their relatives the Seminoles.

Late in August, he arrived in Augusta. He was a dying man. On Sunday, August 30, he would be seventy-three years old. He lived to see his birthday, but he could not live beyond it. On Monday, August 31 he was buried.

It was a long funeral procession that made its way to the burial ground of Saint Paul's Church. The two local companies of militia walked in front of the gun carriage on foot beside their horses. Isaacs and town dignitaries walked behind the coffin. The state militia agreed to wear crepe armbands, and Governor Mitchell issued a proclamation at Milledgeville ordering all military officers in the state to wear similar armbands for thirty days. In his proclamation Mitchell said, "By this demise, another hero of the Revolution is gone. Whatever political errors he may have fallen into in the course of a long public life, let them rest in oblivion. He has carried with him to the grave many scars from the wounds he received fighting battles of the Revolution—let us, therefore, pay that respect which is due to the memory of a soldier who braved death to establish the independence of our country."

The Augusta papers were warmer in their words. They expressed admiration for his "kind, benevolent, sincere, just, tenacious personality." And they noted that "though his heart was stung by some recent transactions," his patriotism had been so strong that he had refused to let his personal resentment outweigh his love of country.

However well or ill he handled the sting in his heart, his last meeting with the Seminole chief had been one of his worst political errors. Kindelan kept making the right noises where Mathews had made the wrong sounds. The threats Mathews made at the final meeting called the Indians' hand. Bowlegs had not forgotten the insults he felt he had suffered at the June meeting. When he heard what had been said at Alachua he gave his father the word that the black messengers from Saint Augustine had brought him. Governor Kindelan deplored the disruption of the Indian trade the white invaders had caused. Because of this, Kindelan had been unable to send the gifts he had for the Seminoles. If the Americans were to succeed in taking Saint Augustine, dire consequences for the Indians would follow; the white men would then take the Indians' lands. Neutrality could not save the Indians; they must strike while they still had Spanish allies. King Payne said he still thought they should keep the peace, but Bowlegs's arguments prevailed at the general council, and finally the old warrior agreed as well. "Go and fight, and if you are able to drive the white people out, go and do it," he said.

On July 26, while George Mathews was making his way toward Augusta, a band of Indian and black warriors killed a white man and five blacks and took thirty-two slaves prisoner at a plantation on the Saint Johns. White men, black men and red men were now at war in Florida. The reason Georgians could not accept Bowlegs's offer of alliance was because they could not accept the black warriors who fought in every Seminole Indian war party. They had been living with that disagreeable and frightening fact for more than sixty years.

In 1750, according to one account, Seacoffee, a chief of a small group of Indians of the Creek confederation, moved into Florida after a dispute with other Creek tribes. Most authorities on the history of these Indians will only say that the move was made about that time. One man who wrote an account of Florida in 1822 and who based his statement on firsthand meetings with Seminole chiefs quoted an old Indian as saying, "An hundred summers have seen the Seminole warrior reposing undisturbed under the shade of his live oak tree." All agree that their name, in the Muskogean language they share with the Creeks, means "runaway" or something similar. They also agree the Seminoles had a close relationship with a number of blacks, a relationship difficult for nineteenth-century Southern Americans to accept or understand. And they agree that the blacks who lived so harmoniously with the Seminoles were themselves runaways or descendants of earlier runaways.

Joshua Giddings, the abolitionist, wrote a book in 1858 in which he made a convincing case for the fact that the word *Seminole*, in the sense of runaway, was first applied to blacks on the run from South Carolina and not Indians. The governor of South Carolina as early as 1738 asked the Spanish governor to return runaways, Giddings pointed out. The governor refused. Spanish sources on the history of Fort Moosa corroborate this and indicate an even earlier arrival of black seminole/runaways. These "exiles of Florida," as Giddings called them, mingled with the Indian later arrivals, and their descendants constituted the force which confronted the patriots in the summer of 1812.

Giddings, of course, is a biased source. The Patriots War of 1812-1813 in Florida was for him a nefarious act of "slave traders and vagabonds" who invaded from Georgia. "Thereafter a struggle ensued for more than two years as the state of Georgia found itself unable to conquer Florida or the Seminoles or capture the exiles." The bitter fight that began in 1812, in Giddings's opinion, led, with a few years' break between them, to the Seminole wars which began in 1818 and were not concluded until 1842. Despite his bias, modern scholars tend to agree with him on that point. In any case, he traced an extended history of bad relations between Georgians and Spanish authorities in Florida over the matter of slaves who, one way or another, continually kept crossing the border from the time Oglethorpe founded his colony.

One of the first acts of the Georgia assembly after it joined forces with the rest of the colonies in declaring independence was to ask the Continental Congress in Philadelphia for troops to help the state militia prevent slaves from deserting their masters and fleeing to Florida. And the first treaty made by the Washington administration, when the new nation began operating under the Constitution, was the treaty signed with the Creeks on August 1, 1790, at Georgia's insistence.

The Creek treaty contained two clauses, Giddings pointed out, which were put in specifically to deal with the fugitive-slave problem. In one conflict with the whites, shortly before the treaty was arranged, the Creeks made off with 110 slaves, property of Georgians. So the treaty said that the Creeks had to return "all prisoners of whatever nature." The second way in which the treaty sought to have slaves returned was the declaration put in the mouths of the Creek chiefs that they were acting for the Seminoles in signing the agreement with the Great White Father. The Seminoles were related to the Creeks, but in 1790 they had been in Florida for at least forty years because of the hatred between them and their Creek cousins.

A key figure in George Mathews's plannng for President Madison's Florida plot, James Seagrove, traveled to Florida in 1792 under that last provision of the Creek Treaty. Enrique White's predecessor listened to Seagrove's plea but refused to give up any of the blacks living in Florida.

By the time of Seagrove's visit the special social arrangement between the Seminoles and the blacks had been worked out. In the last two decades of the eighteenth century, the Seminoles had adapted the whites' system of slavery to suit their way of life. As they settled into north central Florida, Seminole chiefs observed that the British, when they took over Florida from Spain in 1763, considered ownership of blacks a mark of distinction and prosperity. They also saw how the blacks did the work on plantations—raised corn, tended cattle and hogs. There were many cattle still roaming the area where the Creeks settled, near the once vast Spanish cattle ranch at Alachua. So they bought blacks.

When they had done so they found that the task of supervising their work was not something they found they could do well. It took too much time from hunting, so they decided to allow the blacks freedom to plant crops, graze cattle and tend other livestock as the blacks saw fit.

They gave the blacks tools to cut down trees, build houses and establish, beside their Indian villages, black villages that were the blacks' own. The chiefs required a regular payment in kind of corn and livestock, but otherwise the blacks were free to live as they chose.

The Seminoles soon discovered the blacks had other talents beside their skills as agricultural workers. Many of them spoke Spanish and English. So the Georgians had good reason to be concerned about the "exiles of Florida." As word of this freer life-style spread among slaves, the population of the black villages grew. Soon there were more black interpreters available for Seminole chiefs. And by the time the Spanish returned in 1783 blacks were key figures in liaison between red men and white men. They were also some of the Spanish governors' most useful and proficient spies and propaganda agents. Kindelan might not have been as successful as he was in winning over the Seminoles to his side had it not been for the black agents who helped him.

The black villages were prosperous. The blacks dressed in Seminole fashion, which for festive occasions meant moccasins and leather leggings, colorful long smocks, brilliant shawls and bandanna turbans and glittering metal ornaments. Except for having slightly darker skin, they and their Seminole landlords were indistinguishable. They had firearms and hunted too, just as the Indians did. More importantly they gladly joined the Seminoles as comrades-in-arms to defend their joint property. They may have been sharecroppers but they were ready to fight for their homes with the same intense determination as the Indians and other men of the soil. When King Payne and his sons Chief Payne and Bowlegs gave the word, they were ready. They needed no prodding to take the warpath against men who might drag them back to slavery if they lost.

Intensity of feeling on both sides was equal. First McIntosh, then

Mitchell berated the Spanish governor for having black troops and for inciting the Seminoles and their black comrades-in-arms. To them, he was guilty of doing the unthinkable—launching another Santo Domingo. That was an exaggeration, but the action that took place in the summer of 1812 was brutal enough to satisfy the most jaded TV-violence buff.

After the initial attack on July 26 the Indians and blacks rampaged up and down the Saint Johns river as far north as the Saint Marys. War parties kept breaking Smith's supply line between his position near Saint Augustine and Picolata and depots farther north. Early in August they attacked Kingsley's plantation at Laurel Grove. Kingsley and seven men finally held them off, but the red and black party killed three of Kingsley's slaves and captured twenty-six more. Capturing the white men's slaves was a favorite action; it was these red and black warriors' version of Santo Domingo.

Scalping and mutilating were the ways they showed their hatred of their enemies. The men who drove Smith's supply trains and maintained communications were frequent victims. Private Kinnear explained to his mother and brother, his limited education or his horror or both overcoming his punctuation, " . . . the small detachment of two Hundred men and Colonel Smith is scarcely sufficient to maintain its ground against a numerous enemy consisting chiefly of west india Blacks strangers to fear renders our situation extremely critical we have already experienced the loss of ten brave men murdered by Indians and Negros one of them a Mr. Maxwell charged with dispatches for Colonel Smith . . . was way laid and dreadfully tortured and murdered having his nose ears and privites cut off scalped and otherwise barbarously used. Two more of our men likewise charged with dispatches to Piccallatti a fort in our possession on the river St Johns were served in the same manner."

These attacks accomplished all that Kindelan hoped for. The patriots shouldered their muskets and fled Colonel Smith's camp. They had to go home to protect their wives, children and slaves. Some of them stopped at Camp New Hope, as they called the fort near modern Jacksonville that they had taken from the few Spanish soldiers, but most went straight home. Many, once there, packed their families' belongings and headed north for the Saint Marys. As fast as they could find boats they loaded them and crossed the river to Georgia. On August 9 Kindelan declared the investment of Saint Augustine ended. His black troops made contact with the Seminoles and the black cattlemen, and soon cattle were once more being driven into the town as life for the townspeople slowly returned to normal.

The savage war by Indians and blacks aroused strong reaction in Georgia and brought volunteers to Florida, but to no avail. The Savannah Blues and Volunteer Guards, who answered Governor Mitchell's call for help in June, reached the vicinity of Smith's camp on June 26. But they had only signed up for two months' service and had used up one of them getting to this swamp full of lurking scalping parties, with oppressive heat and incessant rain. After two weeks they were demanding transportation home, pointing out they had to be in Savannah on or before sixty days from the date of enlistment to be discharged. On July 24 the Volunteer Guards and some of the Blues arrived back in Savannah. The rest of the Blues slipped quietly into town nine days later.

The men recruited by Colonel Daniel Newnan, who had brought the ethereal tears of patriotism to the eyes of their loved ones, did somewhat better. At least they got into a fight. But in the end they failed too.

As in the case of the men from Savannah, these volunteers from central Georgia had signed up for only sixty days' duty and had used up a month getting as far as Point Petre on July 29. They had not even reached Florida when they began making the same kinds of plans their counterparts from the seacoast had made. Newnan bombarded them with propaganda, one of his most telling points being his appeal to their racial feelings. How could they face Georgians back home, he asked them, so long as Indians and blacks remained in East Florida? He also promised them the Indians' land, reminding them Governor Mitchell had said they could have it once they had killed off the savages. His clincher was producing surveying instruments, actual proof they could go right to work laying out their new farms as soon as the last battle was over. "If reinforcements can reach us by September or October 1st it will be in time," he told them. "Such another opportunity will perhaps never present itself for young men to advance their fortune in so short a time." Most of them signed up for another two-month hitch.

Newnan was not concerned about Saint Augustine. He wanted to carry the fight to the heart of Indian country. He had 250 men, and he planned to march to Alachua and take King Payne's home away from him. After that it would be time to deal with the treacherous Spaniard. But August proved not to be a good month to introduce Georgia boys to Florida. Between heavy rains that soaked them, blistering sun scorched them. The country also disappointed them, although the topsoil seemed deep and filled with humus along the banks of the Saint Johns, thousands of matted roots lay just under the surface. If this was what they were going to take from the Indians it was going to be one hell of a backbreaker to try to farm. Newnan urged them on with tales that the Indians had plenty of already cleared land near their main village. *That* was what they were aiming for.

But of more pressing concern than worrying about the condition of the future farms they would take from the Indians was what they were going to eat until they could accomplish their mission. The patriots had been dispersed by Indian attacks and were not available for foraging or to hand over produce from their own and their neighbors' farms. Newnan could not get enough corn or enough mills to grind what he had. The volunteers soon were thinking about going home again.

The patriots and their cause disgusted them. One volunteer wrote home, "If the whole world were drained to the last dregs, there could never be found such another collection as the constituted authorities of this province, I mean the *PATRIOTS*. Although we protect their lives and property they would willingly receive every soldier's knapsack in the detachment for a quart of milk." By the end of the month 40 of Newnan's men were sick, and 175 refused to go on.

Still, by the end of September Newnan had a force of 117 ready for action, Smith had sent him a detachment of 23 men, 9 Georgians had a change of heart and Captain William Cone of the patriots and 9 of his men volunteered to be guides. On Thursday, September 24, Newnan's troops crossed the Saint Johns and headed southwest for Indian country. Three days later they surprised the Indians, and the biggest battle of the war took place.

In the initial surprise on September 27 the Indians and blacks dropped their packs and lost most of their reserve ammunition. But the outcome was inconclusive. Two more engagements took place between then and October 5 when the volunteers, worn out and unable to destroy their enemies as they had hoped, were ready to retreat, which they did. On October 11, eighteen days after they had set out for Alachua, they reached Kingsley's Laurel Grove. Eight men had been killed, nine wounded and eight were missing. Fourteen of the enemy had been slain.

The Georgia papers painted a glowing picture of the expedition when the news reached north to them, and for more than a hundred years the fiction was told that King Payne had been killed. In fact, although he had been wounded he recovered and died later of old age. Actually, the expedition had been a failure and Newnan admitted it. In doing so he made a surprising statement, one contrary to all accepted local lore among his countrymen. "The Negros," he said, "are their best soldiers."

When Governor Mitchell heard the news of Newnan's retreat on October 10, he exploded. The savages had to be destroyed. He called for ten companies of Georgia militia to be sent to Point Petre to prepare for an invasion of Florida. Not only had Newnan's expedition been forced to turn back, but before that humiliation occurred Colonel Smith had been forced from the camp outside Saint Augustine. In mid-September Captain John Williams with twenty men had tried to get to the Saint Johns to bring supplies to the beleagured American contingent which the harassment of the Seminole warriors had brought to near starvation. As the wagon train of Captain Williams entered the large swamp west of Saint Augustine a band of seventy blacks and six Indians fell on them by surprise. The action lasted only twenty-five minutes, but the Seminoles captured all the wagons, killed one American and wounded eight, including Williams. A marine in the grand tradition of the Corps, he suffered eight wounds before he fell: a broken right arm, a ball in his thigh near the groin, a punctured stomach, three holes in the right hand, one in his shoulder and one in his left leg. He lingered in great pain for two weeks before dying on September 29.

The frustrating of this last attempt to get relief forced Smith to strike camp. On the night of September 14 he burned his thatched-roofed huts and began his retreat to the Saint Johns. Had Kindelan with his superior force attacked the retreating Americans that night he might well have wiped them out. But Kindelan was content. The Indians and the blacks had enabled him to free Saint Augustine without using a single Spanish soldier.

Defeat at the hands of Indians and blacks not only enraged Governor Mitchell, it inflamed the state of Georgia and attracted national attention. *Niles Register* reported in its Southern Frontier section on October 27, "The governor of Georgia intends to raise . . . mounted riflemen for the purpose of punishing the aggression of Seminole Indians. It is an indispensible step, or we shall see our frontier settlers flying before the uplifted tomahawk and the murderous scalping knife reeking with the blood of our women and children.Governor Kinderland [*sic*] has recently augmented his premium for American scalps. He now offers 8 dollars and a bottle of rum for each."

In Georgia reaction was not confined to editorial comment. In Saint Marys, a group of men boarded a boat that ostensibly was loading for Havana. They had discovered that its real destination was Saint Augustine. They ruined the cargo. The following morning they swore an oath to hold up to public scorn and worse anyone directly or indirectly aiding the Spaniards who were employing what they called "savages of different shades" in a war against the Georgia militia. On Sunday night, October 18, hot-tempered young men of Savannah burned the sloop *Alpha*, which had been trading with Saint Augustine. In defending the ship, its crew killed three young Georgians. The Augusta *Chronicle* said this, not the mob's action, had been the real crime because, in instances like those now facing the people of Georgia, taking the law into one's own hand was necessary.

Legislators in Milledgeville sensed the feelings of their constituents and were ready to outdo the governor. On November 9 a bill was introduced in the Georgia Senate authorizing the state militia to invade and conquer Florida. The bill's supporters swept aside the constitutional question that was shackling the war effort in the north. Since the United States Congress had failed to make Florida a fighting front in the war the previous summer, the state of Georgia had to act in its own interest. Not all members of the legislature were ready to go that far, however, and the bill was defeated. In its place were adopted two resolutions. One called on the governor to recruit volunteer cavalry to support the United States invasion of Florida. The other resolution took care of that latter subject, demanding immediate military action by the federal government.

By November 1812 this was no longer a farfetched idea. The disasters on the northern front had badly shaken the country and Madison's administration. Secretary of War Eustis had finally been forced to resign. James Monroe was happy to replace him and wear two hats, secretary of state and of war. In fact, he was pressuring Madison to name him supreme field commander as well. Monroe, after all, had been a colonel in the revolutionary war and had had more field experience than Commander in Chief Dearborn. If given that assignment, his idea was to have Jefferson return to government as secretary of state. That, he felt, would build the country's confidence in the war effort.

Meanwhile, he relieved Mitchell of his Florida assignment in anticipation of real military action in Florida, and wrote General Pinckney, the country's number-two major general and commander of the Southern Department, to get ready to take Florida on the same two conditions that had been given George Mathews; either if offered by local authorities or in case of a threatened foreign power's making any move to touch it.

Two days after Monroe gave Pinckney these orders, December 10, Senator Joseph Anderson, a man Madison could count on, moved in a secret session that a committee be appointed to investigate authorizing the president to occupy and hold Florida. Without waiting for Senate action, the administration began moving troops. Andrew Jackson was told to march from Tennessee to New Orleans and then move east into Mobile, Pensacola and Saint Augustine. Pinckney was ordered to mass troops on the Georgia border ready to move into East Florida.

When they got wind of these developments, John McIntosh and Buckner Harris also took action. They set up a court in December on Bell's River, a tributary of the Amelia River from where they could see Fernandina but safely outside the jurisdiction of Captain Massias. There Judge Buckner Harris passed sentences of confiscation on the property of all those who had fled the province. They were proving the government of the Territory of East Florida had teeth. It was real. It could offer the province to General Pinckney.

As the calendar turned to the new year, January 1813, all the old familiar features in the Florida picture, as George Mathews had seen it, appeared to be back in focus yet again. There was a local authority ready to surrender the country, and American military forces were ready to do their "proper" part.

CHAPTER XIX

SOUND RETREAT

By the time Joseph Anderson introduced his bill to start things moving again to get congressional sanction for an invasion of Florida, James Madison had been reelected. Considering the sorry state of the war effort and the deep division in the country over the war, this was for him a heartening accomplishment. Actually Madison owed it in large measure to the kind of campaign his opponent ran.

DeWitt Clinton from his power base as governor of New York had been scheming for two years to take the presidency from Madison. His plan was to create a clever mixture of the various groups within the Jeffersonian party who were unhappy with the little president. He wanted to get Henry Clay on the ticket with him, but failed when Madison went to war. Undaunted, he sought to put together in 1812 a combination of Jeffersonians-for-peace, Randolph-wing Anglophiles, merchants of New York and New England, hurt by the years of embargo and now war, war hawks other than Henry Clay who were disappointed with the way the war was going and Federalists. His campaign was managed by Martin Van Buren, the first venture into national politics by the man whose feats as a manipulator earned him the name "little magician."

The triumph of the Clinton campaign was getting the Federalists to have all their presidential electors vote for him, a renegade Jeffersonian Republican. The failure was the inherent weakness of Clinton's trying to campaign at the same time for a more vigorous conduct of the war to please the disgruntled hawks, and also denouncing the war's having been declared in the first place to win the votes of the Federalists and the peace Republicans. He threw in a little bank-charter bribery for good measure. Despite his ambivalent and corrupt campaign, Clinton came close. Madison received 128 electoral votes out of a total of 217. New York and all New England as well as New Jersey and Delaware went for Clinton. New York, the most populous state, had hitherto been the Northern anchor of the Jeffersonian party. In the North, only Pennsylvania stood by Madison and only by a slim margin. That and the three votes from Louisiana, the new state Madison had managed to add to the union, enabled him to squeak through.

Although voters found it difficult to trust Clinton *and* Madison, apathy was the main characteristic of the electorate. John Taylor of Caroline wrote to James Monroe that in his part of Virginia only the vigorous effort of two old friends of Madison and Monroe managed to get 130 out of an eligible 700 freeholders to vote for their fellow Virginian. The situation was the same in Pennsylvania and North Carolina. The war was even less popular than the president. Disassociating themselves from it, they called it Mr. Madison's War. Only on the Indian frontier west of the Allegheny Mountains and in Georgia was there much enthusiasm for the war.

It was this that Madison had very much in mind when he decided to try to get congressional support to spread the war to Florida. The total disaster on the northern front, military and political, made him determined to try to give his only supporters something to cheer about. Florida seemed the perfect place to do this and, with luck, perhaps turn around the whole discouraging situation. The war between whites and blacks and reds there had stirred all the southern and western territory.

Already on November 10 Colonel John Williams, adjutant general of the Tennessee militia, had published a call to arms. In making his appeal he nicely mingled the two wars Madison had managed to get into—the undeclared war with the Spanish in Florida and the larger war declared against Great Britian.

"The latest newspaper accounts," read the proclamation, "show a want of troops in East Florida to check the hostile Indians. 'Tis shameful that Georgia alone should bear this burden. All those who have enrolled themselves with me are directed to parade, at Knoxville, on Tuesday the first day of December next, prepared with a supply of provisions to take them to the point of destination. The patriotic freemen of Tennessee are requested on that day to come forward well mounted, and prepare to march to the Saint Johns, where the troops of the United States are stationed, and where the Indians are said to be assembled in such numbers as to threaten the destruction of our troops. . . . War now rages in our land—a deranged Monarch [George III, who had been declared officially insane in 1811], a venal Prince [the Prince Regent, who was declared guardian of his insane father] and a corrupt Ministry have driven us to assert our rights at the point of the bayonnet. They have enlisted under their banners the savages, those hell hounds fitted only for deeds of ferocity. . . . Our females and property are in a place of security—our bretheren in a sister state need our aid."

In response to this appeal 165 men assembled in Knoxville on December 1, 1812. The youngest man was eighteen, the oldest eighty. Pleased with the result, Williams sent off a letter to the president. "A considerable part of the Georgia militia, it is said, have refused to afford relief to the troops of the United States, stationed at St. Johns, from a fatal exposition of the constitution relative to the militia," he wrote. Tennesseans were not inclined to quibble. Williams said he was sure the United States would soon send relief to Florida. In the meantime, Tennessee would volunteer. "Not a man in this corps," he assured Madison, "will entertain constitutional scruples on the subject of boundaries."

Amid cheers and tears, described with the same warmth by the press in Tennessee as by the newspapers in Georgia when Newnan's volunteers started on their earlier ill-fated Florida adventure, the men began their march on December 4. At Asheville, North Carolina, a patriotic farm wife butchered and barbecued her cattle for the hungry men. But it began to snow as the men marched on from Asheville on December 12. A chilling wind blew off the mountain that night, and the temperature dropped to nine above zero. Still they pushed on, and a week later arrived at Washington, Georgia. They were now 240 strong, having added recruits en route. Colonel Williams halted and sent word of their arrival to Governor Mitchell.

Meanwhile back in Tennessee a second volunteer force was being organized. The governor had received word from the War Department in Washington to raise a volunteer force to join General Wilkinson in New Orleans and prepare to move against West Florida, and he asked Andrew Jackson to undertake the job. Jackson published the letter to the governor and on November 14 asked for volunteers. Posters and newspapers spread the word throughout middle Tennessee. People gathered at country courthouses throughout the area for the muster of troops. Enthusiasm to fight the Spaniard who had armed the blacks and incited the Indians was running high. One of the most flame-tongued preachers of the frontier went into his act in the town of Franklin on December 3, when a larger crowd than usual gathered to hear Gideon Blackburn, Presbyterian minister, teacher and Indian fighter. Turning toward the soldiers gathered on the green, he thundered, " . . . touch at Pensacola, and alight, like the Eagle of prey, at St. Augustine—recalling the blood of brave Captain Williams, and the difficulties of Newnan and Smith . . . scale the ramparts and spread the wings of the Eagle of liberty on the summit of their fortifications, chastizing the slaves of monarchy, and eternally enslaving the black renegades."

Despite such divine injunctions, the same winter cold that penetrated the coats of the men who trudged toward Georgia frosted the fingers of the men who mustered at Nashville. On the morning of December 10, the date Jackson had set for the volunteers to gather there, the temperature was two points above zero, but despite the weather eighteen hundred men pitched their tents in the snow on the hills overlooking the town, three hundred more than Jackson had called for.

The bill to authorize action in Florida that Senator Anderson introduced that same day in Washington did not arouse the same kind of enthusiasm. Although Madison had been reelected, so too had many of his old foes and some new ones. Returned Federalists, Clintonians, as well as Samuel Smith and his Invisibles were all highly visible. Timothy Pickering, the man who had dared to flaunt "national security interest" by quoting from diplomatic correspondence the administration wanted to conceal, was back from Massachusetts. The Federalist triumph there had been by a majority of twenty-four thousand votes. Two fresh faces from New England, both strongly anti-Madison, also arrived at the House of Representatives—one the twenty-seven-year-old editor, Alexander Hanson, who had written the stories about the special services for guests Dolley performed at her mother's boardinghouse; the other an eloquent young man from New Hampshire, Daniel Webster. In the Senate, Madison weakened his position considerably when he named William Crawford minister to France to replace the unfortunate Joel Barlow. Barlow had perished of pneumonia in Poland trying to chase down Napoleon, who was fleeting Russia with his armies. Barlow had been determined to get an honest answer from the defeated emperor about the Berlin and Milan Decrees' canceling the blockade against United States ships, and a favorable commercial treaty signed with France.

On December 22 Samuel Smith stood up in the Senate and proposed the Senate kill Anderson's request to authorize action in Florida. His proposal lost by only a narrow vote, and the opposition geared up for another try.

Down on the banks of the Saint Marys River, action was about to begin regardless of how Congress voted. The volunteers Williams had brought to Georgia were restless. They wanted to fight. Governor Mitchell had found himself doubly embarrassed when they arrived and had been stalling their advance. He was embarrassed first by the failure of Georgians to handle their own affairs which the arrival of the Tennessee volunteers implied. And he was embarrassed by the fact the Seminoles were now suing for peace. Having accomplished all the Spanish desired of them, they were ready to retire from the fray and allow their black farmers to concentrate on planting during the coming spring.

Mitchell tried to delay the Tennesseans by a tactful thanks for their willingness to unite with Georgians to share the task of keeping Georgia free from danger. However, he explained to them, since the federal government had not authorized an expedition against the Indians the Georgia militia could not move. He hoped Washington would give a go-ahead and was now waiting for the word. He suggested the Tennesseans wait with him.

Actually, of the two considerations restraining him, Mitchell was motivated more by the second than the first. Since the Indians were suing for peace and negotiating with Indian agent Benjamin Hawkins, he thought more war unnecessary. Public opinion supported him. Georgians were happy the trouble was over. The Georgia *Journal* expressed this feeling, pointing out that the Indians were willing to restore white property and deliver up all "offenders to our laws." In other word, fugitive slaves would be returned. "Could we ask—could they do more?" the paper wanted to know.

The eager Colonel Williams from Tennessee had offered his men to General Pinckney at the same time he offered them to Mitchell, and he now appealed to Pinckney for relief from Mitchell's stalling tactics. Pinckney had been informed by Hawkins of the progress of negotiations. He also on November 27 had been ordered by James Monroe, wearing his secretary-of-war's hat, to prepare to reinforce Smith because "the Seminoles who have committed murders and depredations upon our citizens are to be subdued. . . . "

Although Hawkins had reported to the War Department on his negotiations with the Seminoles, he had heard no reply, so on January 12, 1813, Pinckney informed Monroe that the volunteers would be provisioned and sent against the Seminoles unless contrary orders were sent from President Madison.

Pinckney did not know what was going on in Washington, but the administration's effort to obtain congressional authorization to invade Florida was in serious trouble. The day after Pinckney sent off his letter, Senator William Hunter, Federalist from Rhode Island, made a long, well-reasoned attack on the scheme. It set the tone of the debate and played a key role in the ultimate defeat of Madison's plans for Florida.

First Hunter demolished Madison's favorite argument for claiming Florida, the one the president had liked to use since his days as secretary of state—the right to claim Florida as reimbursement for Spanish spoilations at New Orleans. Hunter pointed out that American merchants had been indemnified by Spain in 1795 for all claims for damage done by Spain to that date. Subsequent claims arose from actions Spain had taken while under control of Napoleon. He suggested Madison's pro-French feelings had prevented the president from accepting this fact.

Next he demolished the other arguments put forth for ordering Pinckney to invade East Florida. The one about refusal of Spanish authorities in Florida to grant total amnesty to the patriots, he called ridiculous. The patriots were only a group of Georgians; and all reports from Florida clearly showed that. That the invasion was justified because of the attack made on Moosa in May was preposterous. "Where is Moosa?" he asked. "Within two miles of Saint Augustine," he answered himself. "If you had the camp of an enemy at Georgetown, threatening the Capitol . . . Would you not attack?"

As for the arming of blacks, Hunter pointed out that black troops had fought in the American Revolution as part of the Rhode Island militia. But his devastating point on the question of the use of blacks by the Spanish was made by turning the fears of the southern proponents of the invasion against them. If he were a Georgian, he said, he would pray for the defeat of the bill, for a war over Florida would surely bring an invasion of Georgia by these black Spanish troops. The blacks in Georgia "aroused to reflection by the sight of black soldiers and black officers, may suspect themselves to be fellow-men . . . Take care that while you are pursuing foreign conquest, your own homes are not devastated."

Finally, regarding the threat of British takeover, he said everyone knew there was not one shred of evidence that such a threat then existed. The threat might very well become reality, however, if Florida, property of England's ally against Napoleon, were invaded.

His strongest words stripped away the mask of all Madison's overt and covert policy toward Florida. He succinctly summarized all the schemes the president had used to take Florida: "I say this is not only war, it is an offensive war; not only an offensive war but an unjust war. I am for the honor of my country forced to say, . . . it is a wicked war, it is robbery."

It was a two-part bill the administration was trying to pass. One merely reiterated the claim to Florida west of Pensacola and the Perdido River; the occupation of this territory had already been authorized by Congress. The second part authorized the invasion of East Florida. At the end of Hunter's speech a vote was demanded. Part two of the bill, the part authorizing the invasion, was defeated. In February the emasculated bill containing only the part dealing with West Florida was passed.

By then, however, an invasion of East Florida was already underway. Madison and Monroe ignored both Hawkins's report of his talks with the Indians and Pinckney's letter of January 12, and so the Tennessee volunteers crossed the Saint Marys on February 3. Once again the president and his chief adviser showed the same manipulators' morality all their previous handling of Florida displayed. By ignoring the fact that the Indian war was over, and allowing the volunteers to fall on the unsuspecting Indians, they calculated Jackson's and Pinckney's troops would not have to fear a Seminole attack when they entered East Florida.

As the volunteers moved south, Colonel Smith's troops moved to rendezvous with them. On Sunday, February 7, the two forces met about thirteen miles from Chief Payne's town. Chief Payne had succeeded his ancient father but ruled only half the tribe. On Sunday night the troops camped about three miles from the Indian settlement. At dawn they charged into the village and found an abandoned town. Friendly Creeks close to Benjamin Hawkins had warned the Indians, and taking their blacks and families with them, they had fled.

The American invaders then went off in search of the village of Bowlegs and his portion of the tribe. Five miles from Bowlegs's town they were met by musket fire from the Indians. Over the course of the next three days, an intermittent battle waged, but again the Indians eluded them. The angry Americans scoured the countryside. They rounded up horses, cattle, pigs and concealed mounds of corn. After all the portable provisions had been secured, they burned every hut and palmetto building they could find. On February 17, Smith ordered a general withdrawal.

In a campaign of three weeks, the volunteers burned 386 Indian houses, consumed or destroyed between fifteen hundred and two thousand bushels of corn, collected three hundred horses and four hundred cattle and took or ruined two thousand deerskins. Twenty Indians had been killed and a number wounded. Nine Indians were captured, five escaped. A wounded Indian woman, an aged black man and one squaw with her infant child were displayed in Georgia as booty.

Governor Mitchell was furious, and worried. He wrote a strong protest to General Pinckney. The Indians attacked were at peace and friendly, he said. This unjust expedition had been sent without consulting or informing him. As a result, Mitchell was afraid the friendly Creeks, with such an example of the white man's treachery at hand, would go on the warpath against the people of western Georgia.

Pinckney replied he was certain the Indians Colonel Smith had attacked were unfriendly, not friendly. As for the volunteers, he had delayed the expedition in the hope of hearing from Washington and receiving an order countermanding the one Monroe had sent him on November 27. When he didn't, he had no choice but to follow his instructions to subdue and chastise the Indians who had caused so much grief to United States troops in East Florida.

By the time news of the affair reached Washington, Madison was making up his mind to change course. He signed the Florida act into law on February 12, well aware that it said nothing new and he couldn't order Pinckney's troops to invade East Florida or permit the Tennessee volunteers of Colonel Williams or those of General Jackson to enter Florida either. He had still not recovered from the bad news that most of General William Henry Harrison's army had been destroyed on the banks of the Raisin River in Ohio in late January. Albert Gallatin had estimated that the nation faced a deficit of $21 million in its effort to finance the war. Congress was refusing all appeals to raise taxes. It would only agree to let the government try to borrow $16 million on any terms the president could negotiate with any available lenders provided that the nominal capital be repaid in twelve years.

In the face of all these pieces of bad news, it seemed to the president about time to get out of Florida. And then another bit of information finally reached Washington. When first broached by the czar to John Quincy Adams, the American minister in Saint Petersburg, and reported in September, 1812, the Russian ruler's offer to mediate with England to bring an end to the war in America had been ignored. On February 24 the Russian minister in Washington presented a formal offer. By then, it was almost time for the president to prepare for his second inauguration on March 4, 1813.

Madison dealt with what confronted him as he assumed office for a second term with characteristic craftiness. He suppressed public announcement of the Russian offer, which he told Monroe he thought should be accepted immediately, until after his inauguration. He wanted to wait until measures he had recommended to strengthen the armed forces got through the final session of the old Congress which adjourned the day before his inauguration. And he wanted to make his inaugural address an appeal for more national fighting spirit.

He had settled the matter of Monroe's military ambition earlier. He had supported it at first because he thought Monroe was popular and his taking charge on the fighting front would strengthen the administration with the public. When he found out differently, he appointed John Armstrong of New York—former minister to Paris and also ambitious to be president—secretary of war.

He still had to face a special session of Congress and try to raise adequate financing for the war, as well as deal with the disaster-ridden major war front in the north.

He decided to cut his losses in Florida.

On March 6, 1813, two days into his new term, he had John Armstrong finally answer General Pinckney's query of January 12. The new secretary of war told the general it was not a good idea to have the Tennessee volunteers attack the Indians. It was not administration policy to harm Indians seeking peace. In a hurt tone, he told Pinckney, "It is the spirit of National policy to give peace to any enemy asking it in sincerity and good faith. The Seminoles do not form an exception."

The next day Armstrong sent the big news. Transmitting a copy of an order of general pardon for the patriots that had been passed by the Cortes in Spain and given Monroe by Onís, he told Pinckney it was administration policy to welcome this good fortune and get all American troops out of Florida. Pinckney was to contact Kindelan. If Kindelan verified and proclaimed this amnesty, Pinckney was to withdraw Smith's troops from the Saint Johns and turn Fernandina back to the Spanish governor.

General Pinckney received this new order on March 18. He was at his general headquarters of the United States Army's Southern Department in Charleston. At once he dispatched an aide to Saint Augustine. Kindelan welcomed the general's emissary warmly and told him that indeed he was ready to promulgate the amnesty order. He said he would be happy to meet the American general but did not think it appropriate while American troops were still on Spanish soil.

The aide, returning with Kindelan's letter and a copy of the governor's proclamation, met Pinckney in Savannah. The general had decided to go to Saint Marys to supervise the final settlement of the mess set off by George Mathews's mission. As soon as he finished reading the document, he sent word to Kindelan that he accepted the statement in good faith and would withdraw the American troops with all possible speed.

Three days before Pinckney received his orders from Washington initiating this sequence of events, on March 15, Andrew Jackson received word from Secretary Armstrong at Natchez that "the causes of embodying and marching to New Orleans the corps under your command having ceased to exist, you will, on receipt of this letter, consider it as dismissed from public service." Jackson was stunned. After the initial muster at Nashville he had rallied a total of more than two thousand men, procured them boats, going personally heavily into debt to do so, and had sailed with them down the Cumberland River to the Ohio and then the Mississippi to Natchez. It had been a bitter cold journey on the ice-covered rivers, but not so bitter or cold as this note. Were his men to be simply left eight hundred miles from home?

Jackson sent off a blistering reply. He told the secretary of war that he would march his men back to Nashville, where he expected to be met by government agents prepared to pay them and all the expenses incurred, "after which I will dismiss them to their homes and families."

The Florida adventures James Madison had initiated in 1810 were now winding rapidly to a close. Before Pinckney reached Saint Marys he dismissed the other Tennessee volunteers. As some of Colonel Williams men desired to return home by different routes, he gave Williams two thousand dollars to cover the expenses of his several detachments. It was a better dismissal than Jackson's men got.

As soon as Pinckney reached Saint Marys Kindelan's aide was waiting. Kindelan wanted to know exact dates for the withdrawal of the United States Army. Kindelan said he wished Spanish soldiers to march in at the same moment the Americans marched out to prevent bloodshed or robbery "by persons of no character or vagabonds from the state of Georgia," who might compromise the peace between Spain and the United States. Pinckney promised to evacuate the troops on the Saint Johns on April 29 and from Amelia Island on May 6.

Kindelan had good reason to worry about the Georgians. The patriot government did not consider itself a group of vagabonds, and they wanted a voice in what was happening. Far from having plans to rob anyone, they feared they were the ones who were going to suffer an even worse fate as soon as the protecting troops left. They did not trust Kindelan.

Buckner Harris in his capacity as "president of the Legislative Council of the Territory of East Florida" called that body together as soon as he learned what was going on. They pledged to defend their territory "to the last extremity." More realistically, they sent a petition to Pinckney. They also gave John McIntosh dictatorial powers as "director of the Territory of East Florida" to handle matters.

McIntosh's action was typical. He issued another strongly worded document in the style of all the other patriot proclamations. "Patriots of East Florida, Weak must be the mind that can have the least dependence on a promise so hollow and deceitful [as the pardon of Kindelan] . . . Can you! Will you become the sport of slaves and the abhorred army of St. Augustine."

Pinckney told McIntosh he thought the proclamation offensive. And he absolutely refused to listen to McIntosh's plea to insist on getting further assurances of pardons for all the patriots before withdrawing the army. He did agree, however, to ask Kindelan to extend the time those patriots who planned to leave Florida could remain before their final departure so that they might harvest their crops. Kindelan had stated in his amnesty order that he would expect such persons to leave by the end of four months—which would mean August. The patriots wanted to stay until October when their crops would all be in. Kindelan refused. He did, however, promise to allow such persons to appoint agents who could supervise their farms and sell their crops after they had left in August. That seemed a good solution to Pinckney.

When Zephaniah Kingsley tried to continue the argument in a letter to him, Pinckney was abrupt. He told Kingsley that the United States had never recognized the acts of George Mathews and since the United States would never allow a foreign power to interpose its authority between that of the government of the United States and its citizens, conversely it could not interpose itself between a foreign power and its subjects. After disavowing Mathews, the United States had used the spoilation claims against Spain as a shield to protect the patriots and keep troops in East Florida. Now after much treasure had been spent and lives lost because of this effort, finally an amnesty had been achieved for the revolutionists. He would regret it if Kindelan did not keep his word, but the United States government could do no more for them. He suggested they appeal to the Spanish government, "the government of your nativity or of your choice," for protection.

The evacuation was carefully planned by Pinckney to look like what was happening was a restoration of neutral territory which the United States troops had held until the Spanish officials complied with the orders issued long before to Mitchell and repeated to him. Monroe had said, when he turned the Florida problem over to Mitchell after dismissing Mathews, that the participants in the rebellion were not to be harmed. The amnesty meant those orders had been complied with. Pinckney ordered his officers to act as disinterested neutrals as they turned over the territory to Kindelan's officers, and to make sure that no property was removed or destroyed.

At Camp New Hope on the Saint Johns, things did not go as planned. The American major in charge left the camp April 26, three days before the date set for the ceremony. The patriots moved in immediately. They burned camp huts, set fire to nearby plantation houses, destroyed farm tools, and killed animals. Kindelan complained, and an embarrassed Pinckney rebuked the major. This officer said his order had been dated April 26. Pinckney requested a formal inquiry leading to a possible court-martial to try to smooth things over.

At Fernandina, Captain Massias saw to it that all went well. On May 6 he had cannons boom a welcome to Captain Rivera, the officer Kindelan sent from Saint Augustine to receive the return of the town. The retreating troops from both posts were loaded on the gunboats of Commodore Campbell, the man whose inability to decide precisely what to do had been the main cause of its capture. As they sailed away, they signaled the Madison administration's official withdrawal from the phony war its covert-action operation had set in motion fourteen months earlier.

By the time Campbell's ships left Fernandina, James Madison

had his mind on other matters. Since February the British had blockaded the entire coast from New England to Norfolk. In March and April Admiral Sir George Cockburn's squadrons entered Delaware and Chesapeake bays and burned towns on the eastern shore of Maryland. He had to think about the defense of Washington. As Henry Adams later observed, not a defensible fort or picket fence stood within ten miles of Washington. He was also wrestling with Congress trying to get an agreement on new taxes and he was busily preparing to send off Albert Gallatin to head the negotiating team to meet with the British to try to end the larger war which had proved an even greater disaster than the Florida affair. He did not forget Florida entirely, however. As the warship *Neptune* sailed for Europe on May 9 with Gallatin and the rest of the delegation, Payne Todd tagging along as Gallatin's secretary, he gave them instructions which included his long-time favorite point on the subject. They should insist that Spain, England's ally, cede Florida as compensation for the ancient spoilations claims. Gallatin thought this was as ridiculous as Senator Hunter had said it was. He reluctantly agreed, however, to include it as a bargaining chip.

Soon his greater problems overtook Madison. In June he fell ill with bilious fever and lingered on the verge of death for four weeks. The opposition press crowed that "he would soon appear at the bar of Immortal Justice," and printed more stories about the amount of laudanum he was taking. He recovered but only to continue to face increasing bad news. By the following summer in August 1814 Washington's buildings had been burned by the British, and Madison was riding around the Maryland countryside trying to find Dolley, who had fled.

Madison never again had time for Florida.

Along the Saint Marys River the patriots were confused and divided after the American troops left. John McIntosh, Lodowick Ashley and his brother William, William Craig and others left Florida. Zephaniah Kingsley stayed but began insisting he had never really been a member of the group. Only Buckner Harris was determined to carry on. He went to Georgia too, but his purpose was to try to rally a *new* patriot army.

Governor Kindelan had been worried about what might happen when he took back Fernandina and the rest of the area the conflict had desolated. He refused to give the town the status of a muncipality to which its distance from Saint Augustine and its size entitled it under Spanish law. He explained his action to the captain general in Cuba on the grounds that, although there were more than six hundred persons living there, only twenty-five were Spanish. Therefore he made Fernandina and the rest of the area north of Saint Augustine districts to be run by appointees responsible directly to him for law and order. "I am only a barracks solider," he wrote his superior, "who does not claim much administrative sophistication." What he was doing, of course, was preparing for a possible return of trouble stirred up by the patriots.

Buckner Harris had just such plans. With a group of fifteen faithful followers he moved from plantation to plantation in Georgia in the old George Mathews manner, promising land and a prosperous settlement in frontier Florida free from Spanish rule. He explained his idea to Governor Mitchell and asked for a loan. He would settle at Alachua, push the Seminoles farther into Florida and, he assured the governor, Georgians would then never again need fear that fugitive slaves would find a haven there. Meanwhile, his former patriot colleague, William Ashley, Lodowick's brother, pumped out propaganda. According to Ashley, former patriots still in Florida feared daily for their lives. Black troops of the Spanish governor were running wild, scouring the countryside for horses, cattle and provisions.

On the Florida side of the river Harris was putting out feelers to invite the Indians to a conference at which he hoped to use his wits, and some of the money he hoped he'd get from either the governor of Georgia or friendly Georgians, to get them to give him land to start his colony. But nothing worked. The Indians wouldn't come to a conference and Governor Mitchell told him frankly he didn't believe the propaganda. "I hear that the utmost cordiality and friendly intercourse subsists," Mitchell said.

Harris then decided on more desperate actions. Gathering a group of sixty men, he crossed the Saint Marys and began to pillage plantations and seize property and slaves along the Saint Johns. His idea was to destroy the cordiality and friendly relationships Mitchell said existed by causing incidents that would inflame the residents of East Florida. Samuel Alexander, a fugitive from the law in Georgia, led the slave stealers for Harris. From September to December, 1813, they preyed on settlers. Such actions hurt Harris's cause more than they helped. He didn't care. And he still pursued his dream of a colony in Seminole country. By January 1814 he managed to induce some seventy colonists to join him in establishing a settlement at Alachua. They built a blockhouse and named it Fort Mitchell, and on January 25 Harris became the new director of the Republic of East Florida.

Harris's settlers then decided to reenact the script Mathews had prepared. They wrote a letter to James Monroe, commissioned one of their number "foreign minister," and sent him north with it and a document ceding the "District of Elotchaway" to the United States. On April 19, 1814, Monroe acknowledged their letter. His reply was the Madison administration's final denial of what had once been its covert-action plan.

"The United States being at peace with Spain," Monroe said, "no countenance can be given by their government to the proceedings of the revolutionary party in East Florida, if it is composed of Spanish subjects—and still less can it be given to them if it consists of American citizens, who, so far as their conduct may fall within the scope of existing laws long enacted and well known and understood, will be liable to censure."

On May 5 a scouting party of Indians and blacks waylaid and killed Buckner Harris. The settlers broke and fled back to Georgia, and the Indians and blacks burned Fort Mitchell.

The patriot movement died with Buckner Harris.

James Madison and James Monroe were also long in their graves before the damage Harris did, and the destruction caused by the war in Florida Madison originally sponsored, disappeared from the American agenda.

Diplomacy succeeded where warfare, overt and covert, failed, and treaties ended the conflict with Great Britain and settled the

Florida question. The treaty of Ghent was completed after peace talks dragged on from June of 1813 until the day before Christmas in 1814, rivaling the Vietnam peace talks of a century and a half later in false starts, bad temper and length. They settled nothing except to end the fighting, but that was progress. When they began, the British were demanding that the boundaries granted the United States at the end of the Revolution be redrawn, and a large Indian buffer state, carved out of what are now the states of Michigan, Illinois and Indiana, be established. The progress was largely due to the skill of John Quincy Adams, aided by Albert Gallatin. It was Adams, one of the few truly great American diplomatists, who arranged to get Florida from Spain in 1819. He did it by swallowing Madison's pet $5 million worth of spoilations claims. The United States government agreed to pay them itself. But it was a clause he allowed to slip into Article 9 that enabled the ghost of the failed covert-action operation in Florida to keep appearing in United States courts for more than half a century.

The clause provided that the United States would make "satisfaction" for the injuries suffered "by the Spanish officers and individual Spanish inhabitants by the late operation of the American army in Florida." After some quibbling about what precisely was meant, in 1834 Congress finally agreed it would pay the people who could prove they suffered losses at the hands of Mathews's patriots as well as the United States Army. The act named the judge of the superior court at Saint Augustine in the new Florida territory as the judicial authority who could determine the validity of the cases and fix damages. It also specified that those damaged had to be able to prove they were subjects of Spain at the time they suffered the losses.

Dozens of claims were filed. And lawyers were finally able to get around the proof-of-Spanish-citizenship problem. Two of the major claimants were John Houstoun McIntosh and Zephaniah Kingsley. They sought more than one hundred thousand dollars. Of course, both of them met the residency requirement, thanks to their royal land grants. It was when other hundred-percent Georgians like the Ashleys showed the same gall and demanded compensation for losses caused by the rebellion they had started that the best sophistry of the legal profession had to come into play. The indiscriminate acts of Buckner Harris's companions enabled the lawyers to make the successful claim that the United States government owed its citizens for the damages. After all, everyone involved in the courts by the 1850s was an American citizen. The old Spanish subjects of Florida became Americans when the United States Army finally legitimately occupied the territory in 1821, and, by 1845, Florida was a full-fledged state.

And they all were paid, the small claimants and the large ones, those who had huts and those who had large two-story plantation homes destroyed. One of the largest group of claimants were those whose case was finally decided on on August 31, 1851. *Francis P. Ferreira, Administrator of Francis Pass* v. *the United States*, under the Ninth Article of the Florida Treaty, gave damages to many, including Zephaniah Kingsley. Years later the claim of Anna Magigene was denied. She was Zaphaniah Kingsley's black widow.

Isaac Bronson, judge of the district court of the United States for the Northern District of Florida, who ruled in the majority of these cases, said when he gave his decision in the Ferreira case, "It is with no pleasure that I have narrated these transactions, or that I call attention to further details, which I fear only tend to disguise their hue or render them less excusable. It is an episode of the general history of the nation which, as an American citizen, I would have wished might remain unwritten."

As the years passed, Judge Bronson got his wish. The story of the patriots' rebellion of 1811 was buried under the layers of words which created myths about America's past that were easier to live with. The first writers to tell the history of Florida, contemporaries of the men who had participated in the action, began the process. All of them dismissed it as an aberration, something that did not belong in the mainstream of events. As Henry Adams pointed out, a principal development in the years following the War of 1812 was the formation of what Americans wanted to believe was their national character. When they looked in the mirror, they saw people who were new creatures in world history—free from Europe's political and religious superstitions, bold, tough, risk-takers, but honest, fair, and, though sometimes falling prey to temptation, above all, pure in heart. East Florida republics spuriously inaugurated by secrets funds provided by the president of the United States did not fit well into that picture.

By the 1970s, when the latest full-length scholarly biographies of James Monroe and James Madison were written, the covert-action operation in Florida had been lost to history. Harry Ammon's *James Monroe, The Quest for National Identity,* published in 1971, dismisses the matter majestically, saying, "In April [1812] Monroe had to resolve a minor problem arising from long-range American expansionist aims in Florida." Ralph Ketcham's *James Madison*, published the same year, makes no mention of the Florida adventure at all.

But it must be remembered that when these books were published America was bogged down in a war as unpopular as Mr. Madison's War with England. And the year before they appeared, Richard Nixon had ordered a covert operation in Chile to prevent the man whom the Chileans had chosen president from taking office. The operation failed, as Madison's did in Florida. When a Chilean general was assassinated by mistake and an embarrassing outcry arose, Nixon and Kissinger reacted as Madison and Monroe had. They had never authorized any such operation, they said. It was all the fault of the CIA. Echoing James Monroe, Henry Kissinger said CIA officers had acted from an abundance of zeal.

EPILOGUE

The Senate Intelligence Committee's investigation in 1973 and a recent book about Nixon and Kissinger, *The Price of Power*, by Seymour Hersh, disclose Kissinger's attempt to put the blame for what happened in Chile on the president's agent, the CIA, just as James Monroe tried to put the blame on George Mathews, the agent of President Madison. When Salvadore Allende, a socialist who planned to nationalize the holdings of American copper companies in Chile, surprised the CIA and the Nixon administration by winning the presidency in a three-way race, September 4, 1970, "the pudding blew up on the stove," said one person who worked at the White House. On September 15 Nixon ordered Richard Helms to get rid of Allende. Helms was told $10 million would be available to get the job done.

From this order grew a web of activities. Propaganda campaigns were undertaken throughout Latin America and the world to show Allende's election signaled the beginning of Communist takeover of the South American continent. (Actually, the CIA's best intelligence estimate was that no vital United States strategic interests were threatened and that Allende's victory posed no threat to the peace of the region.) Agents were sent into Chile from all over the area. And contact was made with military officers who might be talked into staging a coup d'etat to prevent the newly elected president from being sworn in.

This is where the operation came to grief. The most outspoken advocate of a coup was a Chilean officer, General Roberto Viaux, generally considered an irresponsible incompetent. The United States military attaché in Santiago said, "I always operated on the assumption that there's no substitute for brains, and Viaux didn't have any." The ambassador and others in Chile, including the CIA station chief, warned about Viaux. But so great was the pressure put on Helms and his top staff by the White House, they sent "false flaggers," CIA agents pretending to be non-Americans, into Chile to make the contact. And Nixon and Kissinger ordered that the American ambassador not be informed.

Not only was Viaux a dangerous man to deal with, knowledgeable people, the ambassador, his staff, and other observers were certain a coup would fail. The chief of staff of the Chilean army, General Rene Schneider, was adamantly opposed. He believed firmly that the military must support constitutional government. Viaux could think of an obvious solution to that problem.

Kissinger and Nixon at last began to realize that if there were a failed coup, and possibly an assassination, the trail could lead to the White House. Ambassador Korry, whom they had deceived and from whom they hid their command to the CIA, told them decisively on October 12, just weeks before Allende was to take office, that a coup would fail and that Viaux was a madman. On October 15 they ordered the CIA to tell Viaux to make no move, and told the agency to find more moderate plotters.

One day later CIA headquarters cable its station in Santiago: "It is firm and continuing policy that Allende be overthrown by a coup. . . . We are to continue to generate maximum pressure toward this end using every appropriate resource." Over the next eight days the CIA hunted for the appropriate resource and kept Kissinger's deputy, Alexander Haig and others in the White House informed of their progress. Finally General Camilo Valenzuela, given a gift of fifty thousand dollars for his personal use and sufficient other assistance for the operation, agreed to act.

The plot at this point called for the kidnapping, not the murder, of General Schneider. Unfortunately Valenzuela's men muffed the job, twice. And then some of General Viaux's bullyboys took over. They killed Schneider. Everyone in Washington was devastated by this unplanned outcome. For Nixon and Kissinger it was now clearly time to back away as quickly as they could. The White House built a cover story.

The cover story is fully presented by Henry Kissinger in his memoirs. He first developed the line that the CIA was to blame at the Senate investigation of the affair. At the Senate investigation, Kissinger was treated gently. CIA witnesses had already made plain what the real situation was. Most of the staff members of the Senate committee had already made up their minds who was lying and who was not, but they merely noted the discrepancy between the testimony of the CIA witnesses and that of their celebrity witness, Henry Kissinger. In his memoirs, Kissinger called the agency's efforts in Chile "amateurish, being improvised in panic and executed in confusion." As Seymour Hersh says, what he did not add is that much of the panic originated in the White House and most of the confusion was the result of White House fear of exposure.

History does not repeat itself but history lives by analogy. The analogy between the covert operation of 1812 and the covert operation of 1970 illuminates understanding. The thesis of Hersh's *The Price of Power* is that the men in charge of the government in 1970 refused to believe that there were any limits to their writ, that they could not conceive that they did not have the right to do anything they could think of to achieve their ends. In addition, Richard Nixon and Henry Kissinger are the kind of men who find it almost impossible to admit they make mistakes.

James Madison was greatly like them, but not entirely. He appeared, at least, to know what the problem was when he wrote, "Power lodged as it must be in human hands will ever be liable to abuse." In his conduct of the presidency generally, however, and in his covert operations in Florida, he did not act as though he had written those words. But the analogy of history shows he at least wrote the truth.

BIBLIOGRAPHY

Although footnotes have been omitted, this bibliography is annotated so that scholars can trace the documentation on which the book is based and any reader who wishes can find more information on the subject. The notations will point out the sources used for each part of the story. For example, the dialogues among General Mathews, Major Laval, Colonel Isaacs, Commodore Campbell, George Atkinson, Jose Arredondo, Joseph Hibberson, Lodowick Ashley, John Houstoun McIntosh and others are taken from copies, and sometimes the originals, of reports and other correspondence found in several collections noted in the bibliography. The conversations are reproduced either from the verbatim quotations contained in these sources or from accounts graphic enough to permit transcribing into direct quotation without violating the language used.

PRIMARY SOURCES

DOCUMENTS AND MANUSCRIPTS

The most important single collection of documents used in writing this book was the *East Florida Papers*. These are the archives of the entire second Spanish period of Florida's history (1783-1821). It is an unusually complete collection because, in 1821, confusion over interpretations of the Adams-Onís Treaty of 1819 caused United States authorities to seize these papers in Saint Augustine and to refuse to return them to Spain.

They were shipped to the Library of Congress in 1906. A complete microfilm edition, 175 reels of microfilm containing some seventy thousand frames, has recently been calendared by Mr. Bruce Chappell at the P.K. Yonge Library of Florida History, University of Florida, Gainesville, Florida, and now can be used efficiently.

In this book the *East Florida Papers* are the primary source of material on life in Spanish Florida, defense and other governmental affairs, the design and rebuilding of the port of Fernandina and the account of what transpired in northeast Florida in 1811-1812. In particular, Sections 28, 32, 33, 34 and 35 are full of information pertinent to this book.

Also at the P.K. Yonge Library are the *Papelos de Cuba*, like the *East Florida Papers* Spanish archival material. The *Papeles* contain the story of what happened in West Florida in 1810 and before and after. *Legatos* 163, 185, 1561, 1567 and 1568 are the portions of the *Papeles* consulted.

Another collection of documents at the P.K. Yonge Library which contains essential information is the *Joseph B. Lockey Papers*. George Mathews's illiterate letter, written in 1811, on his first arrival at Saint Marys, Georgia, is here, as are copies of the Patriots Manifesto and the Constitution of the Republic of East Florida.

The National Archives in Washington has files which relate some of the main incidents in the Mathews mission and the follow-up military and political events in Florida. Principal of these files are *Teritorial Papers, Record Group 59, Genral Records of the Department of State*. These are items received by the secretary of state concerning the affairs in United States territories until 1873 when the administration of territories was transferred to the secretary of the interior. Vol. I, Microfilm Roll 1, Vol. II, Roll 2, Vol. III, Roll 3, cover the period pertaining to this book.

Microfilmed military records are: *Letters Sent by the Secretary of War*, M-6; *Letters Received by the Secretary of War*, M-22, *Letters Sent to the President by the Secretary of War*, M-127; *Reports to Congress by the Secretary of War*, M-226, *Letters Received by the Office of the Adjutant General*, M-566; *Letters Received by the Secretary of the Navy and Captains' Letters*, M-125.

In Saint Augustine, the Patriot War claims are in the files of the Office of the Clerk of Court of Saint Johns County, Florida. The Saint Augustine Historical Society has full files on Fort San Marcos and Moosa Old Fort. The society also has a complete microfilm edition of the *East Florida Papers*.

At Woodbine, Georgia, the court records, deeds and wills in the Judge of Probate's Office contain much information about people and events in Saint Marys and Camden County, Georgia, in 1812. A printed collection of documents which are important to this story is *Annals of Congress; The*

Debates and Proceedings of the Congress of the United States, March 3, 1789 to May 27, 1824, 42 vols. (Washington, 1834-1856). This predecessor of the *Congressional Record* contains only summaries in places but was used for quotations from debates and for acts of Congress relevant to this book.

Relevant state papers and diplomatic documents are found in *American State Papers: Documents, Legislative and Executive of the Congress of the United States,* 38 vols, (Washington, 1832-1861), especially, Class I, 6 vols, *Foreign Relations.*

William Hunter, *Speech of the Hon. William Hunter in Secret Session of the United States Senate, Feb 2d, 1813, on the Proposal for Seizing and Occupying the Province of East Florida By the Troops of the United States,* (Newport, R.I., 1813).

The P.K. Yonge Library also has two letter collections which are valuable: *The Buckner Harris Letters,* on microfilm, and *The Letterbook of Governor David Mitchell,* also on microfilm.

The following manuscripts have titles which are self-explanatory!

Charles W. Arnade, *Cattle Raising in Spanish Florida, 1513-1713,* undated manuscript, Saint Augustine Historical Society.

Bruce S. Chappell, *A Report on Documentation Relating to the History of the Diego Plains Region in Second Spanish Period Florida (1784-1821),* undated manuscript, P.K. Yonge Library.

Robert Franklin Crider, *The Borderlands of Florida,* Florida State University Ph.D. dissertation, 1979, copy in P.K. Yonge Library.

James David Ghent, *Plantation and Frontier Records of East and Middle Florida,* 1789-1869, 2 vols. University of Michigan Ph.D. dissertation, 1930, copy in P.K. Yonge Library.

Roger C. Harlan, *A Military History of Florida during the Governorship of Enrique White,* Florida State University Master's thesis, 1971, copy in P.K. Yonge Library.

S.C. Hood, *The St Marys in Turmoil,* undated manuscript, P.K. Yonge Library.

Folks Huxford, *The Pioneers of Wire Grass Georgia,* 7 vols, private printing, Jessup, Georgia, 1955, Florida Room, Jacksonville, Florida Public Library.

Juan Marchena, *Guarniciones y poblacion militar en Florida oriental,* undated manuscript, P.K. Yonge Library.

Juan Marchena, *Officiales y soldados en el Ejercito de America,* Ph.D. thesis, University of Sevilla, 1979, copy in P.K. Yonge Library.

Shirley Joiner Thompson, *The People of East Florida During the Revolutionary War–War of 1812 Period,* privately printed, Kingsland, Georgia, 1982.

Shirley Joiner Thompson, *The People of Camden County Prior to 1850*, privately printed, Kingsland, Georgia, 1982.

Abel Poitrineau, *Demography and Political Destiny, Spanish Florida, 1784-1819*, undated manuscript, P.K. Yonge Library.

James C. Vocelle, *History of Camden County Georgia*, undated manuscript, Florida Room, Jacksonville, Florida Public Library.

David Hart White, *Vicente Folch, Governor in Spanish Florida*, (Washington, D.C., University Press of America 1981).

SECONDARY SOURCES

NEWSPAPERS AND OTHER CONTEMPORARY PUBLICATIONS

Newspapers primarily relied upon were: the Savannah *Republican*, Charleston *Courier*, Augusta *Chronicle*, *National Intelligencer*, *The Federal Republican*, and *Niles Register*. Both the Charleston *Courier* and the Savannah *Republican* liberally and frequently quoted other papers whose political opinions agreed with theirs. All these papers are available at the Library of Congress.

Contemporary publications as defined here include pamphlets and books published at about the time of the patriots rebellion in Florida as well as publications written by persons recollecting these events or concerned about aspects such as the damage claims. One such latter is *Claims of Citizens of Florida, House of Representatives Report* 99 (Washington, D.C., 1832). Another key document is Senate Document 55, 1851—*Decision of the Hon. Isaac H. Bronson, Judge of the District Court of the United States for the Northern District of Florida in the Matter of the Claim of Francis P. Ferreira under the Ninth Article of the Florida Treaty.* This document contains official copies in English of all the key correspondence exchanged by the American principals and the Spanish authorities and the first-hand accounts by people claiming damages, including figures such as Zephaniah Kingsley.

In 1860, because litigation was still pending, James Cooper produced a pamphlet to prove the United States government planned the operation—*Secret Acts, Resolutions and Instructions under which East Florida Was Invaded by the United States Troops, Naval Forces and Volunteers in 1812 and 1813* (Washington, D.C., 1860). As the title indicates, this pamphlet contains excerpts of all the pertinent original materials in the story.

Still later, in 1888, Susan L'Engle published in New York her *Notes on My Family*, (The Knickerbocker Press) from which the account of the bullfight in Fernandina is taken.

In 1810 William Walton, Jr., published in London two volumes on *The*

Present State of the Spanish Colonies. From this was taken the advice to merchants trading there.

John Melish's A *Description of East and West Florida and the Bahama Islands, With an Account of the Most Important Places in the United States Bordering Upon Florida and the Gulf of Mexico To Which is Added a Short View of the Recent Transactions Relative to the Taking Possession of Florida* (Philadelphia, 1813) gives a contemporary summary of the Mathews mission.

Four accounts of life in Florida appeared shortly after the territory was acquired in 1821. All are important for an understanding of the are at that time. They are: James G. Forbes, *Sketches Historical and Topographical of the Floridas*, (1821); William Simmons, *Notices of East Florida* (1821), contains a first-hand account of Seminole society; Charles Vignoles, *Observations on the Floridas* (1823); Anonymous, *Narrative of a Voyage to the Spanish Main*, (1819) contains more about Fernandina just after the return of Spanish rule; George R. Fairbanks, *The History of St. Augustine* (1858), dismisses the patriots rebellion with great disdain. All of these titles were reprinted as part of the Bicentennial Floridiana Series in the mid-1970s by the University of Florida Press, Gainesville, Florida.

ARTICLES

The titles of the articles indicate to which part of the book they relate. The *Florida Historical Quarterly* (FHQ) and the *Georgia Historical Quarterly* (GHQ) contain most of the articles cited.

The most important articles in the *Florida Historical Quarterly* are: Rembert W. Patrick, "A New Letter of James Monroe on the Cession of Florida," *FHQ*, Vol. XXIII (1945); *id.*, "Letters of the Invaders of East Florida, 1812", Vol. XXVIII (July, 1949); and with Juline C. Yonge, ed., "The Surrender of Amelia Island," Vol. IV (October, 1925). Louis Bates Hill, "George J.F. Clarke, 1774-1836," Vol. XXI (1943). T. Frederick Davis, "Elotchaway, East Florida, 1814," Vol. VIII (1929). D.C. Corbitt, "The Return of Spanish Rule to the St. Marys and St. Johns, 1813-1821," Vol. XX (1941). Philip May, "Zephaniah Kingsley, Non-Conformist," Vol. XXIII (1945). Amy Bushnell, "The Menendez Marquez Cattle Barony at la Chua and the Determinants of Economic Expansion in 17th Century Florida," Vol. LVI (1978). "East Florida Documents," Vol. XIII (1929). Other references to the patriots rebellion are found in *FHQ* articles in Vols IV, V, XVIII, XXI, XXV and XXX. The most important articles in *GHQ* are: Lee Soltow and Aubrey C. Land, "Housing and Social Standing in Georgia in 1798," Vol. LXIV (1982). Philip J. Green, "William H. Crawford and the War of 1812," Vol. XXVI (1942). William H. Williams, ed. "Ten Letters of William H. Crawford, to Martin Van Buren," Vol.

XLIX (1965). (Two other articles about Crawford are in Vols. XXVI and XXXII.) Daniel M. Smith, "James Seagrove and the Mission to Tuckaubatchee, 1793," Vol. XLIV (1960). Important articles not in either *FHQ* or *GHQ* are: James Steigman, "William H. Crawford, Georgia's Forgotten Man," *Georgia Review*, (1961). Isaac J. Cox, "The Border Missions of George Mathews," *Mississippi Valley Historical Review*, Vol. XII (December, 1925). Paul Kruse, "A Secret Agent in East Florida, General George Mathews and the Patriot War," *Journal of Southern History*, Vol. XVIII (March, 1952). Rufus Kay Wyllys, "The East Florida Revolution of 1812-1814," *Hispanic American Historical Review*, Vol. IX (November, 1929).

Mary J. Adams, "Jefferson's Reaction to the Treaty of San Illdefonso," *Journal of Southern History*, Vol. XXI (May, 1955). This contains the account of Jefferson's scheme to get the Indian chiefs heavily indebted to the government's trading posts in order to get their lands away from them in payment.

Dena Snodgrass, "John Houstoun McIntosh," *Jacksonville Historical Society Papers*," Vol. V (1964).

BOOKS

Rembert W. Patrick, *Florida Fiasco*, (Athens, Georgia, University of Georgia Press 1954). This is the only full scholarly study ever written about the patriots rebellion. It not only covers the subject well but points the way to further research with its excellent bibliography.

Wanjohi Wacuima, *Intervention in Spanish Floridas, 1801-1813, A Study in Jeffersonian Foreign Policy* (Boston, Branden Press 1976). This is an excellent monograph which establishes the thesis that Jefferson and his two successors established the rationale for not only all further continental expansion by the United States but also the fundamental policy of American domination of the Western Hemisphere.

Isaac J. Cox, *The West Florida Controversy, 1798-1813* (Baltimore, Johns Hopkins University Press 1918). This is the classic account of the acquisition of West Florida. It gives a detailed account of Madison's first covert operation in Florida.

J.W. Pratt, *The Expansionists of 1812* (New York, Prentice Hall 1925). The definitive exposition of the thesis that expansionist aims were the cause of the War of 1812.

Much has been written about the War of 1812, but only three other books are cited here:

John Mahon, *The War of 1812* (Gainesville, University of Florida Press 1972). The only book that concentrates on Florida, it unfortunately is mostly concerned with naval affairs.

Gilbert Auchinleck, *A History of the War between Great Britain and the United States* (Toronto, Pendragon Press 1855). This is interesting because it gives a contemporary Canadian reaction to the war.

Henry Adams, *The United States During the Administrations of Thomas Jefferson and James Madison*, 9 vols. (New York, Scribner's 1889-1891). This is one of the great achievements of American historical writing. It covers not only the War of 1812, of course, but is indispensable for an understanding of the first two decades of nineteenth-century America.

James Robinson Ward, *Old Hickory's Town* (Jacksonville, Florida Publishing Co. 1982). Going from the big picture to a small one, this is an unusually fine local history of Jacksonville and northeast Florida. It contains excellent reproductions of old maps, the patriots' flag and drawings of all the defense installations on the Saint Johns River.

James Madison

Irving Brant, *James Madison*, 6 vols (Indianapolis, Bobbs Merrill 1941-1961). This is the most complete biography of Madison. Irving Brant, *James Madison and American Nationalism* (Princeton, 1968). A good perspective on Madison the expansionist. Ralph Ketcham, *James Madison* (New York, MacMillan 1971). The most recent biography, livelier and very thorough in one volume. Robert A. Rutland, *et al*, eds., *The Papers of James Madison*, 13 vols, (University of Virginia 1962-1981). This monumental work, begun at the University of Chicago and now carried on at the University of Virginia, is a meticulously edited collection. The most recent volume in print, Vol. 13, brings the record up to March 1791.

Dolley Madison

Virginia Moore, *The Madisons* (New York, McGraw-Hill 1979) is the most recent biography, enjoyable and thorough.

Katheran S. Anthony, *Dolley Madison, Her Life and Times* (Garden City, Doubleday 1949) is also enjoyable reading. Noel B. Gerson, *The Velvet Glove* (Nashville, T. Nelson 1975) is filled with insight about her personality.

Gaillard Hunt, reprinted. *Margaret Smith's The First Forty Years of Washington Society*, (New York, P. Unger Publishing Co. 1906); and Lucia B. Cutts, *Memoirs and Letters of Dolley Madison by Her Grandniece* (New York, Scribner's 1886). These two books are vital for a feel of the times. The first was written by the wife of the editor of the *National Intelligencer*.

James Monroe

Harry Ammon, *James Monroe and the Quest for National Identity* (New York, McGraw-Hill 1971). The most recent and thorough account of Monroe's life.

Stuart Gerry Brown, ed., *Autobiography of James Monroe* (Syracuse, New York, Syracuse University Press 1959). Harry Ammon comments that James Monroe almost never touched on any subject in his personal letters except politics. He calls Monroe "America's first professional politician." This curious volume bears him out. Monroe, desperate for money in his final years, wrote four hundred pages of autobiography in the third person in the hope of getting a government pension. Unfortunately he never got as far as the War of 1812. Nevertheless, these carefully selected incidents of his career shed light on his character.

Stanislaus Murray Hamilton, ed., *The Writings of James Monroe*, 7 vols. (New York, Scribner's 1898-1903). An old but reliable collection of Monroe papers.

Robert Smith

C.C. Tansill, *Robert Smith*, Vol 3 in Samuel Flagg Bemis's *American Secretaries of State and Their Diplomacy* (Vol. 3 published in New York in 1917, Cooper Square Publishing Co.). The only life of Smith, and, at that, containing practically nothing on the man's career except his official positions. Tansill, however, in researching this book, made the important discovery of Madison's falsifying the date of the receipt of the West Florida Convention's documents.

George Mathews

There is no biography of George Mathews. A search of *American Doctoral Dissertations* and the *Accessions Registry*, Georgia Depository turned up nothing. Some biographical information is contained in *Dictionary of American Biography*, Allen Johnson and Dumas Malone, 20 vols. (New York, Scribner's 1928-36). Also *Biographical Dictionary of the Governors of the United States, 1789-1978*, 4 vols, (Westport, Connecticut, Greenwood Press 1978) contains information. George Gilman Smith, *The Story of Georgia and the Georgia People*, (Atlanta, Byrd 1970); Lucian Knight, *A Standard History of Georgia and the Georgians*, 6 vols, (Chicago, University of Chicago Press 1917), *id.*, *Georgia's landmarks, Memorials and Legends*, 2 vols.; (Atlanta, A.B. Caldwell 1913) and William F. Northern, ed. *Men of Mark in Georgia*, 2 vols (Atlanta, A.B. Caldwell 1931) all contain some bits on Mathews and the other Georgians as well as material on Georgia life in the early nineteenth century.

William H. Crawford

Several items on Crawford are mentioned in the Articles section of this bibliography. Chase C. Mooney, *William H. Crawford* (Lexington, Kentucky, University of Kentucky Press 1974) is a full-length modern biography. Philip Jackson Green, *The Life of William Harris Crawford*, Ph.D. dissertation (University of Chicago, 1935), is another.

Biographical material on the other participants, except for the items mentioned in the Articles section and the books on Georgia referred to above, is nowhere in print.

SPECIAL SUBJECTS

Material on the Seminoles and their relations with blacks is found in:

Joshua Reed Giddings, *The Exiles in Florida* (1858). This is available in the Floridiana Bicentennial Series.

William Simmons's contemporary account has already been referred to.

John Titcomb Sprague, *The Florida War* (1847) is another contemporary account available in the Bicentennial Series.

Charles Henry Coe, *Red Patriots* (1856), also in the Bicentennial Series, is a glowing defense of the Seminoles' fight for their land.

Edwin C. McReynolds, *The Seminoles* (Norman, Oklahoma, University of Oklahoma Press 1959) is a general account of the tribe.

Daniel F. Littlefield, *Africans and Seminoles from Removal to Emancipation* (Westport, Connecticut, Greenwood Press 1977) deals with a later period than covered by this book, but is the most recent discussion of the subject.

Two articles are important. They are: Kenneth W. Porter, "Negros in the East Florida Annexation," *Journal of Negro History*, Vol. XXX (1945), and Edwin L. Williams, "Negro Slavery in Florida," *FHQ*, Vol VIII (1949).

The Slave Trade

Daniel P. Mannix and Malcolm Cowley, *Black Cargoes* (New York, 1962) is based on the exhaustive study by Elizabeth Donnan, *Documents Illustrative of the American Slave Trade*, 4 vols, (Washington, 1935).

The Henry Letters

Adams, *History*, Ketcham, *Madison*, and Patrick, *Fiasco* contain accounts. Edwin A. Cruickshank, *The Political Adventures of John Henry* (Toronto, Pendragon Press 1936) is a full-length account. Samuel Eliot Morrison's paper, "The Henry Crillon Affair of 1812," in *By Land and By sea* (New York, Knopf 1953) is, of course, the best reading.

The Bay of Pigs

Peter Wyden, *Bay of Pigs* (New York, Simon & Schuster 1979) is a thorough and objective account.

David Atlee Philips, *The Night Watch* (New York, Atheneum 1977).

Philips ran the propaganda side of the Bay of Pigs operation and is quoted by Wyden.

E. Howard Hunt, *Give Us This Day* (New Rochelle, New York, Arlington House 1973). As might be expected, Hunt's book about the Bay of Pigs reveals the level of deep emotion felt by covert operators who feel betrayed.

The Chilean Operation

William Colby, *Honorable Men, My Life in the* CIA (New York, Simon & Schuster 1978) gives a guarded account of the operation.

Thomas Powers, *The Man Who Kept the Secrets, Richard Helms and the* CAA (New York, Knopf 1979) is more revealing.

Seymour M. Hersh, "The Price of Power, Kissinger, Nixon, and Chile," *The Atlantic Monthly*, December, 1982, and Hersh's *The Price of Power, Kissinger in Nixon's White House*, (New York, Summit Books, 1983), tell what really happened.

INDEX

Adair, John, 52–53
Adams, Abigail, 26
Adams, Henry, 40, 109, 286, 290–291
Adams, John, 80, 228
Adams, John Quincy, 29, 281, 289
Alabama, 13, 73
Alachua, 263, 287, 288
Alcoholic beverages, 25–26, 143–144
Alexander, Samuel, 288
Alexander I, 29
Allende, Salvador, 16, 173, 292–293
Amelia Island, 73, 87, 88, 100, 104, 139, 140, 141, 147, 185, 197, 198
American Revolution, 83
Ammon, Henry, *James Monroe, The Quest for National Identity*, 291
Anderson, Joseph, 270–271, 272, 276
Anglos, 90
Anti-Semitism, 257
Appling, Daniel, 166, 167, 168, 204
Arbenz government, 13–14
Armstrong, John, 281, 282, 283
Arredondo, Jose, 185, 187, 189, 190, 193, 247, 256
Ashley, Lodowick, 84, 86, 145, 176–177, 183, 187–189, 190–191, 193, 197, 202–204, 255, 286
Ashley, Nathaniel, 84, 145
Ashley, William, 84, 86, 145, 286, 287
Atkinson, George, 88, 182, 185, 187, 189–190, 195, 197, 198–199, 200, 202–203
Augusta *Chronicle*, 269–270
Aviles, Don Pedro Menendez de, 100
Aztecs, 49

Baltimore *American*, 131
Baltimore *Federal Republican*, 225, 226
Bank of Columbia (Washington, D.C.), 225, 226
Barlow, Joe, 276
Baton Rouge, 52, 53, 60, 67, 106
Baton Rouge Convention of 1810, 61–65, 82
Bay of Pigs, 14, 15, 171, 245
Bayard, James, 30
Bayou Sara region, 60
Bell's River, 195, 196, 197

Bessent, Abraham, 182
Black troops, 252, 258, 265–266, 278
Blackburn, Gideon, 275
Bonaparte, Betsy Patterson, 249–250
Bonaparte, Jérôme, 34, 250
Bonaparte, Joseph, 39–40, 55
Bonaparte, Josephine, 26
Bonaparte, Lucien, 39–40
Bonaparte, Napoleon, 13, 34–35, 39–40, 42, 44, 48, 49, 161
Bowlegs, 258, 261, 264, 280
Bribes, 13, 47, 48, 50, 244
Bronson, Isaac, 290
Browere, J. H. I., 13
Burke, Maj. Thomas, 236
Burr, Aaron, 22, 42, 52

Calhoun, John C., 33
Camden County (Georgia), 83, 84, 85, 90, 133, 136, 148, 155
Camp New Hope, 265–266, 285
Campbell Hugh G., 168–170, 174, 175, 183, 187, 189, 190, 194–196, 199–200, 201, 206–207, 237, 239–240, 285
Canot, Captain Theodore, *Twenty Years of an African Slaver*, 135
Carolina Kings Rangers, 150
Cashen, James, 256
Castro, Fidel, 14, 15, 245
Cattle raising, 100–103
Centerville (Georgia), 142
Central America, 14
Central Intelligence Agency, *see* CIA
Charles IV, 49
Charleston *Courier*, 224, 226–227, 228–229
Chile, 173, 292, 293
Choctaw Indians, 106
CIA, 12, 13–14, 114, 173, 245, 291, 292, 293–294
Claiborne, William C., 50, 55, 56, 57, 58, 59–60, 66, 67, 68, 82
Clark, Archibald, 88
Clark, Jacob, 88
Clark, William, 145
Clarke, Charles, 203
Clarke, George John Frederic, 138–140, 141, 155, 185–187, 189–190, 200, 202–203, 256–257
Clay, Henry, 33, 108–109, 110, 111, 272
Clinton, DeWitt, 272, 273
Coale, Edward J., 227
Cockburn, Sir George, 286
Coleraine (Georgia), 142
Coles, Edward, 249
Cone, Capt. William, 268
Constitution, U.S., 109
Cook, George, 88
Cooper, James, *Secret Acts, Resolutions and Instructions under which East Florida was Invaded*, 115, 187
Coquina, 93
Corn liquor, 143, 144
Cortes, 49, 125
Cowford, 175
Craig, James, 223–224
Craig, William, 150, 205, 255, 286
Crawford, William H., 30, 33, 69, 70–71, 76, 78, 79, 81, 82, 112, 164, 241, 245, 259
Creek Agency, 122
Creek Indians, 72, 122, 261–262, 263, 279, 280
Crillon, Comte Edouard de, 219–222
Criollos, 53–54, 90
Cuba, 55, 56, 93, 245
Cumberland Sound, 201
Cushing, Col., 163
Cuthbert, Col., 247

Dana, Senator, 111
De Lassus, Carlos, 60, 61, 62, 64
Dearborn, Henry, 25, 270
Declaration of Independence, 182
Declaration of the Rights of Man, 177
del Carmen, Maria, 103
Delaney, Daniel, 205, 208
Democratic Party, 33
Diego Plains, 102
Doctrine of *national-security interest*, 108
Drinking, 25–26, 143–144, 256
Dubourg, Father, 29
Duche, Sophia, 223

Early, Peter, 165

East Florida, 13, 14, 17, 41, 48, 52, 57, 63
bill to occupy, 251–252
covert-action plan authorized, 113–118
diplomatic protests of mission, 151–153
government of, 158, 247
and the Indians, 257–259, 261–262
invasion of, 279
law passed to take possession of, 163, 164
manifesto of Republic, 177–182
population of, 85–86, 95
prosperity in, 146–148
U.S. right to, according to Monroe, 153–154
East Florida Papers, 92–93
Eisenhower, Dwight D., 17
Ellicott, Andrew, 80–81
England, 41
Epileptoid hysteria, 22–23
Espinosa, Don Diego, 102
Estrada, Juan, 152, 207–208, 212, 235, 242, 243, 258
Eustis, William, 35–36, 270
Evans, John H., 215

Fatio, Susan, *Notes on my Family*, 141–142
Federalists, 219, 228, 230, 276
Ferdinand II, 247
Ferdinand VII, 49, 55, 62
Fernandez, Domingo, 141
Fernandina, 16, 140, 141, 144, 176, 185–201, 208, 209, 256, 282, 285, 287
"Field marshal's baton," 173
Filibustering, 14–15
Flagler, Henry, 95
Fletcher v. Peck, 74
Flogging, 93
Florida
Americans in, 98–99
becomes a state, 290
British in, 96
cattle raising, 100–103
growth of, 99–100
land grants in, 96
population of, 96, 97, 98
Spanish occupation of, 97, 100–105
value of, 45–46
see also East Florida; West Florida
Florida Patriots War of 1811, 149
Florida Proclamation, 109–110
Florida Treaty, 290
Floridianos, 102
Floyd, John, 87, 88, 145, 158, 168, 192, 241
Folch, Vicente, 52, 54–56, 57, 64, 67–68, 82, 107–109, 112, 116–117, 123–124, 125, 126–128, 132, 244
Forrester, John, 104
Fort George Island, 135
Fort Mitchell, 288
Fort Moosa, 238, 243–244, 247, 262, 278
Fort of Baton Rouge, 64
Fort San Carlos, 176
Fort San Marcos, 94, 95, 149, 158, 211, 212
Fort Stoddert, 163
Foster, Augustus John, 151, 153, 201, 230
Foster, Winslow, 199–200
Founding Fathers, 12
France, 13, 38, 45, 47, 48, 55, 56
Francis P. Ferrẽira, Administrator of Francis Pass v. the United States, 290
Franklin, Benjamin, 20, 72
Fulton, Samuel, 57, 58

Gallatin, Albert, 29, 30, 34, 35, 77, 106–107, 226, 231, 281, 286, 289
George II, 73
George III, 136, 161, 274
Georgia, 15, 71, 72, 74–75, 83, 142–145, 251, 263, 266, 269, 270
Georgia Company, 75
Georgia Land Act, 72
Georgia Union Company, 75
Gerry, Elbridge, 219
Giddings, Joshua, 262
Giles, Senator, 108, 218
Giles bill, 110, 112
Godoy, 49

Gore, Lt. Governor, 223
Gracia Real de Santa Teresa de Mose, 211
Graham, John, 226
Grayson, 199–200
Great Britain, 45–46, 55
Greene, Nathaniel, 72
Guatemala, 13–14

Hacienda de la chua, 100
Haig, Alexander, 294
Hamilton, Alexander, 36
Hamilton, Paul, 36
Hampton, Gen. Wade, 163
Hanson, Alexander, 276
Harris, Buckner, 81, 86–87, 135, 255, 271, 284, 286, 287–288
Harrison, Gen. William Henry, 281
Hawkins, Benjamin, 112, 277, 279
Hawkins, Sir John, 100
Helms, Richard, 16, 17, 173, 292
Henry, John, 216, 217, 219, 220, 222–224, 225
Henry, Patrick, 21, 75
Henry letters, 219–229, 259
Henry spy story, 216–218
Hersh, Seymour, *The Price of Power*, 292, 294
Hibberson, Joseph, 186, 187, 189, 190, 193
Hickey, Philip, 60, 61
Hill, Maria del Carmen, 103
Hodge, Governor, 67
Holmes, 63, 64–65, 69
Horsey, Outerbridge, 109–110
Hunter, William, 278, 279

Iberian Peninsula, 53
Indians, 87, 257–259, 265–266, 280
  and Blacks, 263–264, 265–269
  see also Seminoles
"Invisibles, the," 34, 35, 276
Iran, 171
Irving, Washington, 19, 250
Isaacs, Ralph, 118–119, 120–121, 123–125, 129, 132, 161, 165–166, 176–177, 196, 197, 235–237, 242, 244, 245

Jackson, Andrew, 271, 275, 283
Jai, Anna Madgigene, 135, 138
Jefferson, Thomas, 12–13, 16, 19, 24, 33, 36, 37, 38–39, 40, 41–42, 43, 45, 48, 77, 177, 182
Johnson, William, 88

Kennedy, John F., 245
Kennedy, Joseph, 82
Kennedy, Robert F., 245
Ketcham, Ralph, *James Madison*, 291
Kindelan Sebastian, 158, 175, 205, 247, 252, 253, 255, 258–259, 261, 262, 266, 269, 282, 283–284, 285, 287
King, Thomas, 88
King's Road, 175
Kingsley, Martha, 138
Kingsley, Zephaniah, 135–138, 146, 207, 255, 284, 286, 289, 290
  The Patriarchal Slave System, 137–138
Kinnear, William, 254–255
Kissinger, Henry, 291, 292, 293–294
Korry, Ambassador, 293
Kruschchev, Nikita, 17

La chua, 101
La media palabra, 119, 127, 155
Lafayette, Gen., 161
Latin America, 14
Latrobe, Benjamin, 27, 28
Laudanum, 31, 143, 144
Laval, Jacint, 160–163, 165–168, 170–173, 176, 177, 183, 187, 190, 191–192, 206, 213–214
LeClerc, General, 43
Leon, Ponce de, 100
Leslie, Forbes, Panton and Company, 97–98
Leslie, John, 139
Letters to the Secretary of War, 187
Lewis, James, 103–104
Lincoln, Levi, 77
Livingston, Robert, 44
Lopez, Justo, 86, 87–88, 169, 176, 182–183, 185, 186–187, 188, 190, 193, 194, 196, 200–201, 202–203, 204, 205, 235
Louis XIV, 39
Louisiana, 41–42, 43, 47

Louisiana Purchase, 13, 38–39, 40, 109
Loyalists, 84

Madison, Alfred, 249
Madison, Dolley, 19–25, 286
as fashion leader, 26–27
birth of, 20–21
child of, 22
and Elizabeth Monroe, 37
family of, 21
as hostess, 24–25, 249, 276
marriage to James Madison, 22, 23
marriage to John Todd, 21–22
and Nelly Madison, 23–24
redecorating White House, 27–28
style of dress, 26–27
Madison, James, 12–13, 19–20, 45, 50, 106
and Crillon, 219
drinking habits of, 26
and East Florida, 14, 112–113
elected president, 32–33
elected to House of Representatives, 23
family problems of, 29–31
and Florida act, 280–281
and Florida proclamation, 109–110
health problems of, 31
on J. Henry, 216–217
illness of, 22–23
and Louisiana Purchase, 38–39, 40, 42, 44
marriage to Dolley, 22, 23
and Monroe, compared with Nixon and Kissinger, 17, 291, 294–295
as secretary of state, 77
and R. Smith, 35, 129–132
and West Florida, 47, 48, 57–58, 66, 110–111
Madison, Nelly, 23–24
Madison, Robert, 249
Magigene, Anna, 290
Malinche, 49
Manifesto, East Florida Republic, 177–182
Marquez, Pedro Menendez, 100–101
Marquez, Tomas Menendez, 101, 102
Marshall, John, 74, 78
Massias, Abraham, 166, 167, 168, 171, 172, 212–214, 256, 257, 285
Mather, George, 60, 61
Mathews, George, 68, 80, 81, 88–89, 99, 105, 177
appointed commissioner of East Florida mission, 116–118, 119, 159
and Campbell, 168–171
compared with Helms, 17
confusion in orders given him, 128–129
death of, 260–261
dismissal of, 236, 239, 244–245, 247–248
early life of, 71–72
and Fernandina, 176, 184, 187, 189, 190, 191, 193, 195, 197–199, 201
and Folch, 81–83, 125, 126–128
as governor of Georgia, 73–74, 75–76, 78–79
and the Indians, 237–238, 257–259, 261
and Laval, 160–163, 165, 168, 170–171
and McIntosh, 149–152, 154–155
and Mobile Bay, 127–128
and Monroe, 229–231, 232–234, 236
and "patriot army," 156, 157–158
in Saint Augustine, 174–175, 204–206, 208–211, 213–214
in Saint Marys, 146–148
sets out on mission with McKee and Isaacs, 120–124
and West Florida, 132
and Wyllys letter, 159–160
McIntosh, John Houston, 86, 88, 99, 145, 148–151, 154–155, 177, 183, 187, 197, 202–203, 204, 207, 238, 255–256, 258, 264–265, 271, 284, 286, 289
McKee, John, 106, 107, 112, 116, 120–121, 122, 125–126, 129, 132, 163–164
Media palabra, 119, 127, 155
Mexico, 39, 55, 56, 92, 93
Miles's Law, 159
Milledgeville (Georgia), 251, 270

Minorcans, 95, 96, 97, 98
Miro, Esteban, 52
Mississippi, 13, 73
Mississippi Territory, 80, 107, 112, 163
Mitchell, David, 87, 135, 236–237, 240–243, 244, 246–247, 252, 260, 265, 269, 276–277, 280, 287
Mobile, 68, 106, 107, 127, 180, 209
Mobile Bay, 112, 127–128
Mobile River, 123
Monroe, Elizabeth, 37
Monroe, James, 12–13, 16, 36, 43
  and Crillon, 219–222
  and dismissal of Mathews, 236, 239, 244
  and East Florida, 153–154
  and Henry letters, 219–225, 228
  and Isaacs, 235–237
  and Louisiana Purchase, 38–39, 42, 44
  and Mathews, 205–206, 208–210, 229–231, 232–234, 236
  and Mitchell, 236–237
  as secretary of state, 129, 130–131, 132
  and West Florida, 111
Monroe-Pinckney treaty, 37
Moode, Stephen, 182
Moosa Old Fort, 211–212
Moro Castle, 149, 150
Morris, Phoebe, 249

Napoleon, *see* Bonaparte, Napoleon
National Intelligencer, 25, 131, 225, 229
National Security Act, 114
National Security Council (NSC), 114, 115–116
National-security interest, doctrine, 108
New Orleans, 13, 40, 48
New Orleans Territory, 66, 89, 108
New Smyrna, 96
New York *Morning Post*, 227
Newnan, Col. Daniel, 247, 266–268, 274
Ngo Dinh Diem, 12
Niles *Register*, 269
Niles *Weekly Register*, 67, 229
Nixon, Richard M., 16–17, 108, 291, 292, 293, 294
North Carolina, 72–73
NSC (National Security Council) , 114, 115–116

Oglethorpe, James, 73, 94, 149, 211
Oñis, Luis de, 151, 155, 235
Orange Park, 135
Orders in Council, 250
Orleans Territory, 66, 89, 108
Oswald, Lee Harvey, 245
Otis, Harriet, 217

Panton Leslie trading company, 139
Patriot army, 156, 157–158, 238–239, 246
Patriots War of 1811, 149
Patriots War of 1812–1813, 262
Patterson, Betsy, 34
Payne, Chief, 258, 264, 279
Payne, John C., 249
Payne, King, 208, 258, 259, 261, 264, 268
Payne, Lucy, 22, 249
Pearl River, 53
Peninsulares, 53, 54, 90
Pensacola, 42, 53, 68, 112, 180, 209
Pentagon Papers, 108
Perdido, 48
Petit mal, 23
Philadelphia *Aurora*, 251
Pickering, Timothy, 80, 81, 108, 109, 112, 276
Picolata, 207, 237–238, 257
Pinckney, William, 36–37, 45, 270, 271, 277–278, 280, 282, 283, 284, 285
Plausible presidential denial, 17, 67
Point Petre, 156, 157, 158, 160, 169, 203, 236, 266
Powers, Gary, 17
Pratt, Charles, 83
President's Palace, 27
Preston, William, 250–251
Puebla, 92

Quakers, 21
Quesada, Governor, 40–41

Quesada Battery, 175
Quincy, Josiah, 228

Randolph, John, 33, 36, 37, 48, 74, 77–78, 130
Refuge, The, 148
Republican Blues and Savannah Volunteer Guards, 252–253, 266
Republican Party, 33, 37–38
Rhea, Congressman, 112
Ridgeway, Capt. Fielder, 254
Rivera, Capt. Francisco, 247
Rolles, Denys, 96
Roosevelt, Theodore, 15
Rose's Bluff, 166, 177, 190, 192, 198
Ross, John, 182
Ruddle, Mr., 254
Rush, Richard, 226
Rutland, Robert A., *The Papers of James Madison*, 31
Ryland, Herman W., 223–224

Saint Augustine, 15, 52, 85, 96, 98, 101, 102, 159, 174–175, 192–193, 202–214, 247, 252, 257, 261, 265, 269, 287
Saint Johns, 174, 175, 282, 288
Saint Johns Bluff, 135
Saint Johns River, 73, 212
Saint-Mary, Moreau de, 24–25
Saint Marys, 83, 84, 85, 121, 144, 145, 146–148, 214, 269
Saint Marys River, 15, 83–84, 133, 143, 276
Saint Patrick, 84
San Nicolas, 175
San Vincente Ferrer Battery, 175
Sanchez, Francisco Xavier, 97, 102, 103
Santo Domingo, 43, 44
Savannah Blues and Volunteer Guards, 252–253, 266
Savannah *Republican*, 215–216, 238–239
Schneider, Gen. Rene, 293, 294
Seacoffee, 261
Seagrove, James, 84, 86, 88, 90, 145, 164, 165, 182, 263
Security Act of 1947, 114
Seminole Indians, 15, 253, 257–259, 261, 262, 263–264, 265, 268–269, 277, 279, 287
Server, John, 42
Seven Years War, 41
Situado, 92, 101
Slave trade, 15–16, 97, 133–138, 141, 262
  and prostitution, 144–145
  of Seminoles, 263–264
Smith, Robert, 35, 63, 66–67, 69, 79, 116, 121, 123–124, 129–132, 225, 228–229
  Smith, Samuel, 33, 34, 35, 130, 276
Smith, Samuel Harrison, 25–26
Smith, Thomas Adam, 160, 163, 164–165, 172, 203, 206, 210–211, 212, 236, 243, 244, 247, 252, 253, 257, 265, 279, 280, 282
Someruelos, Marquis de, 107, 127
Sonntage, Dr. Karl, 140–141
Soubiran, 221–222
Spain, 13, 41, 46, 47, 56
Spanish-American territories, 55–56
Spanish Florida, 41
Spanish garrisons, 53, 57
Spanish Main, 92
Sparks, Colonel, 82
Stallings, Elias, 167, 168, 254
Stephens, William, *History of Georgia*, 76
Stevens, William, 73
Stoddert, Benjamin, 123
Sullivan, 74
Summers, Anthony, *Conspiracy*, 245

Tallyrand, 42, 44, 47, 66, 111
Tarleton, Colonel Banastre, 21
Taylor, John, 228, 273
Tennessee volunteers, 274, 275, 277, 279
Territory of Orleans, 66, 89, 108
Third Battalion of the Cuban Infantry Regiment, 93–94
Third Company of militia of Amelia Island, 185
"Three Chopped Way," 123
Todd, John, 21–22
Todd, Payne, 22, 23, 28–30, 249

Tories, 84
Traders Hill (Georgia), 142
Treaty of Ghent, 289
Trollope, Frances, "Day of a Lady in the West," 25
Troup, George, 164, 234–235, 251
Truman, Harry, 114
Tucker, Thomas T., 226
Turnbill, Andrew, 96
Turreau, General Louis, 66
Tuscany, 42, 43

United States Constitution, 109
United States v. Francis P. Ferreira, 187

Valenzuela, Gen. Camilo, 294
Van Buren, Martin, 272
Van Courtland, General, 28
Venezuela, 58
Viaux, Gen. Roberto, 293, 294
Vietnam War, 11, 12
Virginia *Patriot*, 226
Virginia Yazoo Company, 75
Vox Populi, Lex Suprema, 201

Walker, William, 14–15
Walton, William, Jr., *The Present State of the Spanish Colonies*, 104–105
War of 1812, 11–12
War with Great Britain, 248, 250
Washington, George, 40
Washington, Lucy Payne, 249
Washington, Thomas, 74
Webster, Daniel, 276
Weed, Jacob, 84
West Florida, 14, 41, 47, 48, 51–68
  and Baton Rouge Convention of 1810, 61–65
  bill to occupy, 251–252
  colonial Spanish Army in, 53–54
  declaration of independence for, 65
  and Folch, 107, 116–117
  governor of, 54–56
  mission terminated in, 132
  as part of Louisiana Purchase, 13, 108–109, 110–111
  as part of New Orleans Territory, 66, 89
  population of, 52–53
  proclamation to take possession of, 66–67
White, Enrique, 86, 87, 90–92, 93–95, 138, 150
White House, 27, 286
White, Hugh Lawson, 165
White, James, 165
Wilkes, Isaac, 104
Wilkinson, Gen., 275
Willard, Sydney, *Memoirs*, 223
Williams, John, 205, 256, 268, 273–274, 275, 277
Winston, Lucy, 21
Woodruff, Joseph, 168
Woods, James, 27
Wykoff, William, 58–60, 69
Wyllys, William, 150–151, 159–160

Yazoo land sale, 74–77, 78, 79
"Yazoo man," 78
Yonge, Philip, 189, 197, 198–199, 256